The Law of Civilizati

by Brooks Adams

Preface

In offering to the public a second edition of The Law of Civilization and Decay I take the opportunity to say emphatically that such value as the essay may have lies in its freedom from any preconceived bias. All theories contained in the book, whether religious or economic, are the effect, and not the cause, of the way in which the facts unfolded themselves. I have been passive.

The value of history lies not in the multitude of facts collected, but in their relation to each other, and in this respect an author can have no larger responsibility than any other scientific observer. If the sequence of events seems to indicate the existence of a law governing social development, such a law may be suggested, but to approve or disapprove of it would be as futile as to discuss the moral bearings of gravitation.

Some years ago, when writing a sketch of the history of the colony of Massachusetts Bay, I became deeply interested in certain religious aspects of the Reformation, which seemed hardly reconcilable with the theories usually advanced to explain them. After the book bad been published, I continued reading theology, and, step by step, was led back, through the schoolmen and the crusades, to the revival of the pilgrimage to Palestine, which followed upon the conversion of the Huns. As ferocious pagans, the Huns had long closed the road to Constantinople; but the change which swept over Europe after the year 1000, when Saint Stephen was crowned, was unmistakable; the West received an impulsion from the East, I thus became convinced that religious enthusiasm, which, by stimulating the pilgrimage, restored communication between the Bosphorus and the Rhine, was the power which produced the accelerated movement culminating in modern centralization.

Meanwhile I thought I had discovered not only that faith, during the eleventh, twelfth, and early thirteenth centuries, spoke by preference through architecture, but also that in

France and Syria, at least, a precise relation existed between the ecclesiastical and military systems of building, and that the one could not be understood without the other. In the commercial cities of the same epoch, on the contrary, the religious idea assumed no definite form of artistic expression, for the Gothic never flourished in Venice, Genoa, Pisa, or Florence, nor did any pure school of architecture thrive in the mercantile atmosphere. Furthermore, commerce from the outset seemed antagonistic to the imagination, for a universal decay of architecture set in throughout Europe after the great commercial expansion of the thirteenth century; and the inference I drew from these facts was, that the economic instinct must have chosen some other medium by which to express itself. My observations led me to suppose that the coinage might be such a medium, and I ultimately concluded that, if the development of a mercantile community is to be understood, it must be approached through its money.

Another conviction forced upon my mind, by the examination of long periods of history, was the exceedingly small part played by conscious thought in moulding the fate of men. At the moment of action the human being almost invariably obeys an instinct, like an animal; only after action has ceased does he reflect.

These controlling instincts are involuntary, and divide men into species distinct enough to cause opposite effects under identical conditions. For instance, impelled by fear, one type will rush upon an enemy, and another will run away; while the love of women or of money has stamped certain races as sharply as ferocity or cunning has stamped the lion or the fox.

Like other personal characteristics, the peculiarities of the mind are apparently strongly hereditary, and, if these instincts be transmitted from generation to generation, it is plain that, as the external world changes, those who receive this heritage must rise or fall in the social scale, according as their nervous system is well or ill adapted to the conditions to which they are born. Nothing is commoner, for example, than to find families who have been famous in one century sinking into obscurity in the next, not because the children have degenerated, but because a certain field of activity which afforded the ancestor full scope, has been closed against his offspring. Particularly has this been true in revolutionary epochs such as the Reformation; and families so situated have very generally become extinct.

When this stage had been reached, the Reformation began to wear a new aspect, but several years elapsed before I saw whither my studies led. Only very slowly did a sequence of cause and effect take shape in my mind, a sequence wholly unexpected in character, whose growth resembled the arrangement of the fragments of an inscription, which cannot be read until the stones have been set in a determined order. Finally, as the historical work neared an end, I perceived that the intellectual phenomena under examination fell into a series which seemed to correspond, somewhat closely, with the laws which are supposed to regulate the movements of the material universe.

Theories can be tested only by applying them to facts, and the facts relating to successive phases of human thought, whether conscious or unconscious constitute history; therefore, if intellectual phenomenena are evolved in a regular sequence, history, like matter, must be governed by law. In support of such a conjecture, I venture to offer an bypothesis by which to classify a few of the more interesting intellectual phases through which human society must, apparently, pass, in its oscillations between barbarism and civulization, or, what amounts to the same thing, in its movement from a condition of physical dispersion to one of concentration. The accompanying volume contains the evidence which suggested the hypothesis, although, it seems hardly necessary to add, an essay of this size on so vast a subject can only be regarded as a suggestion.

The theory proposed is based upon the accepted scientific principle that the law of force and energy is of universal application in nature, and that animal life is one of the outlets through which solar energy is dissipated.

Starting from this fundamental proposition, the first deduction is, that, as human societies are forms of animal life, these societies must differ among themselves in energy, in proportion as nature has endowed them, more or less abundantly, with energetic material.

Thought is one of the manifestations of human energy, and among the earlier and simpler phases of thought, two stand conspicuous—Fear and Greed. Fear, which, by stimulating the imagination, creates a belief in an invisible world, and ultimately develops a priesthood; and Greed, which dissipates energy in war and trade.

Probably the velocity of the social movement of any community is proportionate to its energy and mass, and its centralization is proportionate to its velocity; therefore, as human movement is accelerated, societies centralize. In the earlier stages of concentration, fear appears to be the channel through which energy finds the readiest outlet; accordingly, in primitive and scattered communities, the imagination is vivid, and the mental types produced are religious, military, artistic. As consolidation advances, fear yields to greed, and the economic organism tends to supersede the emotional and martial.

Whenever a race is so richly endowed with the energetic material that it does not expend all its energy in the daily struggle for life, the surplus may be stored in the shape of wealth; and this stock of stored energy may be transferred from community to community, either by conquest, or by superiority in economic competition.

However large may be the store of energy accumulated by conquest, a race must, sooner or later, reach the limit of its martial energy, when it must enter on the phase of economic competition. But, as the economic organism radically differs from the emotional and martial, the effect of economic competition has been, perhaps invariably, to dissipate the energy amassed by war.

When surplus energy has accumulated in such bulk as to preponderate over productive energy, it becomes the controlling social force. Thenceforward, capital is autocratic, and energy vents itself through those organisms best fitted to give expression to the power of capital. In this last stage of consolidation, the economic, and, perhaps, the scientific intellect is propagated, while the imagination fades, and the emotional, the martial, and the artistic types of manhood decay. When a social velocity has been attained at which the waste of energetic material is so great that the martial and imaginative stocks fail to reproduce themselves, intensifying competition appears to generate two extreme economic types,—the usurer in his most formidable aspect, and the peasant whose nervous system is best adapted to thrive on scanty nutriment. At length a point must be reached when pressure can go no further, and then, perhaps, one of two results may follow: A stationary period may supervene, which may last until ended by war, by exhaustion, or by both combined, as seems to have been the case with the Eastern Empire; or, as in the Western, disintegration may set in, the civilized population may perish, and a reversion may take place to a primitive form of organism.

The evidence, however, seems to point to the conclusion that, when a highly centralized society disintegrates, under the pressure of economic competition, it is because the energy of the race has been exhausted. Consequently, the survivors of such a community lack the power necessary for renewed concentration, and must probably remain inert until supplied with fresh energetic material by the infusion of barbarian blood.

BROOKS ADAMS

QUINCY, August 20, 1896.

Chapter I: The Romans

WHEN the Romans first emerged from the mist of fable, they were already a race of land-owners who held their property in severalty, and, as the right of alienation was established, the formation of relatively large estates had begun. The ordinary family, however, held, perhaps, twelve acres, and, as the land was arable, and the staple grain, it supported a dense rural population. The husbandmen who tilled this land were of the martial type, and, probably for that reason, though supremely gifted as administrators and soldiers, were ill-fitted to endure the strain of the unrestricted economic competition of a centralized society. Consequently their conquests had hardly consolidated before decay set in, a decay whose causes may be traced back until they are lost in the dawn of history.

The Latins had little economic versatility; they lacked the instinct of the Greeks for commerce, or of the Syrians and Hindoos for manufactures. They were essentially land-owners, and, when endowed with the acquisitive faculty, usurers. The latter early developed into a distinct species, at once more subtle of intellect and more tenacious of life than the farmers, and on the disparity between these two types of men, the fate of all subsequent civilization has hinged. At a remote antiquity Roman society divided into creditors and debtors; as it consolidated, the power of the former increased, thus intensifying the pressure on the weak, until, when centralization culminated under the Cæsars, reproduction slackened, disintegration set in, and, after some centuries of decline, the Middle Ages began.

The history of the monarchy must probably always remain a matter of conjecture, but it seems reasonably certain that the expulsion of the Tarquins was the victory of an hereditary monied caste, which succeeded in concentrating the functions of government in a practically self-perpetuating body drawn from their own order. (1) Niebuhr has demonstrated, in one of his most striking chapters, that usury was originally a patrician privilege; and some of the fiercest struggles of the early republic seem to have been decided against the oligarchy by wealthy plebeians, who were determined to break down the monopoly in money-lending. At all events, the conditions of life evidently favoured the growth of the instinct which causes its possessor to suck the vitality of the economically weak; and Macaulay, in the preface to *Virginia* has given so vivid a picture of the dominant class, that one passage at least should be read entire.

> "The ruling class in Rome was a monied class; and it made and administered the laws with a view solely to its own interest. Thus the relation between lender and borrower was mixed up with the relation between sovereign and subject. The great men held a large portion of the community in dependence by means of advances at enormous usury. The law of debt, framed by creditors, and for the protection of creditors, was the most horrible that has ever been known among men. The liberty, and even the life, of the insolvent were at the mercy of the patrician money-lenders. Children often became slaves in consequence of the misfortunes of their parents. The debtor was imprisoned, not in a public gaol under the care of impartial public functionaries, but in a private workhouse belonging to the creditor. Frightful stories were told respecting these dungeons."

But a prisoner is an expense, and the patricians wanted money. Their problem was to exhaust the productive power of the debtor before selling him, and, as slaves have less energy than freemen, a system was devised by which the plebeians were left on their land, and stimulated to labour by the hope of redeeming themselves and their children from servitude. Niebuhr has explained at length how this was done.

For money weighed out a person could pledge himself, his family, and all that belonged to him. In this condition he became *nexus*, and remained in possession of his property until breach of condition, when the creditor could proceed by summary process. (2) Such a contract satisfied the requirements, and the usurers had then only to invent a judgment for debt severe enough to force the debtor to become *nexus* when the alternative was offered him. This presented no difficulty. When an action was begun the defendant had thirty days of grace, and was then arrested and brought before the prætor. If he could neither pay nor find security, he was fettered with irons weighing not less than fifteen pounds, and taken home by the plaintiff. There he was allowed a pound of corn a day, and given sixty days in which to settle. If he failed, he was taken again before the prætor and sentenced. Under this sentence he might be sold or executed, and, where there were several plaintiffs, they might cut him up among them, nor was any individual liable for carving more than his share (3). A man so sentenced involved his descendants, and therefore, rather than submit, the whole debtor class became *nexi* toiling for ever to fulfil contracts quite beyond their strength, and year by year sinking more hopelessly into debt, for ordinarily the accumulated interest soon raised "the principal to many times its original amount."(4) Niebuhr has thus summed up the economic situation:—

> "To understand the condition of the plebeian debtors, let the reader, if he is a man of business, imagine that the whole of the private debts in a given country were turned into bills at a year, bearing interest at twenty per cent or more; and that the non-payment of them were followed on summary process by imprisonment, and by the transfer of the debtor's whole property to his creditor, even though it exceeded what he owed. We do not need those further circumstances, which are incompatible with our manners, the personal slavery of the debtor and of his children, to form an estimate of the fearful condition of the unfortunate plebeians." (5)

Thus the usurer first exhausted a family and then sold it; and as his class fed on insolvency and controlled legislation, the laws were as ingeniously contrived for creating debt, as for making it profitable when contracted. One characteristic device was the power given the magistrate of fining for "offences against order." Under this head "men might include any accusations they pleased, and by the higher grades in the scale of fines they might accomplish whatever they desired."(6) As the capitalists owned the courts and administered justice, they had the means at hand of mining any plebeian whose property was tempting. Nevertheless, the stronghold of usury lay in the fiscal system, which down to the fall of the Empire was an engine for working bankruptcy. Rome's policy was to farm the taxes; that is to say, after assessment, to sell them to a publican, who collected what he could. The business was profitable in proportion as it was extortionate, and the country was subjected to a levy unregulated by law, and conducted to enrich speculators. "Ubi publicanus esset," said Livy, quoting the Senate, "ibi aut jus publicum vanum, aut libertatem sociis nullam esse."

Usury was the cream of this business. The custom was to lend to defaulters at such high rates of interest that insolvency was nearly certain to follow; then the people were taken on execution, and slave-hunting formed a regular branch of the revenue service. In Cicero's time whole provinces of Asia Minor were stripped bare by the traffic. The effect upon the Latin society of the fourth century before Christ was singularly destructive. Italy was filled with petty states in chronic war, the troops were an unpaid militia, which comprised the whole able-bodied population, and though the farms yielded enough for the family in good times, when the males were with the legions labour was certain to be lacking. The campaigns therefore brought want, and with want came the inability to pay taxes.

As late as the Punic War, Regulus asked to be relieved from his command, because the death of his slave and the incompetence of his hired man left his fields uncared for; and if a general and a consul were pinched by absence, the case of the men in the ranks can be imagined. Even in victory the lot of the common soldier was hard enough, for, beside the chance of wounds and disease, there was the certain loss of time, for which no compensation was made. Though the plebeians formed the whole infantry of the line, they received no part of the conquered lands, and even the plunder was taken from them, and appropriated by the patricians to their private use.(7) In defeat, the open country was overrun, the cattle were driven off or slaughtered, the fruit trees cut down, the crops laid waste, and the houses burned. In speaking of the Gallic invasion, Niebuhr has pointed out that the ravaging of the enemy, and the new taxes laid to rebuild the ruined public works, led to general insolvency.(8)

Such conditions fostered the rapid propagation of distinct types of mind, and at a very early period Romans had been bred destitute of the martial instinct, but more crafty and more tenacious of life than the soldier. These were the men who conceived and enforced the usury laws, and who held to personal pledges as the dearest privilege of their order; nor does Livy attempt to disguise the fact "that every patrician house was a gaol for debtors; and that in seasons of great distress, after every sitting of the courts, herds of sentenced slaves were led away in chains to the houses of the nobles." (9)

Of this redoubtable type the Claudian family was a famous specimen, and the picture which has been drawn by Macaulay of the great usurer, Appius Claudius, the decemvir, is so brilliant that it cannot be omitted.

> "Appius Claudius Crassus... was descended from a long line of ancestors distinguished by their haughty demeanour, and by the inflexibility with which they had withstood all the demands of the plebeian order. While the political conduct and the deportment of the Claudian nobles drew upon them the fiercest public hatred, they were accused of

wanting, if any credit is due to the early history of Rome, a class of qualities which, in a military commonwealth, is sufficient to cover a multitude of offences. The chiefs of the family appear to have been eloquent, versed in civil business, and learned after the fashion of their age; but in war they were not distinguished by skill or valor. Some of them, as if conscious where their weakness lay, had, when filling the highest magistracies, taken internal administration as their department of public business, and left the military command to their colleagues. One of them had been entrusted with an army, and had failed ignominiously. None of them had been honoured with a triumph....

"His grandfather, called, like himself, Appius Claudius, had left a name as much detested as that of Sextus Tarquinius. This elder Appius had been consul more than seventy years before the introduction of the Licinian Laws. By availing himself of a singular crisis in public feeling, he had obtained the consent of the commons to the abolition of the tribuneship, and had been the chief of that Council of Ten to which the whole direction of the State had been committed. In a few months his administration had become universally odious. It had been swept away by an irresistible outbreak of popular fury; and its memory was still held in abhorrence by the whole city. The immediate cause of the downfall of this execrable government was said to have been an attempt made by Appius Claudius upon the chastity of a beautiful young girl of humble birth. The story ran that the Decemvir, unable to succeed by bribes and solicitations, resorted to an outrageous act of tyranny. A vile dependant of the Claudian house laid claim to the damsel as his slave. The cause was brought before the tribunal of Appius. The wicked magistrate, in defiance of the clearest proofs, gave judgment for the claimant. But the girl's father, a brave soldier, saved her from servitude and dishonour by stabbing her to the heart in the sight of the whole Forum. That blow was the signal for a general explosion. Camp and city rose at once; the Ten were pulled down; the tribuneship was re-established; and Appius escaped the hands of the executioner only by a voluntary death." (10)

Virginia was slain in 449 B.C., just in the midst of the long convulsion which began with the secession to the Mons Sacer, and ended with the Licinian Laws. During this century and a quarter, usury drained the Roman vitality low. Niebuhr was doubtless right in his conjecture that the mutinous legions were filled with *nexi* to whom the continuance of the existing status meant slavery, and Mommsen also pointed out that the convulsions of the third and fourth centuries, in which it seemed as though Roman society must disintegrate, were caused by "the insolvency of the middle class of land-holders." (11)

Had Italy been more tranquil, it is not inconceivable that the small farmers might even then have sank into the serfdom which awaited them under the Empire, for in peace the patricians might have been able to repress insurrection with their clients; but the accumulation of capital had hardly begun, and several centuries were to elapse before money was to take its ultimate form in a standing army. Meanwhile, troops were needed almost every year to defend the city; and, as the legions were a militia, they were the enemy and not the instrument of wealth. Until the organization of a permanent paid police they were, however, the highest expression of force, and, when opposed to them, the monied oligarchy was helpless, as was proved by the secession to the Mons Sacer. The storm gathered slowly. The rural population was ground down under the usury laws, and in 495 B.C. the farmers refused to respond to the levy. The consul Publius Servilius had to suspend prosecutions for debt and to liberate debtors in prison; but at the end of the campaign the promises he had made in the moment of danger were repudiated by Appius Claudius, who rigorously enforced the usury legislation, and who was, for the time, too strong to be opposed.

That year the men submitted, but the next the legions had again to be embodied; they again returned victorious; their demands were again rejected; and then, instead of disbanding, they marched in martial array into the district of Crustumeria, and occupied the hill which ever after was called the Sacred Mount. (12) Resistance was not even attempted; and precisely the same surrender was repeated in 449. When Virginius stabbed his daughter he fled to the camp, and his comrades seized the standards and marched for Rome. The Senate yielded at once, decreed the abolition of the Decemvirate, and the triumphant cohorts, drawn up upon the Aventine, chose their tribunes.

Finally, in the last great struggle, when Camillus was made dictator to coerce the people, he found himself impotent. The monied oligarchy collapsed when confronted with an armed force; and Camillus, reduced to act as mediator, vowed a temple to Concord, on the passage of the Licinian Laws.(13) The Licinian Laws provided for a partial liquidation, and also for an increase of the means of the debtor class by redistribution of the public land. This land had been seized in war, and had been monopolized by the patricians without any particular legal right. Licinius obtained a statute by which back payments of interest should be applied to extinguishing the principal of debts, and balances then remaining due should be liquidated in three annual instalments. He also limited the quantity of the public domain which could be held by any individual, and directed that the residue which remained after the reduction of all estates to that standard should be distributed in five-acre lots.

Pyrrhus saw with a soldier's eye that Rome's strength did not lie in her generals, who were frequently his inferiors, but in her farmers, whom he could not crush by defeat, and this was the class which was favoured by the Licinian Laws. They multiplied greatly when the usurers capitulated, and, as Macaulay remarked, the effect of the reform was "singularly happy and glorious." It was indeed no less than the conquest of Italy. Rome, "while the disabilities of the plebeians continued... was scarcely able to maintain her ground against the Volscians and Hernicans. When those disabilities were removed, she rapidly became more than a match for Carthage and Macedon." (14)

But nature's very bounty to the Roman husbandman and soldier proved his ruin. Patient of suffering, enduring of fatigue, wise in council, fierce in war, he routed all who opposed him; and yet the vigorous mind and the robust frame which made him victorious in battle, were his weakness when at peace. He needed costly nutriment, and when brought into free economic competition with Africans and Asiatics, he starved. Such competition resulted directly from foreign conquests, and came rapidly when Italy had consolidated, and the Italians began to extend their power over other races. Nearly five centuries intervened between the foundation of the city and the defeat of Pyrrhus, but within little more than two hundred years from the victory of Beneventum, Rome was mistress of the world.

Indeed, beyond the peninsula, there was not much, save Carthage, to stop the march of the legions. After the death of Alexander, in 323 B.C., Greece fell into decline, and by 200, when Rome attacked Macedon, she was in decrepitude. The population of Asia Minor, Syria, and Egypt was not martial, and had never been able to cope in battle with the western races; while Spain and Gaul, though inhabited by fierce and hardy tribes, lacked cohesion, and could not withstand the onset of organized and disciplined troops. Distance, therefore, rather than hostile military force, fixed the limit of the ancient centralization, for the Romans were not maritime, and consequently failed to absorb India or discover America. Thus their relatively imperfect movement made the most material difference between the ancient and modern economic system.

By conquest the countries inhabited by races of a low vitality and great tenacity of life were opened both for trade and slaving, and their cheap labour exterminated the husbandmen of Italy. Particularly after the annexation of Asia Minor this labour overran Sicily, and the cultivation of the cereals by the natives became impossible when the island had been parcelled out into great estates stocked by capitalists with eastern slaves who, at Rome, undersold all competitors. During the second century the precious metals poured into Latium in a flood, great fortunes were amassed and invested in land, and the Asiatic provinces of the Empire were swept of their men in order to make these investments pay. No data remain by which to estimate, even approximately, the size of this involuntary migration, but it must have reached enormous numbers, for sixty thousand captives were the common booty of a campaign, and after provinces were annexed they were depopulated by the publicans.

The best field hands came from the regions where poverty had always been extreme, and where, for countless generations, men had been inured to toil on scanty food. Districts like Bithynia and Syria, where slaves could be bought for little or nothing, had always been tilled by races far more tenacious of life than any Europeans. After Lucullus plundered Pontus, a slave brought only four drachmae, or, perhaps, seventy cents. (15) On the other hand, competition grew sharper among the Italians themselves. As capital accumulated in the hands of the strongest, the poor grew poorer, and pauperism spread. As early as the Marsian War, in 90 B.C., Lucius Marcius Philippus estimated that there were only two thousand wealthy families among the burgesses. In about three hundred years nature had culled a pure plutocracy from what had been originally an essentially martial race.

The primitive Roman was a high order of husbandman, who could only when well fed flourish and multiply. He was adapted to that stage of society when the remnants of caste gave a certain fixity of tenure to the farmer, and when prices were maintained by the cost of communication with foreign countries. As the world centralized, through conquest, these barriers were swept away. Economic competition became free, land tended to concentrate in fewer and fewer hands, and this land was worked by eastern slaves, who reduced the wages of labour to the lowest point at which the human being can survive.

The effect was to split society in halves, the basis being servile, and the freemen being separated into a series of classes, according to the economic power of the mind. Wealth formed the title to nobility of the great oligarchy which thus came to constitute the core of the Empire. At the head stood the senators, whose rank was hereditary unless they lost their property, for to be a senator a man had to be rich. Augustus fixed $48,000 as the minimum of the senatorial fortune, and made up the deficiency to certain favoured families,(16) but Tiberius summarily ejected spendthrifts.(17) All Latin literature is redolent of money. Tacitus, with an opulent connection, never failed to speak with disdain of the base-born, or, in other words, of the less prosperous. "Poppæus Sabinus, a man of humble birth," raised to position by the caprice of two emperors;(18) "Cassius Severus, a man of mean extraction"; (19) and, in the poetry of antiquity, there are few more famous lines than those in which Juvenal has described the burden of poverty:

> "Haud facile emergunt, quorum virtutibus obstat
> Res angusta domi."(20)

Perhaps no modern writer has been so imbued with the spirit of the later Empire as Fustel de Coulanges, and on this subject he has been emphatic. Not only were the Romans not democratic, but at no period of her history did Rome love equality. In the Republic rank was determined by wealth. The census was the basis of the social system. Every citizen had to declare his fortune before a magistrate, and his grade was then assigned him. "Poverty and wealth established the legal differences between men."

The first line of demarcation lay between those who owned land and those who did not. The former were *assidui:* householders rooted in the soil. The latter were *proletarians.* The *proletarians* were equal in their poverty; but the *assidui* were unequal in their wealth, and were consequently divided into five classes. Among these categories all was unequal—taxes, military service, and political rights. They did not mix together.

" If one transports oneself to the last century of the Republic... one finds there an aristocracy as strongly consolidated as the ancient patrician.... At the summit came the senatorial order. To belong to it the first condition was to possess a great fortune.... The Roman mind did not understand that a poor man could belong to the aristocracy, or that a rich man was not part of it." (21)

Archaic customs lingered late in Rome, for the city was not a centre of commercial exchanges; and long after the death of Alexander, when Greece passed its meridian, the Republic kept its copper coinage. Regulus fanned his field with a single slave and a hired servant, and there was, in truth, nothing extraordinary in the famous meeting with Cincinnatus at the plough, although such simplicity astonished a contemporary of Augustus. Advancing centralization swept away these ancient customs, a centralization whose march is, perhaps, as sharply marked by the migration of vagrants to the cities, as by any single phenomenon. Vagrant paupers formed the proletariat for whose relief the "Frumentariæ Leges" were framed; and yet, though poor-laws in some form are considered a necessity in modern times, few institutions of antiquity have been more severely criticised than those regulating charity. From the time of Cato downward, the tendency has been to maintain that at Rome demagogues fed the rabble at the cost of the lives of the free-holders.

Probably the exact converse is the truth; the public gifts of food appear to have been the effect of the ruin of agriculture, and not its cause. After the Italian husbandmen had been made insolvent by the competition of races of lower vitality, they flocked starving to the capital, but it was only reluctantly that the great speculators in grain, who controlled the Senate, admitted the necessity of granting State aid to the class whom they had destroyed.

Long before the Punic Wars the Carthaginians had farmed Sicily on capitalistic principles; that is to say, they had stocked domains with slaves, and had traded on the basis of large sales and narrow profits. The Romans when they annexed the island only carried out this system to its logical end. Having all Asia Minor to draw upon for labour, they deliberately starved and overworked their field-hands, since it was cheaper to buy others than to lose command of the market. The familiar story of the outbreak of the Servile War, about 134 B.C., shows how far the contemporaries of the Sicilian speculators believed them capable of going.

Damophilus, an opulent Sicilian landlord, being one day implored by his slaves to have pity on their nakedness and misery, indignantly demanded why they went hungry and cold, with arms in their hands, and the country before them. Then he bound them to stakes and flayed them with the lash. (22)

The reduction of Syracuse by Marcellus broke the Carthaginian power in the island, and, after the fall of Agrigentum in 210 B.C., the pacification of the country went on rapidly. Probably from the outset, even in the matter of transportation, the provinces of the mainland were at a disadvantage because of the cheapness of sea freights, but at all events the opening of the Sicilian grain trade had an immediate and disastrous effect on Italy. The migration of vagrants to Rome began forthwith, and within seven years, 203B.C., a public distribution of wheat took place, probably by the advice of Scipio. Nevertheless the charity was private and not gratuitous. On the contrary, a charge of four sesterces, or seventeen cents the bushel, was made, apparently near half the market rate, a price pretty regularly maintained on such occasions down to the Empire. This interval comprehended the whole period of the Sicilian supremacy in the corn trade, for in 30 B.C. Egypt was annexed by Augustus.

The distress which followed upon free trade with Egypt finally broke down the resistance of the rich to gratuitous relief for the poor. Previously the opposition to State aid had been so stubborn that until 123B.C. no legal provision whatever was made for paupers; and yet the account left by Polybius of the condition of Lombardy toward the middle of the second century shows the complete wreck of agriculture.

"The yield of corn in this district is so abundant that wheat is often sold at four obols a Sicilian medimnus [about seven cents and a quarter, or a little less than two sesterces], barley at two, or a metretes of wine for an equal measure of barley.... The cheapness and abundance of all articles of food may also be clearly shown from the fact that travellers in these parts, when stopping at inns, do not bargain for particular articles, but simply ask what the charge is per head for board. And for the most part the innkeepers are content" with half an as (about half a cent) a day. (23)

These prices indicate a lack of demand so complete, that the debtors among the peasantry must have been ruined, and yet tax-payers remained obdurate. Gratuitous distributions were tried in 58 B.C. by the Lex Clodia, but soon abandoned as costly, and Cæsar applied himself to reducing the outlay on the needy. He hoped to reach his end by cutting down the number of grain-receivers one-half, by providing that no grain should be given away except on presentation of a ticket, and by ordering that the number of ticket-holders should not be increased. The law of nature prevailed against him, for the absorption of Egypt in the economic system of the Empire, marked, in the words of Mommsen "the end of the old and the beginning of a new epoch." (24)

Among the races which have survived through ages upon scanty nutriment, none have, perhaps, excelled the Egyptian fellah. Even in the East no peasantry has probably been so continuously over-worked, so under-paid, and so taxed.

> "If it is the aim of the State to work out the utmost possible amount from its territory, in the Old World the Lagids were absolutely the masters of statecraft. In particular they were in this sphere the instructors and the models of the Cæsars."(25)

In the first century Egypt was, as it still is, pre-eminently a land of cheap labour; but it was also something more. The valley of the Nile, enriched by the overflow of the river, returned an hundred-fold, without manure; and this wonderful district was administered, not like an ordinary province, but like a private farm belonging to the citizens of Rome. The emperor reserved it to himself. How large a revenue he drew from it is immaterial; it suffices that one-third of all the grain consumed in the capital came from thence. According to Athenæus, some of the grain ships in use were about 420 feet long by 57 broad, or nearly the size of a modern steamer in the Atlantic trade.(26) From the beginning of the Christian era, therefore, the wages of the Egyptian fellah regulated the price of the cereals within the limits where trade was made free by Roman consolidation, and it is safe to say that, thenceforward, such of the highly nourished races as were constrained to sustain this competition, were doomed to perish. It is even extremely doubtful whether the distributions of grain by the government materially accelerated the march of the decay. Spain should have been far enough removed from the centre of exchanges to have had a certain local market of her own, and yet Martial, writing about 100 A.D., described the Spanish husbandman eating and drinking the produce he could not sell, and receiving but four sesterces the bushel for his wheat, which was the price paid by paupers in the time of Cicero. (27)

Thus by economic necessity great estates were formed in the hands of the economically strong. As the value of cereals fell, arable land passed into vineyards or pasture, and, the provinces being unable to sustain their old population, eviction went on with gigantic strides. Had the Romans possessed the versatility to enable them to turn to industry, factories might have afforded a temporary shelter to this surplus labour, but manufactures were monopolized by the East; therefore the beggared peasantry were either enslaved for debt, or wandered as penniless paupers to the cities, where gradually their numbers so increased as to enable them to extort a gratuitous dole. Indeed, during the third century, their condition fell so low that they were unable even to cook the food freely given them, and Aurelian had their bread baked at public ovens.(28)

As centralization advanced with the acceleration of human movement, force expressed itself more and more exclusively through money, and the channel in which money chose to flow was in investments in land. The social system fostered the growth of large estates. The Romans always had an inordinate respect for the landed magnate, and a contempt for the tradesman. Industry was reputed a servile occupation, and, under the Republic, the citizen who performed manual labour was almost deprived of political rights. Even commerce was thought so unworthy of the aristocracy that it was forbidden to senators. "The soil was always, in this Roman society, the principal source and, above all, the only measure of wealth."

A law of Tiberius obliged capitalists to invest two-thirds of their property in land. Trajan not only exacted of aspirants to office that they should be rich, but that they should place at least one-third of their fortune in Italian real estate; and, down to the end of the Empire, the senatorial class "was at the same time the class of great landed proprietors." (29)

The more property consolidated, the more resistless the momentum of capital became. Under the Empire small properties grew steadily rarer, and the fewer they were, the greater the disadvantage at which their owners stood. The small farmer could hardly sustain himself in competition with the great landlord. The grand domain of the capitalist was not only provided with a full complement of labourers, vine-dressers, and shepherds, but with the necessary artisans. The poor farmer depended on his rich neighbour even for his tools. "He was what a workman would be to-day who, amidst great factories, worked alone." (30) He bought dearer and sold cheaper, his margin of profit steadily shrunk; at last he was reduced to a bare subsistence in good years, and the first bad harvest left him bankrupt.

The Roman husbandman and soldier was doomed, for nature had turned against him; the task of history is but to ascertain his fate, and trace the fortunes of his country after he had gone.

Of the evicted, many certainly drifted to the cities and lived upon charity, forming the proletariat, a class alike despised and lost to self-respect: some were sold into slavery, others starved; but when all deductions have been made, a surplus is left to be accounted for, and there is reason to suppose that these stayed on their farms as tenants to the purchasers.

In the first century such tenancies were common. The lessee remained a freeman, under no subjection to his landlord, provided he paid his rent; but in case of default the law was rigorous. Everything upon the land was liable as a pledge, and the tenant himself was held in pawn unless he could give security for what he owed. In case, therefore, of prolonged agricultural depression, all that was left of the ancient rural population could hardly fail to pass into the condition of serfs, bound to the land by debts beyond the possibility of payment.

That such a depression actually occurred, and that it extended through several centuries, is certain. Nor is it possible that its only cause was Egyptian competition, for had it been so, an equilibrium would have been reached when the African exchanges had been adjusted, whereas a continuous decline of prices went on until long after the fall of the Western Empire. The only other possible explanation of the phenomenon is that a contraction of the currency began soon after the death of Augustus, and continued without much interruption down to Charlemagne. Between the fall of Carthage and the birth of Christ, the Romans plundered the richest portions of the world west of the Indus; in the second century, North Africa, Macedon, Spain, and parts of Greece and Asia Minor; in the first, Athens, Cappadocia, Syria, Gaul, and Egypt. These countries yielded an enormous mass of treasure, which was brought to Rome as spoil of war, but which was not fixed there by commercial exchanges, and which continually tended to flow back to the natural centres of trade. Therefore, when conquests ceased, the sources of new bullion dried up, and the quantity held in Italy diminished as the balance of trade grew more and more unfavourable.

Under Augustus the precious metals were plenty and cheap, and the prices of commodities were correspondingly high; but a full generation had hardly passed before a dearth began to be felt, which manifested itself in a debasement of the coinage, the surest sign of an appreciation of the currency.

Speaking generally, the manufactures and the more costly products of antiquity came from countries to the east of the Adriatic, while the West was mainly agricultural; and nothing is better established than that luxuries were dear under the Empire, and food cheap.(31) Therefore exchanges were unfavourable to the capital from the outset; the exports did not cover the imports, and each year a deficit had to be made good in specie.

The Romans perfectly understood the situation, and this adverse balance caused them much uneasiness. Tiberius dwelt upon it in a letter to the Senate as early as 22 A.D. In that year the ædiles brought forward proposals for certain sumptuary reforms, and the Senate, probably to rid itself of a delicate question, referred the matter to the executive. Most of the emperor's reply is interesting, but there is one particularly noteworthy paragraph. "If a reform is in truth intended, where must it begin? and how am I to restore the simplicity of ancient times?... How shall we reform the taste for dress?... How are we to deal with the peculiar articles of female vanity, and, in particular, with that rage for jewels and precious trinkets, which drains the Empire of its wealth, and sends, in exchange for bawbles, the money of the Commonwealth to foreign nations, and even to the enemies of Rome?" (32) Half a century later matters were, apparently, worse, for Pliny more than once returned to the subject. In the twelfth book of his Natural History, after enumerating the many well-known spices, perfumes, drugs, and gems, which have always made the Eastern trade of such surpassing value, he estimated that at the most moderate computation 100,000,000 sesterces, or about $4,000,000 in coin, were annually exported to Arabia and India alone; and at a time when silk was worth its weight in gold, the estimate certainly does not seem excessive. He added, "So dear do pleasures and women cost us."(33)

The drain to Egypt and the Asiatic provinces could hardly have been much less serious. Adrian almost seems to have been jealous of the former, for in his letter to Servianus, after having criticised the people, he remarked that it was also a rich and productive country "in which no one was idle," and in which glass, paper and linen were manufactured.(34) The Syrians were both industrial and commercial. Tyre, for example, worked the raw silk of China, dyed and exported it. The glass of Tyre and Sidon was famous; the local aristocracy were merchants and manufacturers, "and, as later the riches acquired in the

East flowed to Genoa and Venice, so then the commercial gains of the West flowed back to Tyre and Apamea." (35)

Within about sixty years from the final consolidation of the Empire under Augustus, this continuous efflux of the precious metals began to cause the currency to contract, and prices to fall; and the first effect of shrinking values appears to have been a financial crisis in 33 A.D. Probably the diminution in the worth of commodities relatively to money, had already made it difficult for debtors to meet their liabilities, for Tacitus has prefaced his story by pointing out that usury had always been a scourge of Rome, and that just previous to the panic an agitation against the money-lenders had begun with a view to enforcing the law regarding interest. As most of the senators were deep in usury they applied for protection to Tiberius, who granted what amounted to a stay of proceedings, and then, as soon as the capitalists felt themselves safe, they proceeded to take their revenge. Loans were called, accommodation refused, and mortgagors were ruthlessly sold out. "There was great scarcity of money... and, on account of sales on execution, coin accumulated in the imperial, or the public treasury. Upon this the Senate ordered that every one should invest two-thirds of his capital on loan, in Italian real estate; but the creditors called in the whole, nor did public opinion allow debtors to compromise." Meanwhile there was great excitement but no relief, "as the usurers hoarded for the purpose of buying low. The quantity of sales broke the market, and the more liabilities were extended, the harder liquidation became. Many were ruined, and the loss of property endangered social station and reputation." (36) The panic finally subsided, but contraction went on and next showed itself, twenty-five years later, in adulterated coinage. From the time of the Punic Wars, about two centuries and a half before Christ, the silver denarius, worth nearly seventeen cents, had been the standard of the Roman currency, and it kept its weight and purity unimpaired until Nero, when it diminished from 1/84 to 1/96 of a pound of silver, the pure metal being mixed with 1/10 of copper. (37) Under Trajan, toward 100 A.D., the alloy reached twenty per cent; under Septimius Severus a hundred years later it had mounted to fifty or sixty per cent, and by the time of Elagabalus, 220 A.D., the coin had degenerated into a token of base metal, and was repudiated by the government.

Something similar happened to the gold. The aureus, though it kept its fineness, lost in weight down to Constantine. In the reign of Augustus it equalled one-fortieth of a Roman pound of gold, in that of Nero one forty-fifth, in that of Caracalla but one-fiftieth, in that of Diocletian one-sixtieth, and in that of Constantine one seventy-second, when the coin ceased passing by tale and was taken only by weight.(38)

The repudiation of the denarius was an act of bankruptcy; nor did the financial position improve while the administration remained at Rome. Therefore the inference is that, toward the middle of the third century, Italy had lost the treasure she had won in war, which had gradually gravitated to the centre of exchanges. This inference is confirmed by history. The movements of Diocletian seem to demonstrate that after 250A.D. Rome ceased to be either the political or commercial capital of the world.

Unquestionably Diocletian must have lived a life of intense activity at the focus of affairs, to have raised himself from slavery to the purple at thirty-nine; and yet Gibbon thought he did not even visit Rome until he went thither to celebrate his triumph, after he had been twenty years upon the throne. He never seemed anxious about the temper of the city. When proclaimed emperor he ignored Italy and established himself at Nicomedia on the Propontis, where he lived until he abdicated in 305. His personal preferences evidently did not influence him, since his successors imitated his policy; and everything points to the conclusion that he, and those who followed him, only yielded to the same resistless force which fixed the economic capital of the world upon the Bosphorus. In the case of Constantine the operation of this force was conspicuous, for it was not only powerful enough to overcome the habit of a lifetime, but to cause him to undertake the gigantic task of building Constantinople.

Constantine was proclaimed in Britain in 306, when only thirty-two. Six years later he defeated Maxentius, and then governed the West alone until his war with Licinius, whom he captured in 323 and afterward put to death. Thus, at fifty, he returned to the East, after an absence of nearly twenty years, and his first act was to choose Byzantium as his capital, a city nearly opposite Nicomedia.

The sequence of events seems plain. Very soon after the insolvency of the government at Rome, the administration quitted the city and moved toward the boundary between Europe and Asia; there, after some forty years of vacillation, it settled permanently at the true seat of exchanges, for Constantinople remained the economic centre of the earth for more than eight centuries.

Similar conclusions may be drawn from the fluctuations of the currency. At Rome the coin could not be maintained at the standard, because of adverse exchanges; but when the political and economic centres had come to coincide, at a point upon the Bosphorus, depreciation ceased, and the aureus fell no further.

This migration of capital, which caused the rise of Constantinople, was the true opening of the Middle Ages, for it occasioned the gradual decline of the rural population, and thus brought about the disintegration of the West. Victory carried wealth to Rome, and wealth manifested its power in a permanent police; as the attack in war gained upon the defence, and individual resistance became impossible, transportation grew cheap and safe, and human movement was accelerated. Then economic competition began, and intensified as centralization advanced, telling always in favour of the acutest intellect and the cheapest labour. Soon, exchanges became permanently unfavourable, a steady drain of bullion set in to the East, and, as the outflow depleted the treasure amassed at Rome by plunder, contraction began, and with contraction came that fall of prices which first ruined, then enslaved, and finally exterminated, the native rural population of Italy.

In the time of Diocletian, the ancient silver currency had long been repudiated, and, in his well-known edict, he spoke of prices as having risen nine-fold, when reckoned in the denarii of base metal; the purchasing power of pure gold and silver had, however, risen very considerably in all the western provinces. Nor was this all. It appears to be a natural law that when social development has reached a certain stage, and capital has accumulated sufficiently, the class which has had the capacity to absorb it shall try to enhance the value of their property by legislation. This is done most easily by reducing the quantity of the currency, which is a legal tender for the payment of debts. A currency obviously gains in power as it shrinks in volume, and the usurers of Constantinople intuitively condensed to the utmost that of the Empire. After the insolvency under Elagabalus, payments were exacted in gold by weight, and as it grew scarcer its value rose. Aurelian issued an edict limiting its use in the arts; and while there are abundant reasons for inferring that silver also gained in purchasing power, gold far outstripped it. Although no statistics remain by which to establish, with any exactness, the movement of silver in comparison with commodities, the ratio between the precious metals at different epochs is known, and gold appears to have doubled between Caesar and Romulus Augustulus.

47 B.C.	_gold stood to silver as 1: 8.9
1 A.D under Augustus,	" " " 1: 9.3
100-200, Trajan to Severus,	" " " 1: 9-10
310, Constantine,	" " " 1:12.5
450, Theodosius II.,	" " " 1:18

As gold had become the sole legal tender, this change of ratio represents a diminution, during the existence of the Western Empire, of at least fifty percent in the value of property in relation to debt, leaving altogether out of view the appreciation of silver itself, which was so considerable that the government was unable to maintain the denarius.(39)

Resistance to the force of centralized wealth was vain. Aurelian's attempt to reform the mints is said to have caused a rebellion, which cost him the lives of seven thousand of his soldiers; and though his policy was continued by Probus, and Diocletian coined both metals again at a ratio, expansion was so antagonistic to the interests of the monied class that, by 360, silver was definitely discarded, and gold was made by law the only legal tender for the payment of debts.(40) Furthermore, the usurers protected themselves against any possible tampering with the mints by providing that the solidus should pass by weight and not by tale; that is to say, they reserved to themselves the right to reject any golden sou which contained less than one seventy-second of a pound of standard metal, the weight fixed by Constantine.(41)

Thus, at a time when the exhaustion of the mines caused a failure in the annual supply of bullion, the old composite currency was split in two, and the half retained made to pass by weight alone, so as to throw the loss by clipping and abrasion upon the debtor. So strong a contraction engendered a steady fall of prices, a fall which tended rather to increase than diminish as time went on. But in prolonged periods of decline in the market value of agricultural products, farmers can with difficulty meet a money rent, because the sale of their crops leaves a greater deficit each year, and finally a time comes when insolvency can no longer be postponed.

In his opening chapter Gibbon described the Empire under the Antonines as enjoying "a happy period of more than fourscore years" of peace and prosperity; and yet nothing is more certain than that this halcyon age was in reality an interval of agricultural ruin. On this point Pliny was explicit, and Pliny was a large land-owner.

He wrote one day to Calvisius about an investment, and went at length into the condition of the property. A large estate adjoining his own was for sale, and he was tempted to buy, "for the land was fertile, rich, and well watered," the fields produced vines and wood which promised a fair return, and yet this natural fruitfulness was marred by the misery of the husbandmen. He found that the former owner "had often seized the 'pignora,' or pledges [that is, all the property the tenants possessed]; and though, by so doing, he had temporarily reduced their arrears, he had left them "without the means of tilling the soil. These tenants were freemen, who had been unable to meet their rent because of falling prices, and who, when they had lost their tools, cattle, and household effects, were left paupers on the farms they could neither cultivate nor abandon. Consequently the property had suffered, the rent had declined, and for these reasons and "the general hardness of the times," its value had fallen from five million to three million sesterces.(42)

In another letter he explained that he was detained at home making new arrangements with his tenants, who were apparently insolvent, for "in the last five years, in spite of great concessions, the arrears have increased. For this reason most [tenants] take no trouble to diminish their debt, which they despair of paying. Indeed, they plunder and consume what there is upon the land, since they think they cannot save for themselves." The remedy he proposed was to make no more money leases, but to farm on shares.(43)

The tone of these letters shows that there was nothing unusual in all this. Pliny nowhere intimated that the tenants were to blame, or that better men were to be had. On the contrary, he said emphatically that in such hard times money could not be collected, and therefore the interest of the landlord was to cultivate his estates on shares, taking the single precaution to place slaves over the tenants as overseers and receivers of the crops.

In the same way the digest referred to such arrears as habitual.(44) In still another letter to Trajan, Pliny observed, "Continuae sterilitates cogunt me de remissionibus cogitare."(45) Certainly these insolvent farmers could have held no better position when working on shares than before their disasters, for as bankrupts they were wholly in their creditors' power, and could be hunted like slaves, and brought back in fetters if they fled. They were tied to the property by a debt which never could be paid, and they and their descendants were doomed to stay for ever as *coloni* or serfs, chattels to be devised or sold as part of the realty. In the words of the law, "they were considered slaves of the land."(46) The ancient martial husbandman had thus "fallen from point to point, from debt to debt, into an almost perpetual subjection." (47) Deliverance was impossible, for payment was out of the question. He was bound to the soil for his life, and his children after him inherited his servitude with his debt.

The customs, according to which the *coloni* held, were infinitely varied; they differed not only between estates, but between the hands on the same estate. On the whole, however, the life must have been hard, for the serfs of the Empire did not multiply, and the scarcity of rural labour became a chronic disease. Yet, relatively, the position of the *colonus* was good, for his wife and children were his own; slavery was the ulcer which ate into the flesh, and the Roman fiscal system, coupled as it was with usury, was calculated to enslave all but the oligarchy who made the laws.

The taxes of the provinces were assessed by the censors and then sold for cash to the publicans who undertook the collection. Italy was at first exempted, but after her bankruptcy she shared the common fate. Companies were formed to handle these ventures. The knights usually subscribed the capital and divided the profits, which corresponded with the severity of their administration; and, as the Roman conquests extended, these companies grew too powerful to be controlled. The only officials in a position to act were the provincial governors, who were afraid to interfere, and preferred to share in the gains of the traffic, rather than to run the risk of exciting the wrath of so dangerous an enemy.(48)

According to Pliny the collection of a rent in money had become impossible in the reign of Trajan. The reason was that with a contracting currency prices of produce fell, and each year's crop netted less than that of the year before; therefore a rent moderate in one decade was extortionate in the next. But taxes did not fall with the fall in values; on the contrary, the tendency of centralization is always toward a more costly administration. Under Augustus, one emperor with a moderate household sufficed; but in the third century Diocletian found it necessary to reorganize the government under four Cæsars, and everything became specialized in the same proportion.

In this way the people were caught between the upper and the nether millstone. The actual quantity of bullion taken from them was greater, the lower prices of their property fell, and arrears of taxes accumulated precisely as Pliny described the accumulation of arrears of rent. These arrears were carried over from reign to reign, and even from century to century; and Petronius, the father-in-law of Valens, is said to have precipitated the rebellion of Procopius, by exacting the tribute unpaid since the death of Aurelian a hundred years before.

The processes employed in the collection of the revenue were severe. Torture was freely used,(49) and slavery was the fate of defaulters. Armed with such power, the publicans held debtors at their mercy. Though usury was forbidden, the most lucrative part of the trade was opening accounts with the treasury, assuming debts, and charging interest sometimes as high as fifty per cent. Though, as prices fell, the pressure grew severer, the abuses of the administration were never perhaps worse than toward the end of the Republic. In his oration against Verres, Cicero said the condition of the people had become intolerable: "All the provinces are in mourning, all the nations that are free are complaining; every kingdom is expostulating with us about our covetousness and injustice." (50)

The well-known transactions of Brutus are typical of what went on wherever the Romans marched. Brutus lent the Senate of Salaminia at forty-eight per cent a year. As the contract was illegal, he obtained two decrees of the Senate at Rome for his protection, and then to enforce payment of his interest, Scaptius, his man of business, borrowed from the governor of Cilicia a detachment of troops. With this he blockaded the Senate so closely that several members starved to death. The Salaminians, wanting at all costs to free themselves from such a load, offered to pay off both interest and capital at once; but to this Brutus would not consent, and to impose his own terms upon the province he demanded from Cicero more troops, "only fifty horse." (51)

When at last, by such proceedings, the debtors were so exhausted that no torment could wring more from them, they were sold as slaves; Nicodemus, king of Bithynia, on being reproached for not furnishing his contingent of auxiliaries, replied that all his able-bodied subjects had been taken by the farmers of the revenue.(52) Nor, though the administration doubtless was better regulated under the Empire than under the Republic, did the oppression of the provinces cease. Juvenal, who wrote about 100, implored the young noble taking possession of his government to put some curb upon his avarice, "to pity the poverty of the allies. You see the bones of kings sucked of their very marrow."(53) And though the testimony of Juvenal may be rejected as savouring too much of poetical licence, Pliny must always be treated with respect. When Maximus was sent to Achaia, Pliny thought it well to write him a long letter of advice, in which he not only declared that to wrest from the Greeks the shadow of liberty left them would be "durum, ferum, barbarumque;" but adjured him to try to remember what each city had been, and not to despise it for what it was. (54)

Most impressive, perhaps, of all, is the statement of Dio Cassius that the revolt led by Boadicea in Britain in 61 A.D., which cost the Romans seventy thousand lives, was provoked by the rapacity of Seneca, who, having forced a loan of ten million drachmas ($1,670,000) on the people at usurious interest, suddenly withdrew his money, thereby inflicting intense suffering.(55) As Pliny said with bitterness and truth, "The arts of avarice were those most cultivated at Rome."(56)

The stronger type exterminated the weaker; the money-lender killed out the husbandman; the race of soldiers vanished, and the farms, whereon they had once flourished, were left desolate. To quote the words of Gibbon: "The fertile and happy province of Campania... extended between the sea and the Apennines from the Tiber to the Silanis. Within sixty years after the death of Constantine, and on the evidence of an actual survey, an exemption was granted in favour of three hundred and thirty thousand English acres of desert and uncultivated land; which amounted to one-eighth of the whole surface of the province." (57)

It is true that Gibbon, in this paragraph, described Italy as she was in the fourth century, just before the barbarian invasions, but a similar fate had overtaken the provinces under the Caesars. In the reign of Domitian, according to Plutarch, Greece had been almost depopulated.

> "She can with much difficulty raise three thousand men, which number the single city of Megara sent heretofore to the battle of Platæa.... For of what use would the oracle be now, which was heretofore at Tegyra or at Ptous? For scarcely shall you meet, in a whole day's time, with so much as a herdsman or shepherd in those parts." (58)

Wallon has observed that Rome, "in the early times of th Republic, was chiefly preoccupied with having a numero and strong population of freemen. Under the Empire she had but one anxiety—taxes."(59)

To speak with more precision, force changed the channel through which it operated. Native farmers and native soldiers were needless when such material could be bought cheaper in the North or East. With money the cohorts could be filled with Germans; with money, slaves and serfs could be settled upon the Italian fields; and for the last century, before the great inroads began, one chief problem of the imperial administration was the regulation of the inflow of new blood from without, lacking which the social system must have collapsed.

The later campaigns on the Rhine and the Danube were really slave-hunts on a gigantic scale. Probus brought back sixteen thousand men from Germany, "the bravest and most robust of their youth," and distributed them in knots of fifty or sixty among the legions. "Their aid was now become necessary.... The infrequency of marriage, and the ruin of agriculture, affected the principles of population; and not only destroyed the strength of the present, but intercepted the hope of future generations." (60)

His importations of agricultural labour were much more considerable. In a single settlement in Thrace, Probus established one hundred thousand Bastarnæ; Constantius Chlorus is said to have made Gaul flourish by the herds of slaves he distributed among the landlords; in 370, large numbers of Alemanni were planted in the valley of the Po, and on the vast spaces of the public domain there were barbarian villages where the native language and customs were preserved.

Probably none of these Germans came as freemen. Many, of course, were captives sold as slaves, but perhaps the majority were serfs. Frequently a tribe, hard pressed by enemies, asked leave to pass the frontier, and settle as tributaries, that is to say as *coloni*. On one such occasion Constantius II. was nearly murdered. A body of Limigantes, who had made a raid, surrendered, and petitioned to be given lands at any distance, provided they might have protection. The emperor was delighted at the prospect of such a harvest of labourers, to say nothing of recruits, and went among them to receive their submission. Seeing him alone, the barbarians attacked him. and he escaped with difficulty. His troops slaughtered the Germans to the last man.

This unceasing emigration gradually changed the character of the rural population, and a similar alteration took place in the army. As early as the time of Cæsar, Italy was exhausted; his legions were mainly raised in Gaul, and as the native farmers sank into serfdom or slavery, and then at last vanished, recruits were drawn more and more from beyond the limits of the Empire. At first they were taken singly, afterwards in tribes and nations, so that, when Aëtius defeated Attila at Chalons, the battle was fought by the Visigoths under Theodoric, and the equipment of the Romans and Huns was so similar that when drawn up the lines "presented the image of civil war."

This military metamorphosis indicated the extinction of the martial type, and it extended throughout society. Rome not only failed to breed the common soldier, she also failed to produce generals. After the first century, the change was marked. Trajan was a Spaniard, Septimius Severus an African, Aurelian an Illyrian peasant, Diocletian a Dalmatian slave, Constantius Chlorus a Dardanian noble, and the son of Constantius, by a Dacian woman, was the great Constantine.

All these men were a peculiar species of military adventurer, for they combined qualities which made them, not only effective chiefs of police, but acceptable as heads of the civil bureaucracy, which represented capital. Severus was the type, and Severus has never been better described than by Machiavelli, who said he united the ferocity of the lion to the cunning of the fox. This bureaucracy was the core of the consolidated mass called the Empire; it was the embodiment of money, the ultimate expression of force, and it recognized and advanced men who were adapted to its needs. When such men were to be found, the administration was thought good; but when no one precisely adapted for the purple appeared, and an ordinary officer had to be hired to keep the peace, friction was apt to follow, and the soldier, even though of the highest ability, was often removed. Both Stilicho and Aëtius were murdered.

The monied oligarchy which formed this bureaucracy was a growth as characteristic of the high centralization of the age, as a sacred caste is characteristic of decentralization. Perhaps the capitalistic class of the later Empire has been better understood and appreciated by Fustel de Coulanges than by any other historian.

> "All the documents which show the spirit of the epoch show that this noblesse was as much honoured by the government as respected by the people.... It was from it that the imperial government chose ordinarily its high functionaries."

These functionaries were not sought among the lower classes. The high offices were not given as a reward of long and faithful service; they belonged by prescriptive right to the great families. The Empire made the wealthy, senators, prætors, consuls, and governors; all dignities, except only the military, were practically hereditary in the opulent class.

> "This class is rich and the government is poor. This class is mistress of the larger part of the soil; it is in possession of the local dignities, of the administrative and judicial functions. The government has only the appearance of

power, and an armed force which is continually diminishing....

> "The aristocracy had the land, the wealth, the distinction, the education, ordinarily the morality of existence; it did not know how to fight and to command. It withdrew itself from military service; more than that, it despised it. It was one of the

characteristic signs of this society to have always placed the civil functions not on a level with, but much above, the grades of the army. It esteemed much the profession of the doctor, of the professor, of the advocate; it did not esteem that of the officer and the soldier, and left it to men of low estate."(61)

This supremacy of the economic instinct transformed all the relations of life, the domestic as well as the military. The family ceased to be a unit, the members of which cohered from the necessity of self-defence, and became a business association. Marriage took the form of a contract, dissoluble at the will of either party, and, as it was somewhat costly, it grew rare. As with the drain of their bullion to the East, which crushed their farmers, the Romans were conscious, as Augustus said, that sterility must finally deliver their city into the hand of the barbarians.(62) They knew this and they strove to avert their fate, and there is little in history more impressive than the impotence of the ancient civilization in its conflict with nature. About the opening of the Christian era the State addressed itself to the task. Probably in the year 4 A.D., the emperor succeeded in obtaining the first legislation favouring marriage, and this enactment not proving effective, it was supplemented by the famous Leges Julia and Papia Poppæa of the year 9. In the spring, at the games, the knights demanded the repeal of these laws, and then Augustus, having called them to the Forum, made them the well-known speech, whose violence now seems incredible. Those who were single were the worst of criminals, they were murderers, they were impious, they were destroyers of their race, they resembled brigands or wild beasts. He asked the *equites* if they expected men to start from the ground to replace them, as in the fable; and declared in bitterness that while the government liberated slaves for the sole purpose of keeping up the number of citizens, the children of the Marcii, of the Fabii, of the Valerii, and the Julii, let their names perish from the earth.(63)

In vain celibacy was made almost criminal. In vain celibates were declared incapable of inheriting, while fathers were offered every bribe, were preferred in appointments to office, were even given the choice seats at games; in the words of Tacitus, "not for that did marriage and children increase, for the advantages of childlessness prevailed."(64) All that was done was to breed a race of informers, and to stimulate the lawyers to fresh chicane.(65)

When wealth became force, the female might be as strong as the male; therefore she was emancipated. Through easy divorce she came to stand on an equality with the man in the marriage contract. She controlled her own property because she could defend it; and as she had power, she exercised political privileges. In the third century Julia Domna, Julia Mamæa, Soæmias and others, sat in the Senate, or conducted the administration.

The evolution of this centralized society was as logical as every other work of nature. When force reached the stage where it expressed itself exclusively through money, the governing class ceased to be chosen because they were valiant or eloquent, artistic, learned, or devout, and were selected solely because they had the faculty of acquiring and keeping wealth. As long as the weak retained enough vitality to produce something which could be absorbed, this oligarchy was invincible; and for very many years after the native peasantry of Gaul and Italy had perished under the load, new blood injected from more tenacious races kept the dying civilization alive.

The weakness of the monied class lay in their very power, for they not only killed the producer, but in the strength of their acquisitiveness they failed to propagate themselves. The State feigned to regard marriage as a debt, and yet the opulent families died out. In the reign of Augustus all but fifty of the patrician houses had become extinct, and subsequently the emperor seemed destined to remain the universal heir through bequests of the childless.

With the peasantry the case was worse. By the second century barbarian labour had to be imported to till the fields, and even the barbarians lacked the tenacity of life necessary to endure the strain. They ceased to breed, and the population dwindled. Then, somewhat suddenly, the collapse came. With shrinking numbers, the sources of wealth ran dry, the revenue failed to pay the police, and on the efficiency of the police the life of this unwarlike civilization hung.

In early ages every Roman had been a land-owner, and every land-owner had been a soldier, serving without pay. To fight had been as essential a part of life as to plough. But by the fourth century military service had become commercial; the legions were as purely an expression of money as the bureaucracy itself.

From the time of the Servian constitution downward, the change in the army had kept pace with the acceleration of movement which caused the economic competition that centralized the State. Rome owed her triumphs over Hannibal and Pyrrhus to the valour of her infantry, rather than to the genius of her generals; but from Marius the census ceased to be the basis of recruitment, and the rich refused to serve in the ranks.

This was equivalent in itself to a social revolution; for, from the moment when the wealthy succeeded in withdrawing themselves from service, and the poor saw in it a trade, the citizen ceased to be a soldier, and the soldier became a mercenary. From that time the army could be used for "all purposes, provided that they could count on their pay and their booty."(66)

The administration of Augustus organized the permanent police, which replaced the mercenaries of the civil wars, and this machine was the greatest triumph and the crowning glory of capital. Dio Cassius has described how the last vestige of an Italian army passed away. Up to the time of Severus it had been customary to recruit the Prætorians either from Italy itself, from Spain, Macedonia, or other neighbouring countries, whose population had some affinity with that of Latium. Severus, after the treachery of the guard to Pertinax, disbanded it, and reorganized a corps selected from the bravest soldiers of the legions. These men were a horde of barbarians, repulsive to Italians in their habits, and terrible to look upon.(67) Thus a body of wage-earners, drawn from the ends of the earth, was made cohesive by money. For more than four hundred years this corps of hirelings crushed revolt within the Empire, and regulated the injection of fresh blood from without, with perfect promptitude and precision; nor did it fail in its functions while the money which vitalized it lasted.

But a time came when the suction of the usurers so wasted the life of the community that the stream of bullion ceased to flow from the capital to the frontiers; then, as the sustaining force failed, the line of troops along the Danube and the Rhine was drawn out until it broke, and the barbarians poured in unchecked.

The so-called invasions were not conquests, for they were not necessarily hostile; they were only the logical conclusion of a process which had been going on since Trajan. When the power to control the German emigration decayed, it flowed freely into the provinces.

By the year 400 disintegration was far advanced; the Empire was crumbling, not because it was corrupt or degenerate, but because the most martial and energetic race the world had ever seen had been so thoroughly exterminated by men of the economic type of mind, that petty bands of sorry adventurers might rove whither they would, on what had once been Roman soil, without meeting an enemy capable of facing them, save other adventurers like themselves. Goths, not Romans, defeated Attila at Châlons.

The Vandals, who, in the course of twenty years, wandered from the Elbe to the Atlas, were not a nation, not an army, not even a tribe, but a motley horde of northern barbarians, ruined provincials, and escaped slaves—a rabble whom Caesar's legions would have scattered like chaff, had they been as many as the sands of the shore; and yet when Genseric routed Boniface and sacked Carthage, in 439, he led barely fifty thousand fighting men.

Footnotes

(1) *History of Rome*, Mommsen, Dickson's trans., i. 288, 290.

(2) *History of Rome*, Niebuhr, Hare's trans., i. 576. Niebuhr has been followed in the text, although the "nexum" is one of the vexed points of Roman law. (See *Über das altrömische Schuldreckt*, Savigny.) The precise form of the contract is, however, perhaps, not very important for the matter in hand, as most scholars seem agreed that it resembled a mortgage, the breach of whose condition involved not only the loss of the pledge, but the personal liberty of the debtor. See *Gaius*, iv. 21.

(3) *History of Rome*, Niebuhr, Hare's trans., ii. 599. But compare *Aulus Gellius*, xx. 1.

(4) *Ibid.*, i. 582.

(5) *History of Rome*, Niebuhr, Hare's trans., i. 583.

(6) *History of Rome*, Mommsen, Dickson's trans., i. 472.

(7) *History of Rome*, Niebuhr, Hare's trans., i. 583.

(8) *Ibid.*, ii. 603.

(9) *History of Rome*, Niebuhr, Hare's trans., i. 574.

(10) Preface to *Virginia*.

(11) *History of Rome*, Mommsen, Dickson's trans., i. 484.

(12) See *History of Rome*, Mommsen, Dickson's trans., i. 298-9.

(13) See *History of Rome*, Niebuhr, Hare's trans., iii. 22, 30.

(14) Preface to *Virginia*, Macaulay.

(15) *Histoire de l'Esclavage*, Wallon, ii. 38.

(16) Suet. *Aug.*, ii. 41.

(17) Tacitus, *Ann.*, ii. 48.

(18) *Ann.*, vi. 39.

(19) *Ibid.*, iv. 21.

(20) *Sat.*, iii. 164.

(21) *L'Invasion Germanique*, Fustel de Coulanges, 146-157.

(22) Diod. xxxiv. 38. On the subject of the Sicilian slavery, see *Histoire d'Esclavage*, Wallon, ii. 300 *et seq.*

(23) Polybius, ii. 15, Shuckburgh's trans.

(24) *Provinces of the Roman Empire*, Mommsen, ii. 233.

(25) *Ibid.*, ii. 239.

(26) *Deipnosophists*, v. 37.

(27) Martial, *Ep.*, xii. 76.

(28) Vopiscus, *Aurelianus*, 35.

(29) *L'Invasion Germanique*, Fustel de Coulanges, 190.

(30) *Le Colonat Romain: Recherches sur quelques Problèmes d'Histoire*, Fustel de Coulanges, 143.

(31) *Organisation Financière chez les Romaines*, Marquardt, 65 *et seq.*

(32) Tacitus, *Ann.*, Murphy's trans., iii. 53.

(33) *Nat Hist.*, xii. 18.

(34) Vopiscus, *Saturninus*, 8.

(35) *Provinces of the Roman Empire*, Mommsen, ii. 140.

(36) *Ann.*, vi. 16, 17.

(37) See *Geschichte des Römischen Münswesens*, Mommsen, 756.

(38) *Monnaies Byzantines*, Sabatier, i. 51, 52.

(39) *Monnaies Byzantines*, Sabatier, i. 50.

(40) *Geschichte des Römischen Münswesens*, Mommsen, 837.

(41) *Monnaies Byzantines*, Sabatier, i. 51, 52.

(42) Pliny's *Letters*, iii. 19.

(43) Ibid., ix. 37.

(44) *Digest*, xix. 2, 15, and xxxiii. 7, 20.

(45) *Letters*, x. 24. On this whole subject see *Le Colonat Romaine: Recherches sur quelques Problèmes d'Histoire*, Fustel de Coulanges, ch. i.

(46) *Code of Justinian*, xi. 51, 1.

(47) *Le Colonat Romaine*, Fustel de Coulanges, 21.

(48) *Organisation Financière chez les Romaines*, Marquardt, 240.

(49) See *Decline and Fall*, ch. xvii.

(50) In *C. Verrem*, IV. lxxxix.

(51) *Cicero's Letters*, Ad Att. v. 21, and vi. 1.

(52) On this whole subject see *Histoire de l'Esclavage*, Wallon, ii. 42,44.

(53) *Satire*, viii. 89, 90.

(54) *Satire*, viii. 24.

(55) *Dio Cassius*, lxii. 2.

(56) *Nat. Hist.*, xiv., *Prœmium*.

(57) *Decline and Fall*, ch. xvii.

(58) *Morals, Trans.* of 1718, 4, 11.

(59) *Histoire de l'Esclavage*, iii. 268.

(60) *Decline and Fall*, ch. xii.

(61) *L'Invasion Germanique*, 200, 204, 223.

(62) *Dio Cassius*, lvi. 7.

(63) *Dio Cassius*, lvi. 5-8.

(64) *Ann.* iii. 25.

(65) *Ibid.*, xxviii. Latin literature is full of references to these famous laws. Tacitus, Pliny, Juvenal, and Martial constantly speak of them. There were also many commentaries on them by Roman jurists.

(66) *L'Organisation Militaire chez les Romaines*, Marquardt, 143.

(67) *Dio Cassius*, lxxiv. 2.

Chapter II: The Middle Age

PROBABLY the appreciation of the Roman monetary standard culminated during the invasion of the Huns toward the middle of the fifth century. In the reign of Valentinian III. gold sold for eighteen times its weight of silver, and Valentinian's final catastrophe was the murder of Aëtius in 454, with whose life the last spark of vitality at the heart of Roman centralization died. The rise of Ricimer and the accession of Odoacer, mark the successive steps by which Italy receded into barbarism, and, in the time of Theoderic the Ostrogoth, she had become a primitive, decentralized community, whose poverty and sluggishness protected her from African and Asiatic competition. The Ostrogoths subdued Italy in 493, and by that date the barbarians had overrun the whole civilized world west of the Adriatic, causing the demand for money to sustain a consolidated society to cease, the volume of trade to shrink, the market for eastern wares to contract, and gold to accumulate at the centre of exchanges. As gold accumulated, its value fell, and during the first years of the sixth century it stood at a ratio to silver of less than fifteen to one, a decline of eighteen per cent.(1) As prices correspondingly rose, the pressure on the peasantry relaxed, prosperity at Constantinople returned, and the collapse of the Western Empire may have prolonged the life of the European population of the Eastern for above one hundred and fifty years. The city which Constantine planted in 324 on the shore of the Bosphorus, was in reality a horde of Roman capitalists washed to the confines of Asia by the current of foreign exchanges; and these emigrants carried with them, to a land of mixed Greek and barbarian blood, their language and their customs. For many years these monied potentates ruled their new country absolutely. All that legislation could do for them was done. They even annexed rations to their estates, to be supplied at the public cost, to help their children maintain their palaces. As long as prices fell, nothing availed; the aristocracy grew poorer day by day. Their property lay generally in land, and the same stringency which wasted Italy and Gaul operated, though perhaps less acutely, upon the Danubian peasantry also. By the middle of the fifth century the country was exhausted and at the mercy of the Huns.

Wealth is the weapon of a monied society; for, though itself lacking the martial instinct, it can, with money, hire soldiers to defend it. But to raise a revenue from the people, they must retain a certain surplus of income after providing for subsistence, otherwise the government must trench on the supply of daily food, and exhaustion must supervene. Finlay has explained that chronic exhaustion was the normal condition of Byzantium under the Romans.

"The whole surplus profits of society were annually drawn into the coffers of the State, leaving the inhabitants only a bare sufficiency for perpetuating the race of tax-payers. History, indeed, shows that the agricultural classes, from the labourer to the landlord, were unable to retain possession of the savings required to replace that depreciation which time is constantly producing in all vested capital, and that their numbers gradually diminished." (2)

Under Theodosius II., when gold reached its maximum, complete prostration prevailed. The Huns marched whither they would, and one swarm "of barbarians followed another, as long as anything was left to plunder." The government could no longer keep armies in the field. A single example will show how low the community had fallen. In 446, Attila demanded of Theodosius six thousand pounds of gold as a condition of peace, and certainly six thousand pounds of gold, equalling perhaps $1,370,000, was a small sum, even when measured by the standard of private wealth. The end of the third century was not a prosperous period in Italy, and yet before his election as emperor in 275, the fortune of Tacitus reached 280,000,000 sesterces, or upwards of $11,000,000.(3) Nevertheless Theodosius was unable to wring this inconsiderable indemnity from the people, and he had to levy a private assessment on the senators, who were themselves so poor that to pay they sold at auction the jewels of their wives and the furniture of their houses.

Almost immediately after the collapse of the Western Empire the tide turned. With the fall in the price of gold the peasantry revived and the Greek provinces flourished. In the reign of Justinian, Belisarius and Narses marched from end to end of Africa and Europe, and Anastasius rolled in wealth.

Anastasius, the contemporary of Theoderic, acceded to the throne in 491. He not only built the famous long wall from the Propontis to the Euxine, and left behind him a treasure of three hundred and twenty thousand pounds of gold, but he remitted to his subjects the most oppressive of their taxes, and the reign of Justinian, who succeeded him at an interval of only ten years, must always rank as the prime of the Byzantine civilization. The observation is not new, it has been made by all students of Byzantine history.

"The increased prosperity... infused into society soon displayed its effects; and the brilliant exploits of the reign of Justinian must be traced back to the reinvigoration of the body politic of the Roman Empire by Anastasius." (4)

Justinian inherited the throne from his uncle Justin, a Dardanian peasant, who could neither read nor write. But the barbarian shepherd was a thorough soldier, and the army he left behind him was probably not inferior to the legions of Titus or Trajan. At all events, had Justinian's funds sufficed, there seems reason to suppose he might have restored the boundaries of the Empire. His difficulty lay not in lack of physical force, but in dearth of opulent enemies; in the sixth century conquest had ceased to be profitable. The territory open to invasion had been harried for generations, and hardly a country was to be found rich enough to repay the cost of a campaign by mercenaries. Therefore, the more the emperor extended his dominions, the more they languished; and finally to provide for wars, barbarian subsidies, and building, Justinian had to resort to over-taxation. With renewed want came renewed decay, and perhaps the completion of Saint Sophia, in 558, may be taken as the point whence the race which conceived this masterpiece hastened to its extinction.

In the seventh century Asiatic competition devoured the Europeans in the Levant, as three hundred years before it had devoured the husbandmen of Italy; and this was a disease which isolation alone could cure. But isolation of the centre of exchanges was impossible, for the vital principle of an economic age is competition, and, when the relief afforded by the collapse of Rome had been exhausted, competition did its work with relentless rapidity. Under Heraclius (610-640) the population sank fast, and by 717 the western blood had run so low that an Asiatic dynasty reigned supreme. Everywhere Greeks and Romans vanished before Armenians and Slavs, and for years previous to the accession of Leo the Isaurian the great waste tracts where they once lived were systematically repeopled by a more enduring race. The colonists of Justinian II. furnished him an auxiliary army. At Justinian's death in 711 the revolution had been completed; the population had been renovated, and Constantinople had become an Asiatic city.(5) The new aristocracy was Armenian, as strong an economic type as ever existed in western Asia; while the Slavic peasantry which underlay them were among the most enduring of mankind. There competition ended, for it could go no further; and, apparently, from the accession of Leo in 717, to the rise of Florence and Venice, three hundred and fifty years later, Byzantine society, in fixity, almost resembled the Chinese. Such movement as occurred, like Iconoclasm, came from the friction of the migrating races with the old population. As Texier has observed of architecture: "From the time of Justinian until the end of the Empire we cannot remark a single change in the modes of construction." (6)

Only long after, when the money which sustained it was diverted toward Italy during the crusades, did the social fabric crumble; and Gibbon has declared that the third quarter of the tenth century "forms the most splendid period of the Byzantine annals."(7)

The later Byzantine was an economic civilization, without aspiration or imagination, and perhaps the most vivid description which has survived of that ostentatious, sordid, cowardly, and stagnant race, is the little sketch of the Jew, Benjamin of Tudela, who travelled to the Levant in 1173.

Benjamin called the inhabitants of Constantinople Greeks, because of their language, and he described the city as a vast commercial metropolis, "common to all the world, without distinction of country or religion." Merchants from the East and West flocked thither—from Babylon, Mesopotamia, Media, and Persia, as well as from Egypt, Hungary, Russia, Lombardy, and Spain. The rabbi thought the people well educated and social, liking to eat and drink, "every man under his vine and under his fig tree." They loved gold and jewels, pompous display, and gorgeous ceremonial; and the Jew has dwelt with delight on the palace, with its columns of gold and silver, and the wonderful crown so studded with gems that it lighted the night without a lamp. The Greeks also roused his enthusiasm for the splendour of their clothes and of their horses' trappings, for when they went abroad they resembled princes; but on the other hand, he remarked with a certain scorn, that they were utterly cowardly, and, like women, had to hire men to protect them.

> "The Greeks who inhabit the country are extremely rich and possess great wealth of gold and precious stones. They dress in garments of silk, ornamented by gold and other valuable materials.... Nothing upon earth equals their wealth."
> "The Greeks hire soldiers of all nations whom they call barbarians, for the purpose of carrying on... wars with... the Turks." "They have no martial spirit themselves and like women are unfit for war." (8)

The movement of races in the Eastern Empire proceeded with automatic regularity. The cheaper organism exterminated the more costly, because energy operated through money strongly enough to cause free economic competition; nor is the evidence upon which this conclusion rests to be drawn from books alone. Coinage and architecture, sculpture and painting, tell the tale with equal precision.

When, in the fourth century, wealth, ebbing on the Tiber, floated to the Bosphorus the core of the Latin aristocracy, it carried with it also the Latin coinage. For several generations this coinage underwent little apparent alteration, but after the final division of the Empire, in 395, between the sons of Theodosius, a subtle change began in the composition of the ruling class; a change reflected from generation to generation in the issues of their mints. Sabatier has described the transformation wrought in eight hundred years with the minuteness of an antiquary.

If a set of Byzantine coins are arranged in chronological order, those of Anastasius, about 500, show at a glance an influence which is not Latin. Strange devices have appeared on the reverse, together with Greek letters. A century later, when the great decline was in progress under Heraclius, the type had become barbarous, and the prevalence of Greek inscriptions proves the steady exhaustion of the Roman blood. Another fifty years, and by 690, under Justinian II., the permanent and conventional phase had been developed. Religious emblems were used; the head of Christ was struck on the golden sou, and fixity of form presaged the Asiatic domination. The official costumes, the portraits of the emperors, certain consecrated inscriptions, all were changeless; and in 717, an Armenian dynasty ascended the throne in the person of Leo the Isaurian.(9) This motionless period lasted for full three hundred and fifty years, as long as the exchanges of the world centred at Byzantium, and the monied race who dwelt there sucked copious nutriment from the pool of wealth in which it lay. But even before the crusades the tide of trade began to flow to the south, and quitting Constantinople passed directly from Bagdad to the cities of Italy. Then the sustenance of the money-changers gradually failed. From the reign of Michael VI. effigies of the saints were engraved upon the coin, and after the revolution led by Alexius Comnenus, in 1081, the execution degenerated and debasement began. This revolution marked the beginning of the end. Immediately preceding the crusades, and attended by sharp distress, it was probably engendered by an alteration in the drift of foreign exchanges. Certainly the currency contracted sharply, and the gold money soon became so bad that Alexius had to stipulate to pay his debts in the byzants of his predecessor Michael.(10) For the next hundred years, as the Italian cities rose, the Empire languished, and with the thirteenth century, when Venice established its permanent silver standard by coining the "grosso," Constantinople crumbled into ruin.

In architecture the same phenomena appear, only differently clothed. Though the Germans, who swarmed across the Danube, often surged against the walls of Constantinople, they never became the ruling class of the community, because they were of the imaginative type. Money retained its supremacy, and while it did so energy expressed itself through the economic mind. Though Justinian was of barbarian blood, the nephew of a barbarian shepherd, the aristocracy about him, which formed the core of society, was neither imaginative nor devotional. Hardly Christian, it tended toward paganism or scepticism. The artists were of the subject caste, and they earned their living by gratifying the tastes of the nobles; but the nobles loved magnificence and gorgeous functions; hence all Byzantine architecture favoured display, and nowhere more so than in Saint Sophia. "Art delighted in representing Christ in all the splendour of power.... To glorify him the more all the magnificence of the imperial court was introduced into heaven.... Christ no longer appeared under the benevolent aspect of the good shepherd, but in the superb guise of an oriental monarch:

he is seated on a throne glittering with gold and precious stones." (11) Here then lay the impassable gulf between Byzantium and Paris; while Byzantium remained economic and materialistic, Paris passed into the glory of an imaginative age.

The Germans who overran the Roman territory were of the same race as the Greeks, the Latins, or the Gauls, but in a different stage of development. They tilled farms and built villages and perhaps fortresses, but they were not consolidated, and had neither nations nor federations. They were substantially in the condition in which the common family had been, when it divided many centuries before, and their minds differed radically from the minds of the inhabitants of the countries beyond the Danube and the Rhine. They were infinitely more imaginative, and, as the flood of emigration poured down from the north, the imagination came more and more to prevail.

Although the lowest of existing savages are relatively advanced, they suggest that the strongest passion of primeval man must have been fear; and fear, not so much of living things, as of nature, which seemed to him resolutely hostile. Against wild beasts, or savages like himself, he might prevail by cunning or by strength; but against drought and famine, pestilence and earthquake, he was helpless, and he regarded these scourges as malevolent beings, made like himself, only more formidable. His first and most pressing task was to mollify them, and above the warrior class rose the sacred caste, whose function was to mediate between the visible and the invisible world.

Originally these intercessors appear to have been sorcerers, rather than priests, for spirits were believed to be hostile to man; and perhaps the first conception of a god may have been reached through the victory of a clan of sorcerers in fight. As Statius said eighteen hundred years ago, "Primus in orbe deos fecit timor." (12) Probably the early wizards won their power by the discovery of natural secrets, which, though they could be transmitted to their descendants, might also be discovered by strangers. The later discoverers would become rival medicine men, and battle would be the only test by which the orthodoxy of the competitors could be determined. The victors would almost certainly stigmatize the beings the vanquished served, as devils who tormented men. There is an example of this process in the eighteenth chapter of 1 Kings:—

"And Elijah... said, How long halt ye between two opinions? if the Lord be God, follow him: but if Baal, then follow him. And the people answered him not a word."

Then Elijah proposed that each side should dress a bullock, and lay it on wood, and call upon their spirit; and the one who sent down fire should be God. And all the people answered that it was well spoken. And Jezebel's prophets took their bullock and dressed it, and called on "Baal from morning even until noon, saying, O Baal, hear us!" But nothing came of it.

Then Elijah mocked them, "and said, Cry aloud:... either he is talking, or he is pursuing, or he is in a journey, or peradventure he sleepeth, and must be awaked."

And they cried aloud, and cut themselves with knives till "blood gushed out upon them. And... there was neither voice, nor any to answer." Then Elijah built his altar, and cut up his bullock and laid him on wood, and poured twelve barrels of water over the whole, and filled a trench with water.

And "the fire of the Lord fell, and consumed the burnt sacrifice, and the wood, and the stones, and the dust, and licked up the water that was in the trench.

"And when all the people saw it, they fell on their faces: and they said, The Lord, he is the God.

"And Elijah said unto them, Take the prophets of Baal; let not one of them escape. And they took them: and Elijah brought them down to the brook Kishon, and slew them there."

The Germans of the fourth century were a very simple race, who comprehended little of natural laws, and who therefore referred phenomena they did not understand to supernatural intervention. This intervention could only be controlled by priests, and thus the invasions caused a rapid rise in the influence of the sacred class. The power of every ecclesiastical organization has always rested on the miracle, and the clergy have always proved their divine commission as did Elijah. This was eminently the case with the mediaeval Church. At the outset Christianity was socialistic, and its spread among the poor was apparently caused by the pressure of competition; for the sect only became of enough importance to be persecuted under Nero, contemporaneously with the first signs of distress which appeared through the debasement of the denarius. But socialism was only a passing phase, and disappeared as the money value of the miracle rose, and brought wealth to the Church. Under the Emperor Decius, about 250, the magistrates thought the Christians opulent enough to use gold and silver vessels in their service, and, by the fourth century, the supernatural so possessed the popular mind, that Constantine not only allowed himself to be converted by a miracle, but used enchantment as an engine of war.

In one of his marches, he encouraged the belief that he saw a luminous cross in the sky, with the words "By this conquer." The next night Christ appeared to him, and directed him to construct a standard bearing the same design, and, armed with this, to advance with confidence against Maxentius.

The legend, preserved by Eusebius, grew up after the event; but, for that very reason, it reflects the feeling of the age. The imagination of his men had grown so vivid that, whether he believed or not, Constantine found it expedient to use the Labarum as a charm to ensure victory. The standard supported a cross and a mystic monogram; the army believed its guards to be invulnerable, and in his last and most critical campaign against Licinius, the sight of the talisman not only excited his own troops to enthusiasm, but spread dismay through the enemy.

The action of the Milvian Bridge, fought in 312, by which Constantine established himself at Rome, was probably the point whence nature began to discriminate decisively against the monied type in Western Europe. Capital had already abandoned Italy; Christianity was soon after officially recognized, and during the next century the priest began to rank with the soldier as a force in war.

Meanwhile, as the population sank into exhaustion, it yielded less and less revenue, the police deteriorated, and the guards became unable to protect the frontier. In 376, the Goths, hard pressed by the Huns, came to the Danube and implored to be taken as subjects by the emperor. After mature deliberation, the Council of Valens granted the prayer, and some five hundred thousand Germans were cantoned in Mœsia. The intention of the government was to scatter this multitude through the provinces as *coloni*, or to draft them into the legions; but the detachment detailed to handle them was too feeble, the Goths mutinied, cut the guard to pieces, and having ravaged Thrace for two years, defeated and killed Valens at Hadrianople. In another generation the disorganization of the Roman army had become complete, and Alaric gave it its deathblow in his campaign of 410.

Alaric was not a Gothic king, but a barbarian deserter, who, in 392, was in the service of Theodosius. Subsequently, he sometimes held imperial commands, and sometimes led bands of marauders on his own account, but was always in difficulty about his pay. Finally, in the revolution in which Stilicho was murdered, a corps of auxiliaries mutinied and chose him their general. Alleging that his arrears were unpaid, Alaric accepted the command, and with this army sacked Rome.

During the campaign the attitude of the Christians was more interesting than the strategy of the soldiers. Alaric was a robber, leading mutineers, and yet the orthodox historians did not condemn him. They did not condemn him because the sacred class instinctively loved the barbarians whom they could overawe, whereas they could make little impression on the materialistic intellect of the old centralized society. Under the Empire the priests, like all other individuals, had to obey the power which paid the police; and as long as a revenue could be drawn from the provinces, the Christian hierarchy were subordinate to the monied bureaucracy who had the means to coerce them.

> "It was long since established, as a fundamental maxim of the Roman constitution, that every rank of citizen were alike subject to the laws, and that the care of religion was the right as well as duty of the civil magistrate." (13)

Their conversion made little change in the attitude of the emperors, and Constantine and his successors continued to exercise a supreme jurisdiction over the hierarchy. The sixteenth book of the Theodosian Code sufficiently sets forth the plenitude of their authority. In theory, bishops were elected by the clergy and the people, but in practice the emperor could control the patronage if it were valuable; and whether bishops were elected or appointed, as long as they were created and paid by laymen, they were dependent. The priesthood could only become autocratic when fear of the miracle exempted them from arrest; and toward the middle of the fifth century this point was approaching, as appears by the effect of the embassy of Leo the Great to Attila.

In 452 the Huns had crossed the Alps and had sacked Aquileia. The Roman army was demoralized; Aëtius could not make head against the barbarians in the field; while Valentinian was so panic-stricken that he abandoned Ravenna, which was thought impregnable, and retreated to the capital, which was indefensible. At Rome, finding himself helpless in an open city, the emperor conceived the idea of invoking the power of the supernatural. He proposed to Leo to visit Attila and persuade him to spare the town. The Pope consented without hesitation, and with perfect intrepidity caused himself to be carried to the Hun's tent, where he met with respect not unalloyed by fear. The legend probably reflects pretty accurately the feeling of the time. As the bishop stood before the king, Peter and Paul appeared on either side, menacing Attila with flaming swords; and though this particular form of apparition may be doubted, Attila seems beyond question to have been oppressed by a belief that he would not long survive the capture of Rome. He therefore readily agreed to accept a ransom and evacuate Italy.

From the scientific standpoint the saint and the sorcerer are akin; for though the saint uses the supernatural for man's benefit, and the sorcerer for his hurt, both deal in magic. The mediæval saint was a powerful necromancer. He healed the sick, cast out devils, raised the dead, foretold the future, put out fires, found stolen property, brought rain, saved from shipwreck, routed the enemy, cured headache, was sovereign in child-birth, and, indeed, could do almost anything that was asked of him, whether he were alive or dead. This power was believed to lie in some occult property of the flesh, which passed by contact. The woman in the Bible said, "If I may touch but his clothes, I shall be whole." Moreover, this fluid was a substance whose passage could be felt, for "Jesus, immediately knowing in himself that virtue had gone out of him, turned him about in the press, and said, Who touched my clothes?" (14)

Anything which came in contact with the saint was likely to have been impregnated with this magical quality, and thus became a charm, or relic, whose value depended primarily on the power of the man himself, and secondly, on the thoroughness with which the material had been charged.

The tomb, which held the whole body, naturally stood highest; then parts of the body, according to their importance—a head, an arm, a leg, down to hairs of the beard. Then came hats, boots, girdles, cups, anything indeed which had been used. The very ground on which a great miracle-worker had stood might have high value.

The Holy Grail, which had held Christ's blood, would cure wounds, raise the dead, and fill itself with choice food, at the command of the owner. The eucharist, though not properly a relic, and which only became God through an incantation, would, in expert hands, stop fires, cure disease, cast out devils, expound philosophy, and detect perjury by choking the liar.

Every prize in life was to be obtained by this kind of magic. When the kings of France made war, they carried with them the enchanted banner of Saint Denis, and Froissart has told how even in the reign of Charles VI. it decided the battle of Roosebeke.(15)

Disease was treated altogether by miracle, and the Church found the business so profitable that she anathematized experimental practitioners. In the thirteenth century Saint Thomas of Canterbury and Saint James of Compostello were among the most renowned of healers, and their shrines blazed with the gifts of the greatest and richest persons of Europe. When Philip Augustus lay very ill, Louis the Pious obtained leave to visit the tomb of Saint Thomas, then in the height of the fashion, and left as part of his fee the famous regal of France, a jewel so magnificent that three centuries and a half later Henry VIII. seized it and set it in a thumb ring. Beside this wonderful gem, at the pillage of the Reformation, "the king's receiver confessed that the gold and silver and precious stones and sacred vestments taken away... filled six-and-twenty carts."(16) The old books of travel are filled with accounts of this marvellous shrine.

> "But the magnificence of the tomb of Saint Thomas the Martyr, Archbishop of Canterbury, is that which surpasses all belief. This, notwithstanding its great size, is entirely covered with plates of pure gold; but the gold is scarcely visible from the variety of precious stones with which it is studded, such as sapphires, diamonds, rubies, balas-rubies, and emeralds... and agates, jaspers and cornelians set in relievo, some of the cameos being of such a

size, that I do not dare to mention it: but everything is left far behind by a ruby, not larger than a man's thumb-nail, which is set to the right of the altar.... They say that it was the gift of a king of France." (17)

But beside these shrines of world-wide reputation, no hamlet was too remote to possess its local fetish, which worked at cheap rates for the peasantry. A curious list of these was sent to the Government by two of Cromwell's visitors in the reign of Henry VIII.

The nuns of Saint Mary, at Derby, had part of the shirt of Saint Thomas, reverenced by pregnant women; so was the girdle of Saint Francis at Grace Dieu. At Repton, a pilgrimage was made to Saint Guthlac and his bell, which was put on the head for headache. The wimple of Saint Audrede was used for sore breasts, and the rod of Aaron for children with worms. At Bury Saint Edmund's, the shrine of Saint Botulph was carried in procession when rain was needed, "and Kentish men... carry thence... wax candles, which they light at the end of the field while the wheat is sown, and hope from this that neither tares nor other weeds will grow in the wheat that year."(18) Most curious of all, perhaps, at Pontefract, Thomas, Duke of Lancaster's belt and hat were venerated. They were believed to aid women in childbirth, and also to cure headache.

Saint Thomas Aquinas, a great venerator of the eucharist, used it to help him in his lectures. When treating of the dogma of the Supper at the University of Paris, many questions were asked him which he never answered without meditating at the foot of the altar. One day, when preparing an answer to a very difficult question, he placed it on the altar, and cried, "Lord, who really and veritably dwells in the Holy Sacrament, hear my prayer. If what I have written upon your divine eucharist be true, let it be given me to teach and demonstrate it. If I am deceived, stop me from proposing doctrines contrary to the truth of your divine Sacrament." Forthwith the Lord appeared upon the altar, and said to him, "You have written well upon the Sacrament of My body, and you have answered the question which has been proposed to you as well as human intelligence can fathom these mysteries." (19)

Primitive people argue directly from themselves to their divinities, and throughout the Middle Ages men believed that envy, jealousy, and vanity were as rampant in heaven as on earth, and behaved accordingly. The root of the monastic movement was the hope of obtaining advantages by adulation.

"A certain clerk, who had more confidence in the Mother than the Son, continually repeated the Ave Maria as his only prayer. One day, while so engaged, Christ appeared to him and said, 'My mother thanks you very much for your salutations,... *tamen et me salutare memento.*" (20)

To insure perpetual intercession it was necessary that the song of praise and the smoke of incense should be perpetual, and therefore monks and nuns worked day and night at their calling. As a twelfth-century bishop of Metz observed, when wakened one freezing morning by the bell of Saint Peter of Bouillon tolling for matins: "Neither the drowsiness of the night nor the bitterness of a glacial winter [kept them] from praising the Creator of the world." (21)

Bequests to convents were in the nature of policies of insurance in favour of the grantor and his heirs, not only against punishment in the next world, but against accident in this. On this point doubt is impossible, for the belief of the donor is set forth in numberless charters. Cedric de Guillac, in a deed to la Grande-Sauve, said that he gave because "as water extinguishes fire, so gifts extinguish sin."(22) And an anecdote preserved by Dugdale, shows how valuable an investment against accident a convent was thought to be as late as the thirteenth century.

When Ralph, Earl of Chester, the founder of the monasteryof Dieulacres, was returning by sea from the Holy Land, he was overtaken one night by a sudden tempest. "How long is it till midnight?" he asked of the sailors. They answered, "About two hours." He said to them, "Work on till midnight, and I trust in God that you may have help, and that the storm will cease." When it was near midnight the captain said to the earl, "My lord, commend yourself to God, for the tempest increases; we are worn out, and are in mortal peril." Then Earl Ralph came out of his cabin, and began to help with the ropes, and the rest of the ship's tackle; nor was it long before the storm subsided.

The next day, as they were sailing over a tranquil sea, the captain said to the earl, "My lord, tell us, if you please, why you wished us to work till the middle of the night, and then you worked harder than all the rest." To which he replied, "Because at midnight my monks, and others, whom my ancestors and I have endowed in divers places, rise and sing divine service, and then I have faith in their prayers, and I believe that God, because of their prayers and intercessions, gave me more fortitude than I had before, and made the storm cease as I predicted." (23)

Philip Augustus, when caught in a gale in the Straits of Messina, showed equal confidence in the matins of Clairvaux, and was also rewarded for his faith by good weather towards morning.

The power of the imagination, when stimulated by the mystery which, in an age of decentralization, shrouds the operations of nature, can be measured by its effect in creating an autocratic class of miracle-workers. Between the sixth and the thirteenth centuries, about one-third of the soil of Europe passed into the hands of religious corporations, while the bulk of the highest talent of the age sought its outlet through monastic life.

The force operated on all; for, beside religious ecstasy, ambition and fear were at work, and led to results inconceivable when centralization has begot materialism. Saint Bernard's position was more conspicuous and splendid than that of any monarch of his generation, and the agony of terror which assailed the warriors was usually proportionate to the freedom with which they had violated ecclesiastical commands. They fled to the cloister for protection from the fiend, and took their wealth with them.

Gérard le Blanc was even more noted for his cruelty than for his courage. He was returning to his castle one day, after having committed a murder, when he saw the demon whom he served appear to claim him. Seized with horror, he galloped to where six penitents had just founded the convent of Afflighem, and supplicated them to receive him. The news spread, and the whole province gave thanks to God that a monster of cruelty should have been so converted.

A few days after, his example was followed by another knight, equally a murderer, who had visited the recluses, and, touched by their piety and austerity, resolved to renounce his patrimony and live a penitent.(24)

Had the German migrations been wars of extermination, as they have sometimes been described, the imagination, among the new barbaric population, might have been so stimulated that a pure theocracy would have been developed between the time of Saint Benedict and Saint Bernard. But the barbarians were not animated by hate; on the contrary, they readily amalgamated with the old population, amongst whom the materialism of Rome lay like a rock in a rising tide, sometimes submerged, but never obliterated.

The obstacle which the true emotionalists never overcame was the inheritance of a secular clergy, who, down to the eleventh century, were generally married, and in the higher grades were rather barons than prelates. In France the Archbishop of Rheims, the Bishops of Beauvais, Noyon, Langres, and others, were counts; while in Germany the Archbishops of Mayence, of Treves, and of Cologne were princes and electors, standing on the same footing as the Dukes of Saxony and Bavaria.

As feudal nobles these ecclesiastics were retainers of the king, owed feudal service, led their vassals in war, and some of the fiercest soldiers of the Middle Ages were clerks. Milo of Treves was a famous eighth-century bishop. Charles Martel gave the archbishopric of Rheims to a warrior named Milo, who managed also to obtain the see of Treves. This Milo was the son of Basinus, the last incumbent of the preferment. He was a fierce and irreligious soldier, and was finally killed hunting; but during the forty years in which he held his offices, Boniface, with all the aid of the crown and the pope, was unable to prevail against him, and in 752 Pope Zachary wrote advising that he should be left to the divine vengeance.(25)

Such a system was incompatible with the supremacy of a theocracy. The essence of a theocracy is freedom from secular control, and this craving for freedom was the dominant instinct of monasticism. Saint Anselm, perhaps the most perfect specimen of a monk, felt it in the marrow of his bones; it was the master passion of his life, and he insisted upon it with all the fire of his nature: "Nihil magis diligit Deus in hoc mundo quam libertatem ecclesiæ suæ.... Liberam vult esse Deus sponsam suam, non ancillam."

Yet only very slowly, as the Empire disintegrated, did the theocratic idea take shape. As late as the ninth century the pope prostrated himself before Charlemagne, and did homage as to a Roman emperor. (26)

Saint Benedict founded Monte Cassino in 529, but centuries elapsed before the Benedictine order rose to power. The early convents were isolated and feeble, and much at the mercy of the laity, who invaded and debauched them. Abbots, like bishops, were often soldiers, who lived within the walls with their wives and children, their hawks, their hounds, and their men-at-arms; and it has been said that, in all France, Corbie and Fleury alone kept always something of their early discipline.

Only in the early years of the most lurid century of the Middle Ages, when decentralization culminated, and the imagination began to gain its fullest intensity, did the period of monastic consolidation open with the foundation of Cluny. In 910 William of Aquitaine drew a charter (27) which, so far as possible, provided for the complete independence of his new corporation. There was no episcopal visitation, and no interference with the election of the abbot. The monks were put directly under the protection of the pope, who was made their sole superior. John XI. confirmed this charter by his bull of 932, and authorized the affiliation of all convents who wished to share in the reform. (28)

The growth of Cluny was marvellous; by the twelfth century two thousand houses obeyed its rule, and its wealth was so great, and its buildings so vast, that in 1245 Innocent IV., the Emperor Baldwin, and Saint Louis were all lodged together within its walls, and with them all the attendant trains of prelates and nobles with their servants.

In the eleventh century no other force of equal energy existed. The monks were the most opulent, the ablest, and the best organized society in Europe, and their effect upon mankind was proportioned to their strength. They intuitively sought autocratic power, and during the centuries when nature favoured them, they passed from triumph to triumph. They first seized upon the papacy and made it self-perpetuating; they then gave battle to the laity for the possession of the secular hierarchy, which had been under temporal control since the very foundation of the Church.

About the year 1000 Rome was in chaos. The Counts of Tusculum, who had often disposed of the tiara, on the death of John XIX., bought it for Benedict IX. Benedict was then a child of ten, but he grew worse as he grew older, and finally he fell so low that he was expelled by the people. He was succeeded by Sylvester; but, a few months after his coronation, Benedict re-entered the city, and crowned John XX. with his own hands. Shortly after, he assaulted the Vatican, and then three popes reigned together in Rome. In this crisis Gregory VI. tried to restore order by buying the papacy for himself; but the transaction only added a fourth pope to the three already consecrated, and two years later he was set aside by the Emperor Henry, who appointed his own chancellor in his place.

It was a last triumph for the laity, but a triumph easier to win than to sustain. When the soldier created the high priest of Christendom, he did indeed inspire such terror that no man in the great assembly dared protest; but in nine months Clement was dead, his successor lived only twenty-four days, poisoned, as it was rumoured, by the perfidious Italians; and when Henry sought a third pope among his prelates, he met with general timidity to accept the post. Then the opportunity of the monks came: they seized it, and with unerring instinct fixed themselves upon the throne from which they have never been expelled. According to the picturesque legend, Bruno, Bishop of Toul, seduced by the flattery of courtiers and the allurements of ambition, accepted the tiara from the emperor, and set out upon his journey to Italy with a splendid retinue, and with his robe and crown. On his way he turned aside at Cluny, where Hildebrand was prior. Hildebrand, filled with the spirit of God, reproached him with having seized upon the seat of the vicar of Christ by force, and accepted the holy office from the sacrilegious hand of a layman. He exhorted Bruno to cast away his pomp, and to cross the Alps humbly as a pilgrim, assuring him that the priests and people of Rome would recognize him as their bishop, and elect him according to canonical forms. Then he would taste the joys of a pure conscience, having entered the fold of Christ as a shepherd and not as a robber. Inspired by these words, Bruno dismissed his train, and left the convent gate as a pilgrim. He walked barefoot, and when after two months of pious meditations he stood before Saint Peter's, he spoke to the people and told them it was their privilege to elect the pope, and since he had come unwillingly he would return again, were he not their choice.

He was answered with acclamations, and on February 2, 1049, he was enthroned as Leo IX. His first act was to make Hildebrand his minister.

The legend tells of the triumph of Cluny as no historical facts could do. Ten years later, in the reign of Nicholas II., the theocracy made itself self-perpetuating through the assumption of the election of the pope by the college of cardinals, and in 1073 Hildebrand, the incarnation of monasticism, was crowned under the name of Gregory VII.

With Hildebrand's election, war began. The council of Rome, held in 1075, decreed that holy orders should not be recognized where investiture had been granted by a layman, and that princes guilty of conferring investiture should be excommunicated. The council of the next year, which excommunicated the emperor, also enunciated the famous propositions of Baronius—the full expression of the theocratic idea:—

> "That the Roman pontiff alone can be called universal.
> "That he alone can depose or reconcile bishops.
> "That his legate, though of inferior rank, takes precedence of all bishops in council, and can pronounce sentences of deposition against them.
> ....
> "That all princes should kiss the pope's feet alone.
> ....
> "That he may depose emperors.
> ....
> "That his judgments can he overruled by none, and he alone can overrule the judgments of all.
> "That he can be judged by no one.
> "That the Roman Church never has, and never can err, as the Scriptures testify.
> ....
> "That by his precept and permission it is lawful for subjects to accuse their princes.
> ....

"That he is able to absolve from their allegiance the subjects of the wicked." (29)

The monks had won the papacy, but the emperor still held his secular clergy, and, at the diet of Worms, where he undertook to depose Hildebrand, he was sustained by his prelates. Without a moment of hesitation the enchanter cast his spell, and it is interesting to see, in the curse which he launched at the layman, how the head of monasticism had become identified with the spirit which he served. The priest had grown to be a god on earth.

> "So strong in this confidence, for the honour and defence of your Church, on behalf of the omnipotent God, the Father, the Son, and the Holy Ghost, by your power and authority, I forbid the government of the German and Italian kingdoms, to King Henry, the son of the Emperor Henry, who, with unheard-of arrogance, has rebelled against your Church. I absolve all Christians from the oaths they have made, or may make to him, and I forbid that any one should obey him as king." (30)

Henry marched on Italy, but in all European history there has been no drama more tremendous than the expiation of his sacrilege. To his soldiers the world was a vast space, peopled by those fantastic beings which are still seen on Gothic towers. These demons obeyed the monk of Rome, and his army, melting from the emperor under a nameless horror, left him helpless.

Gregory lay like a magician in the fortress of Canossa; but he had no need of carnal weapons, for when the emperor reached the Alps he was almost alone. Then his imagination also took fire, the panic seized him, and he sued for mercy.

For three days long he stood barefoot in the snow at the castle gate; and when at last he was admitted, half-naked and benumbed, he was paralyzed rather by terror than by cold. Then the great miracle was wrought, by which God was made to publicly judge between them.

Hildebrand took the consecrated wafer and broke it, saying to the suppliant, "Man's judgments are fallible, God's are infallible; if I am guilty of the crimes you charge me with, let Him strike me dead as I eat." He ate, and gave what remained to Henry; but though for him more than life was at stake, he dared not taste the bread. From that hour his fate was sealed. He underwent his penance and received absolution; and when he had escaped from the terrible old man, he renewed the war. But the spell was over him, the horror clung to him, even his sons betrayed him, and at last his mind gave way under the strain and he abdicated. In his own words, to save his life he "sent to Mayence the crown, the sceptre, the cross, the sword, the lance."

On August 7, 1106, Henry died at Liege, an outcast and a mendicant, and for five long years his body lay at the church door, an accursed thing which no man dared to bury.

Such was the evolution ot the medieval theocracy, the result of that social disintegration which stimulates the human imagination. and makes men cower before the unknown. The force which caused the rise of an independent priesthood was the equivalent of magic, and it was the waxing of this force through the dissolution of the Empire of the West which made the schism which split Christendom in two. The Latin Church divided from the Greek because it was the reflection of the imaginative mind. While the West grew emotional, Constantinople stayed the centre of exchanges, the seat of the monied class; and when Cluny captured Rome, the antagonism between these irreconcilable instincts precipitated a rupture. The schism dated from 1054, five years after the coronation of Leo. Nor is the theory new; it was explained by Gibbon long ago.

> "The rising majesty of Rome could no longer brook the insolence of a rebel; and Michael Cerularius was excommunicated in the heart of Constantinople by the pope's legates....

"From this thunderbolt we may date the consummation of the schism. It was enlarged by each ambitious step of the Roman pontiffs; the emperors blushed and trembled at the ignominious fate of their royal brethren of Germany; and the people were scandalized by the temporal power and military life of the Latin clergy." (31)

Footnotes

(1) *Monnaies Byzantinus*, Sabatier, i. 50.

(2) *History of the Byzantine Empire*, Finlay, 9.

(3) Vopiscus, *Tacitus*, 10.

(4) *Greece under the Romans*, George Finlay, 214.

(5) *Byzantine Empire*, Finlay, 256.

(6) *Byzantine Architecture*, Texier, 24.

(7) *Decline and Fall*, ch. lii.

(8) *Itinerary of Rabbi Benjamin of Tudela*, trans. from the Hebrew by Asher, 54.

(9) *Monnaies Byzantines*, i. 26.

(10) See Treaty with Bohemund. Anna Comnena, xiii. 7.

(11) *L'Art Byzantin*, Bayet, 16, 17.

(12) *Theb.*, iii. 661.

(13) *Decline and Fall*, ch. xx.

(14) Mark v. 28, 30.

(15) *Chronicles*, ii. 124.

(16) *Anglican Schism*, Sander, trans. by Lewis, 143.

(17) *A Relation, or rather a True Account of the Island of England*, Camden Soc. 30.

(18) *Cal.* x. No. 364. References to the calendar of State papers edited by Messrs. Brewer and Gairdner will be made by this word only.

(19) *Histoire du Sacrament de l'Eucharistie*, Corblet, i. 474. See also on this subject *Cæsarii Dialogus Miraculorum; De Corpore Christi.*

(20) *Hist. Lit. de la France*, xxii. 119.

(21) *Les Moines d'Occident*, Montalembert, vi. 34.

(22) *Histoire de la Grande-Sauve* ii. 13.

(23) *Monasticon*, v. 628, Ed. 1846.

(24) *Les Moines d'Occident*, Montalembert, vi. 101.

(25) *Sacerdotal Celibacy*, Lea, 129.

(26) *Annales Lauressenses*, Perz, i. 188.

(27) *Recueil des Chartes de l'Abbeye de Cluny*, Bruel, i. 124.

(28) *Bull. Clun.*, ii. 1. Also *Manuel des Institutions Françaises*, Luchaire, 93, 95, where the authorities are collected.

(29) *Annales Ecclesiastici*, Baronius, year 1076.

(30) Migne, cxlviii. 790.

(31) *Decline and Fall*, ch. lx.

Chapter III: The First Crusade

Until the mechanical arts have advanced far enough to cause the attack in war to predominate over the defence, centralization cannot begin; for when a mud wall can stop an army, a police is impossible. The superiority of the attack was the secret of the power of the monied class who controlled Rome, because with money a machine could be maintained which made individual resistance out of the question, and revolt difficult. Titus had hardly more trouble in reducing Jerusalem, and dispersing the Jews, than a modern officer would have under similar circumstances.

As the barbarians overran the Roman provinces, and the arts declined, the conditions of life changed. The defence gained steadily on the attack, and, after some centuries, a town with a good garrison, solid ramparts, and abundant provisions had nothing to fear from the greatest king. Even the small, square Norman tower was practically impregnable. As Viollet-le-Duc has explained, these towers were mere passive defences, formidable to a besieger only because no machinery existed for making a breach in a wall. The beleaguered nobles had only to watch their own men, see to their doors, throw projectiles at the enemy if he approached too near, counter-mine if mined, and they might defy a great army until their food failed. Famine was the enemy most feared.(1)

By the eleventh century these towers had sprung up all over the West. Even the convents and churches could be defended, and every such stronghold was the seat of a count or baron, an abbot or bishop, who was a sovereign because no one could coerce him, and who therefore exercised all the rights of sovereignty, made war, dispensed justice, and coined money. In France alone there were nearly two hundred mints in the twelfth century.

Down to the close of the Merovingian dynasty the gold standard had been maintained, and contraction had steadily gone on; but, for reasons which are not understood, under the second race, the purchasing power of bullion temporarily declined, and this expansion was probably one chief cause of the prosperity of the reign of Charlemagne. Perhaps the relief was due to the gradual restoration of silver to circulation, for the coinage was then reformed, and the establishment of the silver pound as the measure of value may be considered as the basis of all the monetary systems of modern Europe.

The interval of prosperity was, however, brief; no permanent addition was made to the stock of precious metals, and prices continued to fall, as is demonstrated by the rapid deterioration of the currency. In this second period of relapse disintegration reached its limit.

During the tenth and eleventh centuries the Northmen infested the coasts of France, and sailed up the rivers burning and ravaging, as far as Rouen and Orléans. Even the convents of Saint Martin of Tours and Saint Germain des Près were sacked. The Mediterranean swarmed with Saracenic corsairs, who took Fraxinetum, near Toulon, seized the passes of the Alps, and levied toll on travel into Italy. The cannibalistic Huns overran the Lower Danube, and closed the road to Constantinople. Western Europe was cut off from the rest of the world. Commerce nearly ceased—the roads were so bad and dangerous, and the sea so full of pirates.

The ancient stock of scientific knowledge was gradually forgotten, and the imagination had full play. Upon philosophy the effect was decisive; Christianity sank to a plane where it appealed more vividly to the minds of the surrounding pagans than their own faiths, and conversion then went on rapidly. In 912 Rollo of Normandy was baptized; the Danes, Norwegians, Poles, and Russians followed; and in 997 Saint Stephen ascended the throne of Hungary and reopened to Latin Christians the way to the Sepulchre.

Perhaps the destiny of modern Europe has hinged upon the fact that the Christian sacred places lay in Asia, and therefore the pilgrimage brought the West into contact with the East. But the pilgrimage was the effect of relic-worship, and relic-worship the vital principle of monasticism. In these centuries of extreme credulity monasticism had its strongest growth. A faculty for scientific study was abnormal, and experimental knowledge was ascribed to sorcery. The monk Gerbert, who became pope as Sylvester II., was probably the most remarkable man of his generation. Though poor and of humble birth, he attracted so much attention that he was sent to Spain, where he studied in the Moorish schools at Barcelona and Cordova, and where he learned the rudiments of mathematics and geography. His contemporaries were so bewildered by his knowledge that they thought it due to magic, and told how he had been seen flying home from Spain, borne on the back of the demon he served, and loaded with the books he had stolen from the wizard, his master. Sylvester died in 1003, but long afterwards anatomy was still condemned by the Church, and four separate councils anathematized experimental medicine, because it threatened to destroy the value of the shrines. The ascendency of Cluny began with Saint Hugh, who was chosen abbot in 1049, the year of Leo's election. The corporation then obtained control of Rome, and in another twenty-five years was engaged in its desperate struggle with the remains of the old secular police power. But though Hildebrand crushed Henry, the ancient materialism was too deeply imbedded to be eradicated in a single generation, and meanwhile the imagination had been brought to an uncontrollable intensity. A new and fiercer excitement seethed among the people—a vision of the conquest of talismans so powerful as to make their owners sure of heaven and absolute on earth.

The attraction of Palestine had been very early felt, for in 333 a guide-book had been written, called the *Itinerary from Bordeaux to Jerusalem*, which gave the route through the valley of the Danube, together with an excellent account of the Holy Land. In those days, before the barbaric inroads, the journey was safe enough; but afterwards communication nearly ceased, and when

Stephen was baptized in 997, the relics of Jerusalem had all the excitement of novelty. Europe glowed with enthusiasm. Sylvester proposed a crusade, and Hildebrand declared he would rather risk his life for the holy places "than rule the universe."

Each year the throngs upon the road increased, convents sprang up along the way to shelter the pilgrims, the whole population succoured and venerated them, and by the time Cluny had seized the triple crown, they left in veritable armies. Ingulf, secretary to William the Conqueror, set out in 1064 with a band seven thousand strong.

In that age of faith no such mighty stimulant could inflame the human brain as a march to Jerusalem. A crusade was no vulgar war for a vulgar prize, but an alliance with the supernatural for the conquest of talismans whose possession was tantamount to omnipotence. Urban's words at Clermont, when he first preached the holy war, have lost their meaning now; but they burned like fire into the hearts of his hearers then, for he promised them glory on earth and felicity in heaven, and he spoke in substance thus: No longer do you attack a castle or a town, but you undertake the conquest of the holy places. If you triumph, the blessings of heaven and the kingdoms of the East will be your share; if you fall, you will have the glory of dying where Christ died, and God will not forget having seen you in His holy army.(2)

Urban told them "that under their general Jesus Christ... they, the Christian, the invincible army," would march to certain victory. In the eleventh century this language was no metaphor, for the Cluniac monk spoke as the mouthpiece of a god who was there actually among them, offering the cross he brought from the grave, and promising them triumphs: not the common triumphs which may be won by man's unaided strength, but the transcendent glory which belongs to beings of another world.

So the crusaders rode out to fight, the originals of the fairy knights, clad in impenetrable armour, mounted on miraculous horses, armed with resistless swords, and bearing charmed lives.

Whole villages, even whole districts, were left deserted; land lost its value; what could not be sold was abandoned; and the peasant, loaded with his poor possessions, started on foot with his wife and children in quest of the Sepulchre, so ignorant of the way that he mistook each town upon the road for Zion. Whether he would or no, the noble had to lead his vassals or be forsaken, and riding at their head with his hawks and hounds, he journeyed towards that marvellous land of wealth and splendour, where kingdoms waited the coming of the devoted knight of God. Thus men, women, and children, princes and serfs, priests and laymen, in a countless, motley throng, surged toward that mighty cross and tomb whose possessor was raised above the limitations of the flesh.

The crusaders had no commissariat and no supply train, no engines of attack, or other weapons than those in their hands, and the holy relics they bore with them. There was no general, no common language, no organization; and so over unknown roads, and through hostile peoples, they wandered from the Rhine to the Bosphorus, and from the Bosphorus to Syria.

These earlier crusades were armed migrations, not military invasions, and had they met with a determined enemy, they must have been annihilated; but it chanced that the Syrians and Egyptians were at war, and the quarrel was so bitter that the caliph actually sought the Christian alliance. Even under such circumstances the waste of life was fabulous, and, had not Antioch been betrayed, the starving rabble must have perished under its walls. At Jerusalem, also, the Franks were reduced to the last extremity before they carried the town; and had it not been for the arrival of a corps of Genoese engineers, who built movable towers, they would have died miserably of hunger and thirst. Nor was the coming of this reinforcement preconcerted. On the contrary, the Italians accidentally lost their ships at Joppa, and, being left without shelter, sought protection in the camp of the besiegers just in time.

So incapable were the crusaders of regular operations, that even when the towers were finished and armed, the leaders did not know how to fill the moat, and Raymond of Saint Gilles had nothing better to propose than to offer a penny for every three stones thrown into the ditch.

On July 15, 1099, Jerusalem was stormed; almost exactly three years after the march began. Eight days later Godfrey de Bouillon was elected king, and then the invaders spread out over the strip of mountainous country which borders the coast of Palestine and Syria, and the chiefs built castles in the defiles of the hills, and bound themselves together by a loose alliance against the common enemy.

The decentralization of the colony was almost incredible. The core of the kingdom was the barony of Jerusalem, which extended only from the Egyptian desert to a stream just north of Beyrout, and inland to the Jordan and the spurs of the hills beyond the Dead Sea, and yet it was divided into more than eighteen independent fiefs, whose lords had all the rights of sovereignty, made war, administered justice, and coined money.(3)

Beside these petty states, the ports were ceded to the Italian cities whose fleets helped in the conquest. Venice, Genoa, and Pisa held quarters in Ascalon, Joppa, Tyre, Acre, and Beyrout, which were governed by consuls or viscounts, who wrangled with each other and with the central government.

Such was the kingdom over which Godfrey reigned, but there were three others like it which together made up the Frankish monarchy. To the north of the barony of Jerusalem lay the county of Tripoli, and beyond Tripoli, extending to Armenia, the principality of Antioch. To the east of Antioch the county of Edessa stretched along the base of the Taurus Mountains and spread out somewhat indefinitely beyond the Euphrates.

Thus on the north Edessa was the outwork of Christendom, while to the south the castle of Karak, which commanded the caravan road between Suez and Damascus, held a corresponding position among the hills to the east of the Dead Sea.

Beyond the mountains the great plain sweeps away into Central Asia, and in this plain the Franks never could maintain their footing. Their failure to do so proved their ruin, for their position lay exposed to attack from Damascus; and it was by operating from Damascus as a base that Saladin succeeded in forcing the pass of Banias, and in cutting the Latin possessions in two at the battle of Tiberias.

A considerable body of Europeans were thus driven in like a wedge between Egypt and the Greek Empire, the two highest civilizations of the Middle Ages, while in front lay the Syrian cities of the plain, with whom the Christians were at permanent war. The contact was the closest, the struggle for existence the sharpest, and the barbaric mind received a stimulus not unlike the impulse Gaul received from Rome; for the interval which separated the East from the West, at the beginning of the twelfth century, was probably not less than that which divided Italy from Gaul at the time of Caesar.

When Godfrey de Bouillon took the cross, the Byzantine Empire was already sinking. The Eastern trade which, for so many centuries, had nourished its population, was beginning to flow directly from Asia into Italy, and, as the economic aristocracy of the capital lost its nutriment, it lost its energy. Apparently it fell in 1081, in the revolution which raised Alexius Comnenus to the throne. Because Alexius sacked Constantinople with a following of mongrel Greeks, Slavs, and Bulgarians, he has been called the first Greek emperor, but in reality the pure Greek blood had long since perished. The Byzantine population at the end of the eleventh century was the lees of a multitude of races,—a mixture of Slavs, Armenians, Jews, Thracians, and Greeks; a residuum of the most tenacious organisms, after all that was higher had disappeared. The army was a mixed horde of Huns, Arabs, Italians, Britons, Franks; of all in short who could fight and were for sale, while the Church was servile, the fancy dead, and art and literature were redolent of decaying wealth.

Nevertheless, ever since the fall of Rome, Constantinople had been the reservoir whence the West had drawn all its materialistic knowledge, and therefore, it was during the centuries when the valley of the Danube was closed, that the arts fell to their lowest ebb beyond the Alps and Rhine. After pilgrimages began again in the reign of Stephen, the Bosphorus lay once more in the path of travel, and as the returning palmers spread over the West, a revival followed in their track; a revival in which the spirit of Byzantium may yet be clearly read in the architecture of Italy and France. Saint Mark is a feeble imitation of Saint Sophia, while Viollet-le-Duc has described how long he hesitated before he could decide whether the carving of Vézelay, Autun, and Moissac was Greek or French; and has dwelt upon the laborious care with which he pored over all the material, before he became convinced that the stones were cut by artists trained at Cluny, who copied Byzantine models.(4)

But the great gulf between the economic and the imaginative development, separated the moribund Greek society from the semi-childhood of the Franks; a chasm in its nature impassable because caused by a difference of mind, and which is, perhaps, seen most strikingly in religious architecture; for religious architecture, though always embodying the highest poetical aspirations of every civilization, yet had in the East and West diametrically opposite points of departure.

Saint Sophia is pregnant with the spirit of the age of Justinian. There was no attempt at mystery, or even solemnity, about the church, for the mind of the architect was evidently fixed upon solving the problem of providing the largest and lightest space possible, in which to display the functions of a plutocratic court. His solution was brilliantly successful. He enlarged the dome and diminished the supports, until, nothing remaining to interrupt the view, it seemed as though the roof had been suspended in the air. For his purpose the exterior had little value, and he sacrificed it.

The conception of the architects of France was the converse of this, for it was highly emotional. The gloom of the lofty vaults, dimly lighted by the subdued splendour of the coloured windows, made the interior of the Gothic cathedral the most mysterious and exciting sanctuary for the celebration of the miracle which has ever been conceived by man; while without, the doors and windows, the pinnacles and buttresses, were covered with the terrific shapes of demons and the majestic figures of saints, admonishing the laity of the danger lurking abroad, and warning them to take refuge within.

But if the Greeks and the Franks had little affinity for each other, the case was different with the Saracens, who were then in the full vigour of their intellectual prime, and in the meridian of their material splendour.

In the eleventh century, when Paris was still a cluster of huts cowering for shelter on the islands of the Seine, and the palace of the Duke of Normandy and King of England was the paltry White Tower of London, Cairo was being adorned with those masterpieces which are still the admiration of the world.

Prisse d'Avennes considered that, among the city gates the Bab-el-Nasr stands first in "taste and style," and the famous Bab-el-Zouilyeh is of the same period. He also thought the mosque of Teyloun a "model of elegance and grandeur," and observed, when criticising the mosque of the Sultan Hassan, built in 1356, that though imposing and beautiful, it lacks the unity which is only found in the earlier Arabic monuments, such as Teyloun.(5) Indeed, the signs are but too apparent that, from the twelfth century, the instinct for form began to fail in Egypt, the surest precursor of artistic decay.

The magnificence of the decoration and furnishing of the Arabic palaces and houses has seldom been surpassed, and a few extracts from an inventory of a sale of the collections of the Caliph Mostanser-Billah, held in 1050, may give some idea of its gorgeousness.

Precious Stones.—A chest containing 7 *Mudds* of emeralds; each of these worth at least 300,000 dynars, which makes in all at the lowest estimation, 36,000,000 francs.

A necklace of precious stones worth about 80,000 dynars.

Seven *Waïbah* of magnificent pearls sent by the Emir of Mecca.

....

Glass,—Several chests, containing a large number of vases... of the purest crystal, chased and plain.

Other chests filled with precious vases of different materials.

....

Table Utensils.—A large number of gold dishes, enamelled or plain, in which were incrusted all sorts of colours, forming most varied designs.

....

One hundred cups and other shapes, of bezoar-stone, on most of which was engraved the name of the Caliph Haroun-el-Raschid.

Another cup which was 3½ hands wide and one deep.

Different Articles.—Chests containing inkstands of different shapes, round or square, small or large, of gold or silver, sandal wood, aloe, ebony, ivory, and all kinds of woods, enriched with stones, gold and silver, or remarkable for beauty and elegance of workmanship.

....

Twenty-eight enamel dishes inlaid with gold, which the Caliph Aziz had received as a present from the Greek emperor and each of which was valued at 3000 dynars.

Chests filled with an enormous quantity of steel, china, and glass mirrors, ornamented with gold and silver filagree; some were bordered with stones, and had cornelian handles, and others precious stones. One of them had quite a long and thick handle of emeralds. These mirrors were enclosed in cases made of velvet or silk or most beautiful wood; their locks were of gold or silver.

....

Four hundred large cases, ornamented with gold and filled with all sorts of jewels.

Various silver household goods, and six thousand gold vases, in which were put narcissus or violets.

Thirty-six thousand pieces of crystal, among them a box ornamented with figures in relief, weighing 17 roks.

A large number of knives which, at the lowest price, were sold for 36,000 dynars.

....

A turban enriched with precious stones, one of the most curious and valuable articles in the palace: it was said to be worth 130,000 dynars. The stones which covered it, and whose weight was 17 roks, were divided between two chiefs, who both claimed it. One had in his share a ruby weighing 23 mitqâls, and in the share which fell to the other were 100 pearls each of which weighed 3 mitqâls. When the two generals were obliged to fly from Fostat, all these valuables were given up to pillage.

A golden peacock enriched with the most valuable precious stones: the eyes were rubies, the feathers gilded enamel representing all the colours of peacock feathers.

A cock of the same metal, with a comb of the largest rubies covered with pearls and other stones; the eyes also were made of rubies.

A gazelle whose body was covered all over with pearls and the most precious stones; the stomach was white and composed of a series of pearls of the purest water.

A sardonyx table, with conical feet of the same substance; it was large enough for several people to eat there at the same time.

A garden, the soil made of chased and gilt silver and yellow earth. There were silver trees, with fruits made of precious materials.

A golden palm-tree enriched with superb pearls. It was in a golden chest and its fruit was made of precious stones representing dates in every stage of ripeness. This tree was of inestimable value. (6)

About the time the monk Gerbert was accused of sorcery because he understood the elements of geometry, the Caliph Aziz-Billah founded the university of Cairo, the greatest Mohammedan institution of learning. This was two hundred years before the organization of the university of Paris, and the lectures at the mosque of El-Azhar are said to have been attended by twelve thousand students. Munk was of opinion that Arabic philosophy reached its apogee with Averrhoës, who was born about 1120.(7) Certainly he was the last of a famous line which began at Bagdad three centuries earlier; and Hauréau, in describing the great period of Saint Thomas at Paris, dwelt upon the debt Western learning owed to the Saracens.

The splendour of Haroun-al-Raschid is still proverbial. The tales of his gold and silver, his silks and gems, almost surpass belief, and even in his reign the mechanical arts were so advanced that he sent a clock to Charlemagne.

Humboldt considered the Arabs as the founders of modern experimental science, and they were relatively skilful chemists, for they understood the composition of sulphuric and nitric acid, and of aqua regia, beside the preparation of mercury and of various oxides of metals. As physicians they were far in advance of Europe. While the Church healed by miracles, and put experimental methods under her ban, the famous Rhazes conducted the hospitals of Bagdad, and in the tenth century wrote a work in ten books, which was printed at Venice as late as 1510. Practitioners of all nations have used his treatise on small-pox and measles; he introduced mild purgatives, invented the seton, and was a remarkable anatomist. He died in 932.

William of Tyre stated that the Frankish nobles of Syria preferred the native or Jewish doctors; and though Saladin sent his physician to Richard, Richard never thought of sending an Englishman to Saladin when afterwards attacked by illness.

Even as late as the middle of the thirteenth century little advance seems to have been made in Europe, for one of the most curious phenomena of the crusades was the improvement in the health of the army of Saint Louis after it surrendered. During the campaign various epidemics had been very fatal; but when the soldiers were subjected to the sanitary regulations of the Egyptian medical staff, disease disappeared.

The Arabs had a strong taste for mathematics, and were familiar with most of the discoveries which have been attributed to astronomers of the fifteenth and sixteenth centuries.

As early as 1000 spherical trigonometry was in use, and Aboul-Hassan wrote an excellent treatise on conic sections. In 833 the Caliph El-Mamoun, having founded observatories at Bagdad and Damascus, caused a degree to be measured on the plain of Palmyra. By the thirteenth century the Arabic instruments were comparatively perfect. They had the astrolabe, the gnomon, the sextant, and the mariner's compass, and Aboul-Wafa determined the third lunar variation six hundred years before Tycho Brahe.

To enumerate all the improvements in agriculture and manufactures which came from the mediaeval pilgrimage would take a separate treatise. A French savant thought of writing a book upon the flora of the crusades alone. The mulberry and the silkworm were brought from Greece, the maize from Turkey, the plum from Damascus, the eschalot from Ascalon, and the windmills with which, down to the present century, corn was ground, were one of the importations from the Levant.

It might almost be said that all the West knew of the arts was learned on the road to the sepulchre. The Tyrians taught the Sicilians to refine sugar, and the Venetians to make glass; Damascus steel was a proverb, Damascus potters were the masters of the potters of France; the silk, brocades, and carpets of Syria and Persia were in the twelfth century what they have been down to the present day, at once the admiration and despair of Western weavers, while there can be little doubt that gunpowder was the invention of the chemists of the East.

All the evidence tends to prove that the ogive came from the Levant, and without the ogive Gothic architecture could never have developed.(8) Prior to the council of Clermont the pointed arch was practically unknown west of the Adriatic; but the Arabs had long used it, and it may still be seen in the ninth century mosque of Teyloun.

In Palestine the Franks were surrounded by Saracenic buildings, and employed Saracenic masons, and the attention of Western architects seems no sooner to have been drawn to the possibilities of the ogive, than they saw in it the solution of those problems which had before defied them. An arch formed by two intersecting segments of a circle could be raised to any height from any base, and was perfectly adapted to vaulting the parallelograms formed by the columns of the nave. Therefore, contemporaneously with the building of the church of the Holy Sepulchre, the period of transition between the Romanesque and the Gothic opened in France. The two most important transition buildings were the abbey of Saint

Denis and the cathedral of Noyon, and, while the Holy Sepulchre was dedicated in 1149, the abbey was completed in 1144, and the cathedral was begun almost immediately after.(9)

Thenceforward the movement was rapid, and before the year 1200. Christian sacred architecture was culminating in those marvels of beauty, the cathedrals of Paris, of Bourges, of Chartres, and of Le Mans. Yet, though sacred architecture tells the story of the rise of the imagination as nothing else can, if it be true that centralization hinges on the preponderance of the attack in war, the surest way of measuring the advance toward civilization of rude peoples must be by military engineering.

In the eleventh century, north of the Alps, this science was rudimentary, and nothing can be more impressive than to compare the mighty ramparts of Constantinople with the small square tower which William the Conqueror found ample for his needs in London.

When the crusaders were first confronted with the Greek and Arabic works, they were helpless; nor were their difficulties altogether those of ignorance. Such fortifications were excessively costly, and a feudal State was poor because the central power had not the force to constrain individuals to pay taxes. The kingdom of Jerusalem was in chronic insolvency.

The life of the Latin colony in Syria, therefore, hung on the development of some financial system which should make the fortification of Palestine possible, and such a system grew up through the operation of the imagination, though in an unusual manner.

Fetish worship drew a very large annual contribution from the population in the shape of presents to propitiate the saints, and one of the effects of the enthusiasm for the crusades was to build up conventual societies in the Holy Land, which acted as standing armies. The most famous of the military orders were the Knights of the Temple and the Knights of Saint John. William of Tyre has left an interesting description of the way in which the Temple came to be organized:—

"As though the Lord God sends his grace there where he pleases, worthy knights, who were of the land beyond the sea, proposed to stay for ever in the service of Our Lord, and to live in common, like regular canons. In the hand of the patriarch they vowed chastity and obedience, and renounced all property.... The king and the other barons, the patriarch and other prelates of the Church, gave them funds to live on and to clothe themselves.... The first thing which was enjoined on them in pardon for their sins was to guard the roads by which the pilgrims passed, from robbers and thieves, who did great harm. This penance the patriarch and the other bishops enjoined. Nine years they remained thus in secular habit, wearing such garments as were given them by the knights and other good people for the love of God. In the ninth a council was assembled in France in the city of Troyes. There were assembled the archbishops of Rheims and Sens and all their bishops. The bishop of Albano especially was there as papal legate, the abbots of Citean and Clairvaux, and many other of the religious.

"There were established the order and the rules by which they were to live as monks. Their habit was ordered to be white, by the authority of Pope Honorius and the patriarch of Jerusalem. This order had already existed nine years, as I have told you, and there were as yet only nine brothers, who lived from day to day on charity. From that time their numbers began to increase, and revenues and tenures were given them. In the time of Pope Eugenius it was ordered that they should have sewn upon their copes and on their robes a cross of red cloth, so that they should be known among all men.... From thence have their possessions so increased as you can see, that the order of the Temple is in the ascendant.... Hardly can you find on either side of the sea a Christian land where this order has not to-day houses and brethren, and great revenues." (10)

The council of Troyes was held in 1128, and in the next fifty years, in proportion as the feudal organization of the Latin kingdom decayed, the military orders increased in wealth and power. The Hospital held nineteen thousand manors in Europe, the Temple nine thousand, and each manor could maintain a knight in the field.

At Paris the house of the Temple filled a whole quarter; its donjon was one of the most superb buildngs of the Middle Ages; at a later period, when the corporation took to banking, it served as a place of deposit for both public and private treasure, and in times of danger the king himself was glad to take shelter within its walls.

The creation of this monastic standing army was evidently due to the inferiority of the attack to the defence, which made the civil power incapable of coercing the individual who refused to pay taxes. The petty barons who built the castles throughout Palestine were too poor to erect fortifications capable of resisting the superior engines used in the East. Therefore the whole burden of the war was thrown upon the Church, and in all modern history nothing is more wonderful than the way in which this work was done.

Within fifty years after the conquest the feudal machinery was in ruin, and the strategic points, one after another, passed into the hands of the strongest force of the age, the force which was incarnate imagination.

The fortresses built by the monks were the ramparts of Christendom, and among the remains which have survived the past, perhaps none are more impressive than the huge castles of the crusaders in the gorges of the Syrian mountains; nor do any show so clearly whence came the rationalistic stimulus which revolutionized Europe, shattered the Church, and brought in the economic society which has ruled Europe since the Templars passed away.

Twenty-five miles due west of Homs, at the point where the Lebanon melts into the Ansarieh range, the mountains open, and two passes lead by easy descents to the sea.

Through the southern runs the road to Tripoli, through the northern that to Tortosa. Between them, on a crag a thousand feet above the valleys, still stands the castle of the Krak des Chevaliers, ceded by Count Raymond of Tripoli to the Hospital in 1145. Towering above the plain it can be seen for miles, and no description can give an idea of its gigantic size and power. Coucy and Pierrefonds are among the largest fortresses of Europe, and yet Clucy and Pierrefonds combined are no larger than the Krak.

Compared with it, the works then built in the West were toys, and the engineering talent shown in its conception was equalled by the magnificence of its masonry. The Byzantine system was adopted. A double wall, the inner commanding the outer, with a moat between; and three enormous towers rising from the moat, formed the donjon. There were stone machicoulis and all the refinements of defence which appeared in France under Saint Louis and his son, and a study of this stupendous monument shows plainly whence Europeans drew their military instruction for a century to come.

The Krak was the outwork dominating the plain where the Christians never made their footing good, and stood at the apex of a triangle of fortresses as remarkable as itself. From its ramparts the great white tower of Chastel-Blanc can be seen, midway between the outpost commanding the mountain passes and the base upon the sea held by the Temple; and from that tower the troop of Templars rode to relieve the knights of Saint John, on the day when the crusaders routed the conqueror Nour-ed-Din, and cut his army to pieces as it fled toward the Lake of Homs, which lies in the distance.

But the white tower is unlike the donjons of other lands, and bears the imprint of the force which built it, for it is not a layman's hold, but a church, whose windows are cut in walls thirteen feet thick, whence the dim light falls across the altar where the magicians wrought their miracles.

Within easy supporting distance lay Tortosa, a walled town, the outwork of a donjon at least as strong as the Krak, and built with a perfection of workmanship, and a beauty of masonry, which proves at once the knowledge and the resources of the order. No monarch of the West could, probably, at that time have undertaken so costly an enterprise, and yet Tortosa was but one of four vast structures which lie within a few miles of each other. The place was ceded to the Temple in 1183, just at the beginning of the reign of Philip Augustus, before men dreamed of the more important French fortifications.

At Margat, a day's journey to the north, the Hospital had their base upon the sea: a stronghold whose cost must have been fabulous, for it is perched upon a crag high above the Mediterranean, and so inaccessible that it is not easy to understand how the materials for building were collected. Viollet-le-Duc, who was lost in admiration at Coucy, declared that it was colossal enough to befit a race of giants, and yet Coucy could have stood in the courtyard of Margat.

The Arabs, who were excellent engineers, deemed it a masterpiece, and the Sultan Kalaoun could not endure the thought of injuring it. After he had mined the great tower and was sure of victory, he proved to the garrison his power to destroy it, in order to induce them to accept most liberal terms of surrender, and let him have the prize. Perhaps the best description ever given of the work is in a letter written by the Sultan of Hamah to his vizier to announce its fall:

"The devil himself had taken pleasure in consolidating its foundations. How many times have the Mussulmans tried to reach its towers and fallen down the precipices! Markab is unique, perched on the summit of a rock. It is accessible to relief, and inaccessible to attack. The eagle and the vulture alone can fly to its ramparts." (11)

Footnotes

(1) Dictionnaire de l'Architecture, v. 50.

(2) Annales Ecclesiastici, Baronious, year 1095.

(3) *Les Familles d'Outre-Mer*, ed. Rey, 3.

(4) *Dictionnaire de l'Architecture*, viii. 108.

(5) *L'Art Arabe*, 111 *et seq.*

(6) *L'Art Arabe*, 203.

(7) *Mélanges*, 458

(8) See *Dictionnaire de L'Architecture*, Viollet-le-Duc, vi. 446.

(9) See *Les Églises de la Terre Sainte*, Vogüé, 217; *Notre Dame de Noyon; Études sur l'Histoire de l'Art*, Vitet, ii. 122; *Dictionnaire de L'Architecture*, Viollet-le-Duc, ii. 301.

(10) *Hist. des Croisades*, xii. 7.

(11) See, on the Syrian castles, *Étude sur les Monuments de l'Architecture Militaire des Croisés en Syrie*, Rey.

Chapter IV: The Second Crusade

As the East was richer than the West, the Saracens were capable of a higher centralization than the Franks, and although they were divided amongst themselves at the close of the eleventh century, no long time elapsed after the fall of Jerusalem before the consolidation began which annihilated the Latin kingdom.

The Sultan of Persia made Zenghi governor of Mosul in 1127. Zenghi, who was the first Atabek, was a commander and organizer of ability, and with a soldier's instinct struck where his enemy was vulnerable. He first occupied Aleppo, Hamah, and Homs. He then achieved the triumph of his life by the capture of Edessa. The next year he was murdered, and was succeeded by his still more celebrated son, Nour-ed-Din, who made Aleppo his capital, and devoted his life to completing the work his father had begun.

After a series of brilliant campaigns, by a mixture of vigour and address, Nour-ed-Din made himself master of Damascus, and, operating thence as a base, he conquered Egypt, and occupied Cairo in 1169. During the Egyptian war, a young emir, named Saladin, rose rapidly into prominence. He was the nephew of the general in command, at whose death the caliph made him vizier, because he thought him pliable. In this the caliph was mistaken, for Saladin was a man of iron will and consummate ability. William of Tyre even accused him of having murdered the last Fatimite caliph with his own hands in order to cause the succession to pass to Nour-ed-Din, and to seize on the substance of power himself, as Nour-ed-Din's representative.

Certainly he administered Egypt in his own interest, and not in his master's; so much so that Nour-ed-Din, having failed to obtain obedience to his commands, had prepared to march against him in person, when, on the eve of his departure, he died. Saladin then moved on Damascus, and having defeated the army of El Melek, the heir to the crown, at Hamah, he had himself declared Sultan of Egypt and Syria.

With a power so centralized the Franks would probably, under the best circumstances, have been unable to cope. The weakness of the Christians was radical, and arose from the exuberance of their imagination, which caused them to proceed by miracles, or more correctly, by magical formulas. An exalted imagination was the basis of the characters of both Louis VII. and Saint Bernard, and the faith resulting therefrom led to the defeat of the second crusade.

The Christian collapse began with the fall of Edessa, for the County of Edessa was the extreme northeastern state of the Latin community, and the key to the cities of the plain. When the first crusaders reached Armenia, Baldwin, brother of Godfrey de Bouillon, conceived the idea of carving a kingdom for himself out of the Christian country to the south of the Taurus range. Taking with him such pilgrims as he could persuade to go, he started from Mamistra, just north of the modern Alexandretta, and marched east along the caravan road. Edessa lay sixteen hours' ride beyond the Euphrates, and he reached it in safety.

At this time, though Edessa still nominally formed part of the Greek Empire, it was in reality independent, and was governed by an old man named Theodore, who had originally been sent from Constantinople, but who had gradually taken the position of a sovereign. The surrounding country had been overrun by Moslems, and Theodore only maintained himself by paying tribute. The people, therefore, were ready to welcome any Frankish baron capable of defending them; and Baldwin, though a needy adventurer, was an excellent officer, and well adapted to the emergency.

As he drew near, the townsmen went out to meet him, and escorted him to the city in triumph, where he soon supplanted the old Theodore, whom he probably murdered. He then became Count of Edessa, but he remained in the country only two years, for in 1100 he was elected to succeed his brother Godfrey. He was followed as Lord of Edessa by his cousin Godfrey de Bourg, who, in his turn, was crowned King of Jerusalem in 1119, and the next count was de Bourg's cousin, Joscelin de Courtney, who had previously held as a fief the territory to the west of the Euphrates. This Joscelin was one of the most renowned warriors who ever came from France, and while he lived the frontier was well defended. So high was his prowess that he earned the title of "the great" in an age when every man was a soldier, and in a country where arms were the only path to fortune save the Church.

The story of his death is one of the most dramatic of that dramatic time. As he stood beneath the wall of a Saracenic tower he had mined, it suddenly fell and buried him in the ruins. He was taken out a mangled mass to die, but, as he lay languishing, news came that the Sultan of Iconium had laid siege to one of his castles near Tripoli. Feeling that he could not sit his horse, he called his son and directed him to collect his vassals and ride to the relief of the fortress. The youth hesitated, fearing that the enemy were too numerous. Then the old man, grieving to think of the fate of his people when he should be gone, had himself slung in a litter between two horses, and marched against the foe.

He had not gone far before he was met by a messenger, who told him that when the Saracens heard the Lord of Courtney was upon the march, they had raised the siege and fled. Then the wounded baron ordered his litter to be set down upon the ground, and, stretching out his hands to heaven, he thanked God who had so honoured him that his enemies dared not abide his coming even when in the jaws of death, and died there where he lay.

The second generation of Franks seems to have deteriorated through the influence of the climate, but the character of the younger Joscelin was not the sole cause of the disasters which overtook him. Probably even his father could not permanently have made head against the forces which were combining against him. The weakness of the Frankish kingdom was inherent: it could not contend with enemies who were further advanced upon the road toward consolidation. Had Western society been enough centralized to have organized a force capable of collecting taxes, and of enforcing obedience to a central administration, a wage-earning army might have been maintained on the frontier. As it was, concentration was impossible, and the scattered nobles were crushed in detail.

Antioch was the nearest supporting point to Edessa, and, when Zenghi made his attack, Raymond de Poitiers, one of the ablest soldiers of his generation, was the reigning prince. But he was at feud with the Courtneys; the king at Jerusalem could not force him to do his duty; the other barons were too distant, even had they been well disposed; and thus the key to the Christian position fell without a blow being struck in its defence.

To that emotional generation the loss of Edessa seemed a reversal of the laws of nature; a consequence not of bad organization but of divine wrath. The invincible relics had suddenly refused to act, and the only explanation which occurred to the men of the time was, that there must have been neglect of the magical formulas.

Saint Bernard never doubted that God would fight if duly propitiated; therefore all else must bend to the task of propitiation: "What think ye, brethren? Is the hand of the Lord weakened, or unequal to the work of defence, that he calls miserable worms to guard and restore his heritage? Is he not able to send more than twelve legions of angels, or, to speak truly, by word deliver his country?" (1)

Saint Bernard of Clairvaux, the soul of the second crusade, was born at the castle of Fontaines, near Dijon, in 1091, so that his earliest impressions must have been tinged by the emotional outburst which followed the council of Clermont. The third son of noble parents, he resembled his mother, who had the ecstatic temperament. While she lived she tried to imitate the nuns, and at her death she was surrounded by holy clerks, who sung with her while she could speak, and, when articulation failed, watched her lips moving in praise to God.

From the outset, Bernard craved a monastic life, and when he grew up insisted on dedicating himself to Heaven. His first success was the conversion of his brothers, whom he carried with him to the cloister, with the exception of the youngest, who was then a child. As the brothers passed through the castle courtyard, on their way to the convent, Guy, the eldest, said to the boy, who was playing there with other children, "Well, Nivard, all our land is now yours." "So you will have heaven and I earth," the child answered; "that is an unequal division." And a few years after he joined his brothers.(2) The father and one daughter then were left alone, and at last they too entered convents, where they died.

At twenty-two, when Bernard took his vows at Citeaux, his influence was so strong that he carried with him thirty of his comrades, and mothers are said to have hid their sons from him, and wives their husbands, lest he should lure them away. He actually broke up so many homes that the abandoned wives formed a nunnery, which afterward grew rich.

His abilities were so marked that his superiors singled him out, when he had hardly finished his novitiate, to found a house in the wilderness. This house became Clairvaux, in the twelfth century the most famous monastery of the world.

In the Middle Ages, convents were little patronized until by some miracle they had proved themselves worthy of hire; their early years were often passed in poverty, and Clairvaux was no exception to the rule, for the brethren suffered privations which nearly caused revolt. In the midst of his difficulties, Bernard's brother Gérard, who was cellarer, came to him to complain that the fraternity were without the barest necessities of life. The man of God asked, "How much will suffice for present wants?" Gerard replied, "Twelve pounds." Bernard dismissed him and betook himself to prayer. Soon after Gérard returned and announced that a woman was without and wished to speak with him. "She, when he had come to her, prostrating herself at his feet, offered him a gift of twelve pounds, imploring the aid of his prayers for her husband, who was dangerously sick. Having briefly spoken with her, he dismissed her, saying: 'Go. You will find your husband well.' She, going home, found what she had heard had come to pass. The abbot comforting the weakness of his cellarer, made him stronger for bearing other trials from God." (3)

Although his family were somewhat sceptical about his gifts, and even teased him to tears, the monk William tells, in his chronicle, how he soon performed an astounding miracle which made Clairvaux a "veritable valley of light," and then wealth poured in upon him.

Meanwhile, his constitution, which had never been vigorous, had been so impaired by his penances that he was unable to follow the monastic life in its full rigour, and he therefore threw himself into politics, to which he was led both by taste and by the current of events.

Clairaux was founded in 1115, and fifteen years later Bernard had risen high in his profession. The turning-point in his life was the part he took in the recognition of Innocent II. In 1130, Honorius II. died, and two popes were chosen by the college of cardinals, Anacletus and Innocent II. Anacletus stayed in Rome, but Innocent crossed the Alps, and a council was summoned at Étampes to decide upon his title. By a unanimous vote the question was referred to Bernard, and his biographer described how he examined the evidence with fear and trembling, and how at last the Holy Ghost spoke through his mouth, and he recognized Innocent. His decision was ratified, and soon after he managed to obtain the adhesion of the King of England to the new pontiff.

His success made him the foremost man in Europe, and when, in 1145, one of his monks was raised to the papacy as Eugenius III., he wrote with truth, "I am said to be more pope than you."

Perhaps no one ever lived more highly gifted with the ecstatic temperament than Saint Bernard. He had the mysterious attribute of miracles, and, in the twelfth century, the miracle was, perhaps, the highest expression of force. To work them was a personal gift, and the possessor of the faculty might, at his caprice, use his power, like the sorcerer, to aid or injure other men.

One day as Saint Bernard was on his way to a field at harvest time, the monk who drove the donkey on which he rode, fell in an epileptic fit. "Seeing which the holy man had pity on him, and entreated God that for the future he would not seize him unaware." Accordingly from that day until his death, twenty years after, "whenever he was to fall from that disease, he felt the fit coming for a certain space of time, so that he had an opportunity to lie down on a bed, and so avert the bruises of a sudden fall." (4)

This cure was a pure act of grace, like alms, made to gratify the whim of the saint; and a man who could so control nature was more powerful than any other on earth. Bernard was such a man, and for this reason he was chosen by acclamation to preach the second crusade.

His sermons have perished, but two of his letters have survived,(5) and they explain the essential weakness of a military force raised on the basis of supernatural intervention. He looked upon the approaching campaign as merely the vehicle for a miracle, and as devised to offer to those who entered on it a special chance for salvation. Therefore he appealed to the criminal classes. "For what is it but an exquisite and priceless chance of salvation due to God alone, that the Omnipotent should deign to summon to his service, as though they were innocent, murderers, ravishers, adulterers, perjurers, and those guilty of every crime?" (6)

Even had an army composed of such material been well disciplined and well led, it would have been untrustworthy in the face of an adversary like Nour-ed-Din; but Louis VII. of France was as emotional and as irrational as Saint Bernard. His father had been a great commander, but he himself had been educated in the Abbey of Saint Denis, and justified his wife's scornful jest, who, when she left him for Raymond de Poitiers, said she had married a monk. The whole world held him lightly, even the priests sneered at him, and Innocent II. spoke of him as a child "who must be stopped from learning rebellion."

Indeed, the pope underrated him, for he appointed his own nephew to the See of Bourges in defiance of the king, and the insult roused him to resistance. Louis raised an army and invaded the County of Champagne, where the bishop had taken refuge. There he stormed and burnt Vitry, and some thirteen hundred men, women, and children, who had taken refuge in the church, perished in the flames of the blazing town. Horror seems to have unhinged his mind, absolution did not calm him, and at last he came to believe that his only hope of salvation lay in a pilgrimage to the Sepulchre. On Palm Sunday, 1146, when Bernard harangued a vast throng at Vézelay, the king was the first to prostrate himself, and take the cross from his hands.

With that day began the most marvellous part of the saint's marvellous career, and were the events which followed less well authenticated, they would be incredible. In that age miracles were as common as medical cures are now, and yet Bernard's performances so astonished his contemporaries that they drew up a solemnly attested record of what they saw, that the story of his preaching might never be questioned.

When he neared a town the bells were rung, and young and old, from far and near, thronged about him in crowds so dense that, at Constance, no one saw what passed, because no one dared to venture into the press. At Troyes he was in danger of being suffocated. Elsewhere the sick were brought to him by a ladder as he stood at a window out of reach. What he did may be judged by the work of a single day.

"When the holy man entered Germany he shone so marvellously by cures, that it can neither be told in words, nor would it be believed if it were told. For those testify who were present in the country of Constance, near the town of Doningen, who diligently investigated these things, and saw them with their eyes, that in one day eleven blind received their sight by the laying on of his hands, ten maimed were restored, and eighteen lame made straight." (7)

Thus, literally by thousands, the blind saw, the lame walked, the maimed were made whole. He cast out devils, turned water into wine, raised the dead. But no modern description can give an idea of the paroxysm of excitement; the stories must be read in the chronicles themselves. Yet, strangely enough, such was the strength of the materialistic inheritance from the Empire, that Bernard does not always seem fully to have believed in himself. He was tinged with some shade of scepticism. The meeting at Vézelay was held on March 24, 1146. Four weeks later, on April 21, at a council held at Chartres, the command of the army to invade Palestine was offered to the Abbot of Clairvaux. Had the saint thoroughly believed in himself and his twelve legions of angels, he would not have hesitated, for no enemy could have withstood God. In fact he was panic-stricken, and wrote a letter to the pope which might befit a modern clergyman.

After explaining that he had been chosen commander against his will, he exclaimed, "Who am I, that I should set camps in order, or should march before armed men? Or what is so remote from my profession, even had I the strength, and the knowledge were not lacking?... I beseech you, by that charity you especially owe me, that you do not abandon me to the wills of men." (8)

During 1146 and 1147 two vast mixed multitudes, swarming with criminals and women, gathered at Metz and Ratisbon. As a fighting force these hosts were decidedly inferior to the bands which had left Europe fifty years before, under Tancred and Godfrey de Bouillon, and they were besides commanded by the semi-emasculated King of France.

The Germans cannot be considered as having taken any part in the war, for they perished without having struck a blow. The Greek emperor caused them to be lured into the mountains of Asia Minor, where they were abandoned by their guides, and wasted away from exposure, hunger, and thirst, until the Saracens destroyed them without allowing them to come to battle.

The French fared little better. In crossing the Cadmus Mountains, their lack of discipline occasioned a defeat, which made William of Tyre wonder at the ways of God.

"To no one should the things done by our Lord be displeasing, for all his works are right and good, but according to the judgment of men it was marvellous how our Lord permitted the Franks (who are the people in the world who believe in him and honour him most) to be thus destroyed by the enemies of the faith." (9)

Soon after this check Louis was joined by the Grand Master of the Temple, under whose guidance he reached Atalia, a Greek port in Pamphylia: and here, had the king been a rationalist, he would have stormed the town and used it as a base of operations against Syria. In the eyes of laymen, the undisguised hostility of the emperor would have fully justified such an attack. But Louis was a devotee, bound by a vow to the performance of a certain mystic formula, and one part of his vow was not to attack Christians during his pilgrimage. In his mind the danger of disaster from supernatural displeasure was greater than the strategic advantage; and so he allowed his army to rot before the walls in the dead of winter, without tents or supplies, until it wasted to a shadow of its former strength.

Finally the governor contracted to provide shipping, but he delayed for another five weeks, and when the transports came they were too few. Even then Louis would not strike, but abandoning the poor and sick to their fate, he sailed away with the flower of his troops, and by spring the corpses of those whom he had deserted bred a pestilence which depopulated the city.

When he arrived at Antioch new humiliations and disasters awaited him. Raymond de Poitiers was one of the handsomest and most gifted men of this time. Affable, courteous, brave, and sagacious, in many respects a great captain, his failing was a hot temper, which led him to his ruin. He forsook Joscelin through jealousy, and the fall of Edessa cost him throne and life.

After the successes of Zenghi, a very short experience of Nour-ed-Din sufficed to convince Prince Raymond that Antioch could not be held without re-establishing the frontier; and when Louis arrived, Raymond tried hard to persuade him to abandon his pilgrimage for that season, and make a campaign in the north.

William of Tyre thought the plan good, and believed that the Saracens were, for the moment, too demoralized to resist. Evidently, by advancing from Antioch, Nour-ed-Din could have been isolated, whereas on the south he was covered by Damascus, one of the strongest places in the East.

Such considerations had no weight with Louis, for, to his emotional temperament, military strategy lay in obtaining supernatural aid, without which no wisdom could avail, and with which victory was sure. He therefore insisted on the punctilious performance of the religious rites, and one of the most interesting passages in *William of Tyre* is the account of the interview between him and Raymond, when a movement against the cities of the north was discussed.

"The prince, who had tried the temper of the king several times privately, and not found what he wanted, came one day to him before his barons and made his requests to the best of his power. Many reasons he showed that if he would agree, he would do his soul much good, and would win the applause of his liege; Christendom would lie so benefited by this thing. The king took counsel, and then he answered that he was vowed to the Sepulchre, and had taken the cross particularly to go there; that, since he had left his country, he had met with many hindrances, and that he had no wish to begin any wars until he had perfected his pilgrimage." (10)

This refusal so exasperated Prince Raymond that he threw off all disguise, and became the avowed lover of the queen, who detested her husband. Louis, shortly afterward, escaped by night from Antioch, taking Eleanor with him by force, and thus the only hope for the recovery of Edessa was lost.

For the emotionalist everything yielded to the transcendent importance of propitiatory rites; therefore Louis ascended Calvary, kissed the stones, intoned the chants, received the benediction, and lost Palestine. Thus, by the middle of the twelfth century, the idealist had begun to flag in the struggle for life.

An attempt, indeed, was afterwards made upon Damascus, but it only served to expose the weakness of the men who relied on magic. By the time the advance began, confidence had been restored among the Saracens, the attack was repulsed, and Nour-ed-Din had only to move from the north to throw the crusaders back upon Jerusalem, covered with ridicule. Nothing conveys so vivid an idea of the shock these reverses gave believers, as the words in which Saint Bernard defended his prophecies.

"Do they not say among the pagans, where is their God? Nor is it wonderful. The sons of the Church, who are known by the name of Christians, are laid low in the desert, destroyed by the sword, or consumed by famine. The Lord hath poured contempt upon princes, and hath caused them to wander in the wilderness, where there is no way. Grief and misfortune have followed their steps, fear and confusion have been in the palaces of the kings themselves. How have the feet strayed of those promising peace and blessings. We have said peace and there is no peace, we have promised good fortune and behold tribulation, as if we had acted in this matter with rashness and levity.... Yet if one of two things must be, I prefer to have men murmur against me rather than God. It is good if I am worthy to be used as a shield. I take willingly the slanders of detractors, and the poisoned stings of blasphemers, that they may not reach him. I do not shrink from loss of glory that his may not be attacked, who gives it to me to be glorified in the words of the Psalmist: 'Because for thy sake I have borne reproach; shame hath covered my face.'"(11)

According to the account of William of Tyre, both sides felt the end to be near. After the failure of Louis the Pious, Prince Raymond was the first to go down before the storm he had too late seen gathering. Nour-ed-Din fell upon his country with fire and sword, defeated him, cut off his head and right arm, and sent them to Bagdad as trophies. The wretched Joscelin died in a dungeon at Aleppo, while Nour-ed-Din entered Damascus, and thus consolidated the Syrian cities of the plain. Thenceforward the decentralized Franks lay helpless in the grasp of their compact adversary, and all that was imaginative in the Middle Ages received its death-wound at Tiberias. That action was the beginning of the decay of fetish-worship.

The crusaders believed they had found the cross on which Christ died at Jerusalem. They venerated it as a charm no less powerful than the Sepulchre itself, and having this advantage over the tomb, that it was portable. They thought it invincible, and used it not only as a weapon against living enemies, but as a means of controlling nature. A remarkable example of the magical properties of this relic was given in the retreat from Bosra.

Baldwin III. was crowned in 1144, when only thirteen. The kingdom was then at peace with Damascus, in whose territory Bosra lay; but, notwithstanding, the child's advisers eagerly listened to the offer of the emir in command to betray the town, and hastened forward the departure of an expedition, in spite of the protests of the envoys from Damascus. On the march the troops suffered severely from heat and thirst, and on their arrival were appalled to find a loyal garrison. A siege was out of the question, and a regular retreat so hazardous that the barons besought the king to fly and save the cross; but the boy refused, and stayed with his men to fight to the last. The outlook was terrible, for the vegetation was dry, and when the march began—

"The Turks threw Greek fire everywhere, so that it seemed as if the whole country burned. The high flames and thick smoke blinded our men. Then were they so beset they knew not what to do. But when there is great need, and men's help fails, then should one seek aid of our Lord, and cry to him to care for us; so did our Christians then; for they called the Archbishop Robert of Nazareth, who carried the true cross before them, and begged him that he would pray our Lord, who to save them had suffered death upon that cross, that he would bring them from this peril; for they could not endure it, nor did they look for other help than his. Truly, they were there all black and scorched, like smiths, from the fire and smoke. The archbishop dismounted and kneeled down, and prayed our Lord with many tears that he would have mercy on his people; then he arose and held the true cross toward the fire which the wind brought strongly against them. Our Lord by his great mercy regarded his people in the great peril which they suffered; for the wind changed straightway and blew the fire and smoke into the faces of the enemy who had lighted it, so that they were forced to scatter over the country and fly. Our men, when they saw this, wept for joy, for they perceived that our Lord had not forgotten them."

Even then they were in extreme peril, for but one way was open, for which they had no guide. Suddenly, a "knight appeared before the troop whom no one in the host knew. He sat a white horse, and carried a crimson banner, he wore a hauberk, whose sleeves came only to the elbow. He offered to guide them, and he put himself in front; he brought them to cool sweet springs;... he made them sleep in comfortable and good places. And he so guided them that on the third day they came to the city of Gadre."(12)

The mighty relic of the cross was taken and defiled by the Saracens at Hattin, where the Christians suffered a decisive defeat, caused by the impotence of the central administration at Jerusalem.

Reginald de Chatillon was the type of the twelfth century adventurer. He came to Palestine in the train of Louis the Pious, and he stayed there because he married a princess. He was a brave soldier, but greedy, violent, and rash, and his insubordination precipitated the catastrophe which led to the fall of the capital.

At the siege of Ascalon he so fascinated Constance, Princess of Antioch, widow of Raymond, that she persisted in marrying him, although she was sought by many of the greatest nobles, and he was only a knight. Her choice was disastrous. He had hardly entered on his government in the north before he quarrelled with the Greek emperor, who forced him to do penance with a rope about his neck. Afterward he was taken prisoner by Nour-ed-Din, who only liberated him after sixteen years, when his wife was dead. He soon married again, this time also another great heiress, Etiennette de Milly, Lady of Karak and Montreal, and, as her husband, Reginald became commander of the fortress of Karak to the east of the Dead Sea, which formed the defence against Egypt. But as the commander of so important a post, this reckless and rapacious adventurer defied the authority of his feudal superior, and by plundering caravans on the Damascus road so irritated Saladin that "in 1187 he burst, with a powerful army, into the Holy Land, made King Guy prisoner, and the Prince Reginald, whose head he cut off with his own hand." (13)

Guy de Lusignan had been crowned at Jerusalem the year before Saladin's invasion, and when war broke out he was at feud with the Count of Tripoli. The imminence of the common danger brought about some semblance of cohesion among the nobles, who agreed to put every available man in the field. The castles were stripped of their garrisons so that they were indefensible in case of reverse, and about fifty thousand troops were concentrated at Sepphoris in Galilee.

The contingents of the Temple and Hospital were well organized and well disciplined, but the army, as a whole, was rather a loose gathering of the retainers of thirty or forty independent chiefs, than a compact mass, subject to a single will, such as the Egyptian revenues enabled Saladin to put in the field.

Suddenly news came to Sepphoris, that the Saracens had poured through the pass of Banias and lay before Tiberias. Dissensions broke out at once, which Guy de Lusignan could not control. He was not a man of strong character, and had he been, he was only one among a dozen princes, any one of whom could quit the army and retire to his castle if he felt so disposed. The Count of Tripoli, who seems to have been the ablest soldier among the Franks, saw the folly of leaving water and marching across a burning country under a July sun, instead of waiting to be attacked. As he represented, he of all men was most interested in relieving Tiberias, for it was his town, and his wife was within the walls; yet such was the jealousy of him in the Latin camp that his advice was rejected, and an advance began on July 3, 1187.

Three miles from Tiberias the action opened by a furious attack on the rearguard, formed by the Temple and the Hospital. When they gave ground Guy lost heart and ordered a halt. The night which followed was frightful. The Moslems fired the dry undergrowth, and, amidst flames and smoke, the Franks lay till dawn, tormented by hunger and thirst, and exposed to clouds of arrows which the enemy poured in on them.

At dawn fighting began again, but the demoralized infantry fled to a hill, whence they refused to move. The Count of Tripoli, seeing the battle lost, cut his way out with a band of his followers, but Guy de Lusignan, Reginald de Chatillon, and a multitude of knights and nobles were captured. The orders were practically annihilated, the whole able-bodied population cut to pieces, and the holy cross, which had been borne before the host as an invincible engine of war, was seized and defiled on the mountain where Jesus taught his disciples to love their enemies.

Emmad-Eddin, an Arabic historian, has described the veneration of the Christians for their talisman, their adoration of it in peace, and their devotion to it in battles; and his words help a modern generation to conceive the shock its worshippers received when it betrayed its helplessness.

"The great cross was taken before the king, and many of the impious sought death about it. When it was held aloft the infidels bent the knee and bowed the head. They had enriched it with gold and jewels; they carried it on days of great solemnity, and looked upon it as their first duty to defend it in battle. The capture of this cross was more grievous to them than the capture of their king."

Footnotes

(1) Letter 363, ed. 1877, Paris.

(2) *Sancti Bernardi, Vita et Res Gestae, Auctore Guillelmo,* 1-3.

(3) *Secunda Vita S. Bernardi Auctore Alano,* vi.

(4) *Exordium Magnum Cisterciense,* viii.

(5) Nos. 363 and 423, ed. of 1877, Paris.

(6) Letter 363.

(7) *De Vita S. Bernardi, Auctore Gaufrido,* iv. 5.

(8) Letter 256, ed. of 1877, Paris.

(9) *Hist. des Croisades,* xvi. 25.

(10) *Hist. des Croisades,* xvi. 27.

(11) *De Consideratione* ii. 1.

(12) *Willam of Tyre*, xvi. 11, 12.

(13) *Les Familles d'Outre-Mer*, Du Cange, 405.

Chapter V: The Fall of Constantinople

MOST writers on the crusades have noticed the change which followed the battle of Tiberias. Pigeonneau, for example, in his *History of Commerce* pointed out that, after the loss of Jerusalem, the Christians became more and more intent on economic interests," and the "crusades became more and more political and commercial, rather than religious, expeditions." (1)

In other words, when decentralization reached its limit, the form of competition changed, and consolidation began. With the reopening of the valley of the Danube, the current turned. At first the tide ran feebly, but after the conquest of the Holy Land the channels of trade altered; capital began to accumulate; and by the thirteenth century money controlled Palestine and Italy, and was rapidly subduing France. Heyd remarked that "the commerce to the Levant took a leap, during the crusades, of which the boldest imagination could hardly have dreamed shortly before," (2) because the possession of the Syrian ports brought Europe into direct communication with Asia, and accelerated exchanges.

From the dawn of European history to the rise of modern London, the Eastern trade has enriched every community where it has centred, and, among others, North Italy in the Middle Ages, Venice, Florence, Genoa, and Pisa were its creations.

In the year 452, when the barbarian migrations were flowing over the Roman provinces in steadily increasing volume, the Huns sacked Aquileia, and the inhabitants of the ravaged districts fled for shelter to the islands which lie in the shallow water at the head of the Adriatic. For many generations these fugitives remained poor, subsisting mainly on fish, and selling salt as their only product; but gradually they developed into a race highly adapted to flourish under the conditions which began to prevail after the council of Clermont.

Isolated save toward the sea, without agriculture or mines, but two paths were open to them, piracy and commerce: and they excelled in both. By the reign of Charlemagne they were prosperous; and when the closing of the valley of the Danube forced traffic to go by sea, Venice and Amalfi obtained a monopoly of what was left of the Eastern trade. For many years, however, that trade was not highly lucrative. Though Rome always offered a certain market for brocades for vestments and for altar coverings, for incense, and jewels for shrines, ready money was scarce, the West having few products which Asiatics or Africans were willing to take in exchange for their goods. Therefore it was not through enterprises sanctioned by the priesthood, that Venice won in the economic competition which began to prevail in the eleventh century.

Venetians prospered because they were bolder and more unscrupulous than their neighbours. They did without compunction what was needful for gain, even when the needful thing was a damnable crime in the eyes of the devout.

The valley of the Nile, though fertile, produces neither wood nor iron, nor men of the fighting type; for these the caliphs were ready to pay, and the Venetians provided them all. Even as early as 971 dealings with the common enemy in material of war had reached proportions which not only stimulated the Emperor John Zimisces to energetic diplomatic remonstrance, but made him threaten to burn all the ships he captured laden with suspicious cargoes.

To sell timber for ships, and iron for swords, to the Saracens, was a mortal sin in children of the Church; but such a sin was as nothing beside the infamy of kidnapping believers as slaves for infidels, who made them soldiers to fight against their God. Charlemagne and the popes after him tried to suppress the traffic, but without avail. Slaving was so lucrative that it was carried on in the streets of Rome herself,(3) and in the thirteenth century two thousand Europeans were annually disposed of in

Damietta and Alexandria, from whom the Mamelukes, the finest corps of soldiers in the East, were recruited.

Thus a race grew up in Italy, which differed from the people of France and Germany because of the absence of those qualities which had caused the Germans to survive when the inhabitants of the Empire decayed. The mediæval Italians prospered because they were lacking in the imagination which made the Northern peoples subservient to the miracle-worker, and among mediaeval Italians the Venetians, from their exposed position, came to be the most daring, energetic, and unscrupulous. By the end of the eleventh century their fleet was so superior to the Greek, that the Emperor Alexis had to confide to them the defence of the harbour of Durazzo against Robert Guiscard. Guiscard attacked Durazzo in 1081, at the time of the revolution which immediately preceded the debasement of the Byzantine coinage; and the demonstration that Venice had already absorbed most of the carrying trade, seems to prove that, during the last half of the eleventh century, the centre of exchanges had a pronounced tendency to abandon Constantinople. Moreover, the result of the campaign showed that the Venetian navy was the strongest in the Mediterranean, and this was of vital moment to the success of the crusades twenty years later, for, without the command of the sea, the permanent occupation of Palestine would have been impossible.

After the capture of Jerusalem in 1099, almost the first operations of Godfrey de Bouillon were against the Syrian ports; but as he controlled too small a force to act alone, he made a treaty with Venice, by which, in consideration of two hundred ships, he promised to cede to her a third part of every town taken. Baldwin made a similar arrangement with the Genoese, and, as the coast was subdued, the Italian cities assumed their grants, and established their administrations. In the end the Venetians predominated at Tyre, the Genoese at Acre, and the Pisans at Antioch. Before the discovery of the Cape of Good Hope, the spices, drugs, brocades, carpets, porcelains, and gems of India and China, reached the Mediterranean mainly by two routes. One by way of the Persian Gulf to Bagdad, up the Euphrates to Rakka, and by land to Aleppo, whence they were conveyed by caravan either to Antioch or Damascus. Damascus, beside being the starting-place of caravans for Mecca and Egypt, and the emporium for the products of Persia, had important manufactures of its own. Its glass, porcelain, steel, and brocades were famous, and it was a chief market for furs, which were highly prized throughout the Middle Ages, when heating was not understood.

The second route was by water. Indian merchants usually sold their cargoes at Aden, whence they were taken to a port in Upper Egypt, floated down the Nile to Cairo, and bought by Europeans at Damietta or Alexandria. The products of Egypt itself were valuable, and next to Constantinople, Cairo was the richest city west of the Indus.

What Europe gave to the Orientals in return is not so well known; but, beside raw materials and slaves, her woollens were much esteemed. At all events, exchanges must have become more favourable to her, as is proved by the increased supply of the precious metals.

Why the short period of expansion, which followed upon the re-establishment of the silver standard in the West, should have been succeeded by a sharp contraction is unknown, but the fact seems proved by the coinage. In the reign of Charlemagne a silver pound of 7680 grains was made the monetary unit, which was divided into 240 denarii, or pence.(4)

For some time these pence were tolerably maintained, but as the empire of Charlemagne disintegrated, they deteriorated until, by the end of the twelfth century, those coined at Venice were but a quarter of their original weight and three parts alloy.(5) After Hattin a new expansion began, in which Venice took the lead. The battle was fought in 1187, and some years later, but probably before

1200, the grosso was struck, a piece of fine silver, of good weight, which thereafter was maintained at the standard. Half a century later gold appeared. Florence coined the florin in 1252, Venice the ducat in 1284, and, between the two dates, Saint Louis issued his crowns.

The return of the precious metals to the West indicated a revival of trade and a change in the form of competition. Instead of the imagination, the economic faculty began to predominate, and energy chose money as its vent. Within a generation the miracle fell decisively in power, and the beginning of this most crucial of social revolutions is visible in the third crusade, the famous expedition led by Philip Augustus and Cœur de Lion.

These two great soldiers probably learned the art of fortification at the siege of Acre, the most remarkable passage of arms of the Middle Ages. The siege is said to have cost one hundred thousand lives, and certainly called forth all the engineering skill of the time. Guy de Lusignan, having been liberated by Saladin soon after Hattin, wandered about the country, abandoned and forlorn, until at last he sat down before Acre, in 1189, with a force inferior to the garrison. There he was joined by the kings of France and England, who succeeded in capturing the city after a desperate defence of two years. An immense booty was taken, but the clergy complained that two secular princes had embezzled the heritage of God. On the other hand, the troops had not received the usual assistance from miracles; for though assaults were delivered almost daily, none were worked, and the Virgin herself only appeared once, and then so quietly as to arouse no enthusiasm.

After the surrender Philip went home, while Richard remained in command. The whole country had been overrun, only a few strongholds like the Krak des Chevaliers and Tortosa held out; and Richard, far from following the example of the first crusaders, who marched straight for the relics at Jerusalem, turned his attention to re-establishing the centres of trade upon the coast.

He moved south along the shore, keeping close to his fleet, with the enemy following on the mountains. As he approached Joppa, the Saracens descended into the plain and gave battle. They were decisively defeated, and Richard occupied Joppa without resistance. From Joppa the road ran direct to Jerusalem. The way was not long nor the country difficult, and there is no reason to suppose an attack to have been particularly hazardous. On the contrary, when Richard advanced, the opposition was not unusually stubborn, and he actually pursued the enemy to within sight of the walls. Yet he resolutely resisted the pressure of the clergy to undertake a siege, the inference being that the power which controlled him held Jerusalem to be worthless. That power must have been capital, for the treaty which he negotiated was as frankly mercenary as though made in modern times. The seaboard from Tyre to Joppa was ceded to the Franks; Ascalon, which was the key to Egypt, was dismantled, and the only mention made of Jerusalem was that it should be open to pilgrims in the future, as it had been in the past. Of the cross, which fifty years before had been prized above all the treasures of the East, not a word was said, nor does it appear that, after Hattin, either Infidels or Christians attached a money value to it.

Some chroniclers have insisted that Richard felt remorse at thus abandoning his God; and when, in a skirmish, he saw the walls of Jerusalem, they related that he hid his face and wept. He may have done so, but, during his life, the time came when Christian knights felt naught but exultation at having successfully bartered the Sepulchre for money. After Richard's departure, the situation of the Franks in the Holy Land went rapidly from bad to worse. The decay of faith constantly relaxed the bond which had once united them against the Moslems, while they were divided amongst themselves by commercial jealousies. The Temple and the Hospital carried on perpetual private wars about disputed property, the fourth crusade miscarried, and the garrison of Joppa was massacred, while Europe looked on with indifference.

When this point was reached, the instinct of self-preservation seems to have roused the clergy to the fact that their fate was bound up with the fate of the holy places: if the miracle were discredited, their reign was at an end. Accordingly, Innocent III., on his election, threw himself into a new agitation with all the intensity of his nature. Foulques de Neuilly was chosen to preach, like Saint Bernard; but his success, at first, was not flattering. He was insulted publicly by Richard, and was even accused of having embezzled the funds entrusted to him. At length, in the year 1199, Tybalt, Count of Champagne, and Louis, Count of Blois, took the cross at a tournament they were holding at the castle of Eery. They soon were joined by others, but probably the most famous baron of the pilgrimage was Simon de Montfort.

At the end of the twelfth century the great fiefs had not been absorbed, and the Count of Champagne was a powerful sovereign. He was therefore chosen leader of the expedition, and, at a meeting held at Compiègne, the three chief princes agreed to send a committee of six to Venice to contract for transportation. In this committee, Ville-Hardouin, who wrote the chronicle of the war, represented Tybalt.

The doge was then Henry Dandolo, perhaps the most remarkable man Venice ever produced. Though nearly ninety-five, he was as vigorous as in middle life. A materialist and a sceptic, he was the best sailor, the ablest diplomatist, and the keenest speculator in Europe; and while, as a statesman and a commander, he raised his country to the pinnacle of glory, he proved himself the easy superior of Innocent III. in intrigue. So eminent were his abilities that, by common consent, he was chosen leader of a force which held some of the foremost captains of the age; and when, by his sagacity, Constantinople had been captured, he refused the imperial crown.

Ville-Hardouin always spoke of him with deep respect as "the good duke, exceeding wise and prudent;" and, indeed, without him the Frankish princes would certainly have fallen victims to the cunning of the Greeks, whom he alone knew how to over-reach, and whom he hated because his eyes had been seared by the Emperor Manuel Comnenus, when he had been upon a mission at his court.

In his bands the Frankish envoys were like children, bewildered by the wealth and splendour which surrounded them. After stating their errand to Dandolo, they waited eight days for an answer, and were then tendered a contract which has the look of having been part of a premeditated plan to ensnare the crusaders, and make them serve the republic.

The Venetians bound themselves to provide shipping for 4500 knights with their horses, 9000 squires, and 20,000 foot, with provisions for nine months, for 85,000 marks of silver; probably about equal to $5,500,000 of our money. But beside this the city proposed, "for the love of God," to add fifty galleys, and divide the conquests equally. Whatever its character, and however much such obligations were beyond the ability of the Franks, the contract was executed and sent to Innocent for ratification, who approved it with the proviso that no hostilities should be undertaken against Christians during the crusade. The pilgrims were to meet at Venice in the spring.

When Ville-Hardouin returned, Tybalt was dying, and his loss threw all into confusion. Possibly also the suspicion spread that the Venetians had imposed on the committee, for many of the nobles sailed from other ports where better terms were to be made, among whom was Reginald de Dampierre, to whom Tybalt had confided his treasure. So, in the spring of 1202, hardly more than half the knights presented themselves at Venice, and these found it quite impossible to meet their engagements. Even when the princes had sent their plate and jewels to the Ducal Palace, a deficit, estimated at 34,000 marks, remained.

On their side the Venetians declined to make any abatement of their price, but offered as a compromise to give time, and collect the balance from plunder. As a preliminary they proposed an attack on Zara, an Adriatic port, which had revolted and transferred its allegiance to the King of Hungary.

Few propositions could have been a greater outrage on the Church. Not only were the people of Zara fellow-Christians, against whom the Franks had no complaint, but the King of Hungary was himself a crusader, his dominions were under the protection of the pope, and an attack on him was tantamount to an attack on Rome herself.

On these points difference of opinion was impossible, and the papal legate, with all the other ecclesiastics, denounced the Venetians and threatened them with excommunication. The result showed that force already expressed itself in the West through money, and not through the imagination.

What followed is the more interesting since it can be demonstrated that, when beyond the Alps, and withdrawn from the pressure of capital, the French barons were as emotional as ever. While these very negotiations were pending, the subjects of Philip Augustus had deserted him in a mass, and had grovelled before Innocent as submissively as if he had been Hildebrand.

The first wife of Philip Augustus was Ingeburga, a Danish princess, for whom he had an irrepressible disinclination. In 1195 he obtained a divorce from her, by an assembly of prelates presided over by the Cardinal of Champagne. He then married Agnes de Méranie, to whom he was devotedly attached; Ingeburga appealed to Rome, and Innocent declared the divorce void, and ordered Philip to separate "from his concubine."

Philip refused, and Innocent commanded his legate to put the kingdom under interdict. At Vienne, in the month of January, 1200, at the dead of night, the magical formulas were recited. When the Christ upon the altar had been veiled, the sacred wafer burned, the miracle-working corpses hidden in the crypt, before the shuddering people, the priest laid his curse upon the king until he should put away his harlot.

From that hour all religious rites were suspended. The church doors were barred, the bells were silent, the sick died unshriven, the dead lay unburied. The king summoned his bishops, and threatened to drive them from France: it was of no avail. The barons shrank from him, his very men-at-arms fell off from him; he was alone as Henry had been at Canossa. The people were frenzied, and even went to England to obtain priestly aid. The Count of Ponthieu had to marry Philip's sister at Rouen, within the Norman jurisdiction.

In his extremity Philip called a parliament at Paris, and Agnes, clad in mourning, implored protection, but not a man moved; a mortal terror was in every heart. She was then in the seventh month. The assembly decided that the king must submit, and Agnes supplicated the pope not to divide her from her husband; the crown, she said, was indifferent to her. But this was a struggle for supremacy, and Innocent was inexorable. A council was convened at Néelle, where Philip promised to take back Ingeburga and part from Agnes. He explained that she was pregnant, and to leave the realm might kill her; but the priests demanded absolute submission, and he swore upon the evangelists to see her no more. Agnes, broken by her misery, set forth for a Norman castle, where she died in bearing a son, whom she called Tristan, from her sorrow at his birth.

The soldier, who belonged to the old imaginative society, had been conquered by the Church, which was the incarnation of the imagination; but Dandolo was a different development. He was the creation of economic competition, and he trampled the clergy under his feet.

Although, apparently, profoundly sceptical, as the man must be who is the channel through which money acts, he understood how to play upon the imaginations of others, and arranged a solemn function to glorify the Sepulchre. One Sunday he summoned both citizens and pilgrims to

Saint Mark's, and mounting the pulpit, he addressed the congregation.

"My lords, you are engaged to the greatest people of the world, for the highest enterprise that ever was undertaken; and I am old and feeble, and need repose, and am infirm in body; but I see that none can command and control you as I can, who am your doge. If you will permit me to take

the cross to lead you, and let my son stay here in my place and conduct the government, I will go to live or die with you, and with the pilgrims." (6)

Ville-Hardouin's simple chronicle shows how perfectly the old man knew his audience:—

"There was great pity among the people of the country and the pilgrims, and many tears were shed, because this worthy man had so much cause to stay behind; for he was old and... his sight poor." (7)

Amidst an outburst of enthusiasm assent was given. Then, while the church rang with shouts, Dandolo knelt before the altar, in a passion of tears fixed the cross to the ducal bonnet, and rose, the commander of the finest army in the world.

And Dandolo was a great commander; a commander of the highest stamp. He tolerated no insubordination, and trod the clergy down. When Peter of Capua, the papal legate, interfered, Dandolo sternly told him that the army of Christ lacked not for military chiefs, and that if priests would stay therein they must content themselves with prayers.

A Cistercian monk, named Gunther, who had been appointed to follow his abbot on the pilgrimage, kept a chronicle of what he saw. His superior, named Martin, was so disheartened at Venice that he asked the legate for absolution from his vow, and for permission to return to his convent at Bile; but this request the cardinal refused. The priests had determined to stay by Dandolo and fight him to the last. Therefore the abbot sailed with the Venetians, but he learned a bitter lesson at Zara. There the clergy received a letter from Innocent, explaining the position of the Church, and threatening with excommunication all who should molest the King of Hungary. Simon de Montfort and a portion of the more devout, who had from the first been scandalized at the contract made with Dandolo, then withdrew and camped apart; and, at a meeting called to consider the situation, Guy, Abbot of Vaux-de-Cemay, tried to read the letter. An outbreak followed, and some of the chroniclers assert that the Venetians would have murdered Guy, had not Simon de Montfort stood by him sword in hand.(8)

On the main point there is no doubt. The priests ignominiously failed to protect their ally; the attack was made, and nothing shows that even de Montfort refused to share in it, or to partake of the plunder after the city fell. There was no resistance. The besieged made no better defence than hanging crosses on their walls, and on the fifth day capitulated. First the Franks divided the plunder with the Italians; then they sent an embassy to Rome to ask for absolution.

They alleged that they were helpless, and either had to accept the terms offered by Dandolo, or abandon their enterprise. Innocent submitted. He coupled his forgiveness, indeed, with the condition that the plunder should be returned; (9) yet no record remains that a single mark, of all the treasures taken from Zara, ever found its way back to the original owners.

The Venetians neither asked for pardon nor noticed the excommunication. On the contrary, Dandolo used the time when the envoys were at Rome in maturing the monstrous crime of diverting the crusade from Palestine to Constantinople.

Just before the departure from Venice, an event happened which Ville-Hardouin called "one of the greatest marvels you ever heard of." In 1195 the Greek emperor, named Isaac, had been dethroned, imprisoned, and blinded by his brother Alexis, who usurped the throne. Isaac's son, also named Alexis, escaped, and took shelter with his brother-in-law, Philip of Swabia. Philip could not help him, but suggested to him to apply to the crusaders in Venice, and ask them for aid. Whether or not this application had been arranged by Dandolo, does not appear. Alexis went to Venice, where he was cordially received by the doge; but as the fleet was then weighing anchor, his affairs were postponed until after the attack on Zara, when an embassy from Philip arrived, which brought up the whole situation at Constantinople for consideration. In the struggle which followed between the Venetians and the Church, the Franks lay like a prize destined to fall to the stronger, and in Gunther's narrative the love the priests bore their natural champions can be plainly seen. In the thirteenth century, as in the fifth century, the ecclesiastics recognized that over a monied oligarchy they could never have control; accordingly the monks hated the Venetians, whom Gunther stigmatized as "a people excessively greedy of money," always ready to commit sacrilege for gain.

On his side Dandolo followed his instinct, and tried to bribe the pope by offering him an union of the communions. But Innocent was inflexible. He wrote in indignation that the crusaders had sworn to avenge the wrongs of Christ, and likened those who should turn back to Lot's wife, whom God turned into a pillar of salt for disobeying his commands. (10)

Yet, though the priesthood put forth its whole strength, it was beaten. The power of wealth was too great. No serious defection took place. Ville-Hardouin gave a list of those who left the fleet, among whom was Simon de Montfort, adding contemptuously, "Thus those left the host,... which was great shame to them." (11)

Judging by the words alone, a century might have separated the writer and his comrades from the barons who abandoned Agnes to Innocent; yet they were the same men transplanted to an economic civilization, and excited by the power of wealth.

On Easter Monday, 1203, the fleet sailed for Corfu, where another and more serious split occurred. But the dazzling prize finally prevailed over the fear of the supernatural, and, getting under way once more, the pilgrims crossed the Sea of Marmora, and anchored at the convent of Saint Stephen, about twelve miles from Constantinople. Since exchanges had again returned to Italy, the vitality of the Greek Empire had burned low. It was failing fast through inanition. But Byzantium was still defended by those stupendous fortifications which were impregnable from the land, and only to be assailed from the sea by an admiral of genius.

Such an one was Dandolo, a born seaman, sagacious yet fiery; and, besides, a pilot of the port. At a council of war he laid out a plan of campaign:—

"My lords, I know more of the character of this country than you do, for I have been here before. You have before you the greatest and most perilous enterprise which any men have ever undertaken, and therefore it would be well that we should act prudently." (12)

He then explained how the attack should be made; and had the Franks implicitly obeyed him, the town would have been carried at the first assault. Three days later the allies occupied Scutari, the Asiatic suburb of Constantinople, and lay there ten days collecting supplies. On the twelfth they stormed the tower of Galata, which commanded Pera, the key to the Golden Horn. While the action was going on, Dandolo forced his way into the port. The entrance was defended not only by a great tower, but by a huge iron chain, fastened to piles, and covered by twenty galleys armed with machines.

Nothing stopped the Venetians. Disregarding the fire, the sailors sprang on the chain, and from thence gained the decks of the Greek galleys, whose crews they threw overboard. Meanwhile, one of the Italian ships, provided with steel shears, bore down on the cable, cut it, and led the way into the harbour.

The weakest part of the walls being uncovered, Dandolo insisted that the only hope for success lay in assaulting from ship-board where the battlements were lowest; but the French obstinately refused to depart from their habits, and determined to fight on horseback. The event proved Dandolo's wisdom; for though the attack failed through the mistake of dividing the force, and of attempting the fortifications toward the land, the doge so led his sailors that Ville-Hardouin kindled with enthusiasm as he told the tale.

When the old man saw his ships recoil before the tremendous fire from the battlements,

"so that the galleys could not make the land, then there was seen a strange sight, for the duke of Venice, who was an old man, and saw not well, was fully armed and commanded his galley, and had the gonfalon of Saint Mark's before him; and he cried to his men to put him ashore, or if they would not he would do justice on their bodies; and they brought the galley to shore, and they sallied forth and carried the banner before him to the shore. And when the Venetians saw the gonfalon of Saint Mark's ashore, and the galley of the lord ashore before them, they were all ashamed and made for the land, and rushed out from their ships pell-

mell. Then might one see a marvellous assault. And thus testifies Geoffrey de Ville-Hardouin, the marshal of Champagne, who dictates this book, that more than forty declare they saw the banner of Saint Mark of Venice on one of the towers, and none knew who carried it thither."(13)

Once a foothold on the ramparts had been gained, the Greeks fled, twenty-five towers fell in quick succession, and the Italians had already entered the streets and fired the houses to drive the enemy from the roofs, when news was brought that Alexis was advancing from the gates, and threatened to envelop the French. Indeed, the danger was extreme; for, as Ville-Hardouin explained, the crusaders were wondrous few when compared with the garrison, for they "had so many men we should all have been engulfed amongst them." (14) With the instinct of a great commander, Dandolo instantly sounded a retreat, abandoned the half-conquered town, and hastened to the support of his allies. He reached the ground opportunely, for Alexis, when he saw the reinforcement, retreated without striking a blow.

That night Alexis fled, leaving Constantinople without a government; and the people took the blind Isaac from his dungeon and set him on the throne. In theory, therefore, the work of the crusaders was done, and they were free to embark for Palestine to battle for the Sepulchre. In fact, the thing they came for remained to be obtained, and what they demanded amounted to the ruin of the empire. Young Alexis had promised 200,000 marks of silver, to join the crusade himself, to provide rations for a year, and to recognize the supremacy of Rome; but such promises were impossible to fulfil. During a delay of six months the situation daily grew more strained, a bitter hatred sprang up between the foreigners and the natives, riots broke out, conflagrations followed, and at last the allies sent a deputation to the palace to demand the execution of the treaty.

In despair, Alexis attacked the fleet with fire-ships, and his failure led to a revolution in which he was killed. Isaac died from terror, and one Moursouffle was raised to the throne. In their extremity the Greeks had recourse to treachery, and nearly succeeded in enticing the Frankish princes to a banquet, at which they were to have been assassinated. The plot was frustrated by the sagacity of Dandolo, who would allow no one to trust themselves within the walls; then both sides prepared for war.

Defeat had taught the Franks obedience, and they consented to serve on the galleys. They embarked on April 8, 1204, to be ready for an assault in the morning. But though the attack was made in more than one hundred places at once, "yet for our sins were the pilgrims repulsed." Then the landsmen proposed to try some other part of the walls, but the sailors told them that elsewhere the current would sweep them away; and "know," said the marshal, "there were some who would have been well content had the current swept them away" altogether, "for they were in great peril." (15)

This repulse fell on a Friday; the following Monday the attack was renewed, and at first with small success, but at length—

"Our Lord raised a wind called Boreas... and two ships which were lashed together, the one named the *Pilgrim* and the other the *Paradise*, approached a tower on either side, just as God and the wind brought them, so that the ladder of the Pilgrim was fixed to the tower; and straightway a Venetian and a French knight... scaled the tower, and others followed them, and those in the tower were discomforted and fled." (16)

From the moment the walls were carried, the battle turned into a massacre. The ramparts were scaled in all directions, the gates were burst open with battering rams, the allies poured into the streets, and one of the most awful sacks of the Middle Ages began.

Nothing was so sacred as to escape from pillage. The tombs of the emperors were violated, and the body of Justinian stripped. The altar of the Virgin, the glory of Saint Sophia, was broken in pieces, and the veil of the sanctuary torn to rags. The crusaders played dice on the tables which represented the apostles, and drank themselves drunk in the holy chalices. Horses and mules were driven into the sanctuary, and when they fell under their burdens, the blood from their wounds stained the floor of the cathedral. At last a young prostitute mounted the patriarch's chair, intoned a lewd chant, and danced before the pilgrims. Thus fell Constantinople, by the arms of the soldiers of Christ, on the twelfth day of April, in the year one thousand two hundred and four. Since the sack of Rome by Alaric no such prize had ever fallen to a victor, and the crusaders were drunk with their success. Ville-Hardouin estimated that the share of the Franks, after deducting some fifty thousand marks which the Venetians collected from them, came to four hundred thousand marks of silver, not to speak of masses of plunder of which no account was taken. The gain was so great there seemed no end to the gold and silver, the precious stones, the silks, the ermines, and whatever was costly in the world.

"And Geoffrey de Ville-Hardouin testifies of his own knowledge, that since the beginning of time, there was never so much taken in one town. Every one took what he wanted, and there was enough. Thus were the host of the pilgrims and of the Venetians quartered, and there was great joy and honour for the victory which God had given them, since those who had been poor were rich and happy." (17)

In obedience to the soothsayers, the devotees of Louis the Pious had perished by tens of thousands, and over their corpses the Moslems had marched to victory. The defenders of Christ's cross had been slaughtered like sheep upon the mountains of the Beatitudes, and sold into slavery in herds at Damascus and Aleppo; even the men who, at the bidding of God's vicar, had left Dandolo to fight for the Sepulchre upon the barren hills of Palestine, had been immolated. Five hundred had perished in shipwreck, more had been massacred in Illyria, none had received reward. But those who, in defiance of the supernatural and in contempt of their vow, had followed the excommunicated Venetian to plunder fellow-Christians, had won immeasurable glory, and been sated with incalculable spoil.

The pilgrims who, constant to the end, had been spilling their blood in God's service, came trooping to the Bosphorus to share in the last remaining crumbs; the knights of the Temple and the Hospital set sail for Greece, where money might still be made by the sword, and the King of Jerusalem stood before the Tomb, naked unto his enemies. Innocent himself was cowed; his commands had been disregarded and his curse defied; laymen had insulted his legate, and had, without consulting him, divided among themselves the patronage of the Church; and yet for the strongest there was no moral law. When Baldwin announced that he was emperor, the pope called him "his dearest son," and received his subjects into the Roman communion. (18)

But yesterday, the greatest king of Christendom had stood weeping, begging for the life of his wife; a hundred years earlier an emperor had stood barefoot, and freezing in the snow, at the gate of Canossa, as a penance for rebellion; but in 1204 a Venetian merchant was blessed by the haughtiest of popes for having stolen Christ's army, made war on his flock, spurned his viceregent, flouted his legate, and usurped his patrimony. He had appointed a patriarch without a reference to Rome. All was forgiven, the appointment was confirmed, the sinner was shriven; nothing could longer resist the power of money, for consolidation had begun.

Yet, though nature may discriminate against him, the emotionalist will always be an emotionalist, for such is the texture of his brain; and while he breathes, he will hate the materialist. The next year Baldwin was defeated and captured by the Bulgarians, and then Innocent wrote a letter to the Marquis of Montferrat, which showed how the wound had rankled when he blessed the conqueror.

He said bitterly:—

"You had nothing against the Greeks, and you were false to your vows because you did not fight the Saracens, but the Christians; you did not capture Jerusalem, but Constantinople; you preferred earthly to heavenly treasures. But what was far graver, you have spared neither religion, nor age, nor sex, and you have committed adulteries, fornications and incests before men's eyes.... Nor did the imperial treasures suffice you, nor the plunder alike of rich and poor. You laid your hands on the possessions of the Church, you tore the silver panels from the altars, you broke into the sanctuaries and carried away the images, the crosses and the relics so that the Greeks, though afflicted by persecution, scorn to render obedience to the apostolic chair, since they see in the Latins nothing but an example of perdition and of the works of darkness, and therefore rightly abhor them more than dogs." (19)

For the north and west of Europe the crusade of Constantinople seems to have been the turning point whence the imagination rapidly declined. At the opening of the thirteenth century, everything shows that the genuine ecstatic type predominated in the Church—the quality of mind which believed in the miracle, and therefore valued the amulet more than money. Innocent himself, with all his apparent worldliness, must have been such a man; for, though the material advantages of a union with the Greek Church far outweighed the Sepulchre, his resistance to the diversion of the army from Palestine was unshaken to the last. The same feeling permeated the inferior clergy; and an anecdote told by Gunther shows that even so late as the year 1204 the monks unaffectedly despised wealth in its vulgar form.

"When therefore the victors set themselves with alacrity to spoil the conquered town, which was theirs by right of war, the abbot Martin began to think about his share of the plunder; and lest, when everything had been given to others, he should be left empty-handed, he proposed to stretch out his consecrated hand to the booty. But since he thought the taking of secular things unworthy, he bestirred himself to obtain a portion of the sacred relics, which he knew were there in great quantities." (20)

The idea was no sooner conceived than executed. Although private marauding was punished with death, he did not hesitate, but hastened to a church, where he found a frightened old monk upon his knees, whom he commanded in a terrible voice to produce his relics or prepare for death. He was shown a chest full to the brim. Plunging in his arms, he took all he could carry, hurried to his ship and hid his booty in his cabin; and he did this in a town whose streets were literally flowing with gold and silver. He had his reward. Though a sacrilegious thief, angels guarded him by sea and land until he reached his cloister at Bile. Then he distributed his plunder through the diocese.

Occasionally, when the form of competition has abruptly changed, nature works rapidly. Within a single generation after Hattin, the attitude, not only of the laity but of the clergy, had been reversed, and money was recognized, even by the monks, as the end of human effort.

The relics at Jerusalem had first drawn the crusaders to the East, and, incidentally, the capture of the Syrian seaports led to the reopening of trade and the recentralization of the Western world. As long as imagination remained the dominant force, and the miracle retained its power, the ambition of the Franks was limited to holding the country which contained their talismans; but as wealth accumulated, and the economic type began to supplant the ecstatic, a different policy came to prevail.

Beside the cities of the Holy Land, two other portions of the levant had a high money value—the Bosphorus and the valley of the Nile. In spite of Rome, the Venetians, in 1204, had seized Constantinople; at the Lateran council of 1215, Innocent himself proposed an attack on Cairo. Though conceived by Innocent, the details of the campaign were arranged by Honorius III., who was consecrated in July, 1816; these details are, however, unimportant: the interest of the crusade lies in its close. John of Brienne, King of Jerusalem, nominally commanded, but the force he led little resembled Dandolo's. Far from being that compact mass which can only be given cohesion by money, it rather had the character of such an hysterical mob as Louis the Pious led to destruction.

After some semblance of a movement on Jerusalem, the army was conveyed to the Delta of the Nile, and Damietta was invested in 1218. Here the besiegers amounted to little more than a fluctuating rabble of pilgrims, who came and went at their pleasure, usually serving about six months. Among such material, military discipline could not exist; but, on the contrary, the inflammable multitude were peculiarly adapted to be handled by a priest, and soon the papal legate assumed control. Cardinal Pelagius was a Spaniard who had been promoted by Innocent in 1306. His temperament was highly emotional, and, armed with plenary power by Honorius, he exerted himself to inflame the pilgrims to the utmost. After a blockade of eighteen months Damietta was reduced to extremity, and to save the city the sultan offered the whole Holy Land, except the fortress of Karak, together with the funds needed to rebuild the walls of Jerusalem. King John, and all the soldiers, who understood the difficulty of invading Egypt, favoured a peace; but Pelagius, whose heart was fixed on the plunder of Cairo, prevented the council from reaching a decision. Therefore the siege went on, and presently the ramparts were carried without loss, as the whole population had perished from hunger and pestilence.

This victory made Pelagius a dictator, and he insisted on an advance on the capital. John, and the grand masters of the military orders, pointed out the disaster which must follow, as it was July, and the Nile was rising. In a few weeks the country would be under water. Moreover, the fleet could not ascend the river, therefore the army must be isolated in the heart of a hostile country, and probably overwhelmed by superior numbers.

Pelagius reviled them. He told them God loved not cowards, but champions who valued his glory more than they feared death. He threatened them with excommunication should they hang back. Near midsummer, 1221, the march began, and the pilgrims advanced to the apex of the delta, where they halted, with the enemy on the opposite shore.

The river was level with its banks, the situation was desperate, and yet even then the sultan sent an embassy offering the whole of the Holy Land in exchange for the evacuation of Egypt. The soldiers of all nations were strenuously for peace, the priests as strenuously for war.

They felt confident of repeating the sack of Constantinople at Cairo, nor can there be a greater contrast than Martin spurning the wealth of Constantinople as dross, and Pelagius rejecting the Sepulchre that he might glut himself with Egyptian wealth.

But all history shows that the emotionalist cannot compete with the materialist upon his own ground. In the end, under free economic competition, he must be eliminated. Pelagius tarried idly in the jaws of death until the Nile rose and engulfed him.

Footnotes

(1) *Histoire de la Commerce de la France*, 132.

(2) *Histoire du Commerce du Levant*, Heyd, French trans., i. 163.

(3) *Histoire du Levant*, Heyd, French trans., i. 95.

(4) See, on this question of cheaper money in the Carlovingian period, *Nouveau Manuel de Numismatique*, Blanchet, i. 101; also *Histoire du Commerce de la France*, Pigeonneau, 87 *et seq.*

(5) *Le Monete di Venesia*, Papadopoli, 73.

(6) *Ville-Hardouin*, ed. Wailly, xiv. 65.

(7) *Ibid.*

(8) *Historiens de la France*, xix. 23.

(9) *Patrologiæ Cursus Completus* Migne, ccxiv. 1180.

(10) *Historiens de la France* xix. 421.

(11) *Chronique*, ed. Buchon, 44.

(12) *Ville Hardouin*, ed. Buchon, 51.

(13) *Chronique de Ville-Hardouin*, ed. Buchon, 69.

(14) *Chronique*, ed. Wailly, xxxvii. 178.

(15) *Chronique*, ed. Wailly, lii. 239.

(16) *Chronique*, ed. Buchon, 96.

(17) *Chronique*, ed. Buchon, 99.

(18) *Patrologiæ Cursus Completus*, Migne, ccxv. 454.

(19) Migne, ccxv. 712.

(20) *Historia Captæ a Latinis Constantinopoleos*, Migne, ccxii. 19.

Chapter VI: The Suppression of the Temple

PHYSICAL weakness has always been the vulnerable point of the sacred caste, for priests have rarely been warriors, and faith has seldom been so profound as to guarantee ecclesiastics against attack. This difficulty was marked in the early Middle Ages, when, although disintegration so far prevailed as to threaten the very tradition of centralized power, a strong leaven of the ancient materialism remained.

In the ninth century the trend toward decentralization was resistless. Although several of the descendants of Charlemagne were men of ability and energy, the defence was so superior to the attack that they could not coerce their vassals, and their domains melted away into independent sovereignties until the crown became elective, and the monarchy almost a tradition. During the tenth century it seems possible that the regal authority might have been obliterated, even to the last trace, had it not been for the Church, which was in sore need of a champion. The priesthood cared nothing for the legitimate line; what they sought was a protector, and accordingly they chose, not the descendant of Charlemagne, but him who, in the words of the Archbishop of Rheims, was "distinguished by his wisdom and who found support in the greatness of his soul." Hugh Capet succeeded Louis V. because he was the best chief of police in France.

From such an alliance, between the priest and the soldier, has always sprung the dogma of the divine right of kings. In mediaeval Europe, enchantment was a chief element of the royal power. The monarch was anointed with a magic oil, girt with a sacred sword, given a supernatural banner, and endowed with the gift of miracles. His touch healed disease. In return for these gifts, he fought the battles of the Church, whose property was the natural prey of a predatory baronage. Every diocese and every abbey was embroiled in endless local wars, which lasted from generation to generation, and sometimes from century to century. A good example was the interminable feud between the Abbey of Vézelay and the Counts of Nevers, and a letter of a papal legate named Conon, which described one of the countless raids, gives an idea of the ferocity of the attack.

"The men of the Count of Nevers have burst open the doors of the cloister, have thrown stones on the reliquaries which contain the bodies of Saint Lazanis, of Saint Martha, of Saint Andocious, and of Saint Pontianus; they have not even respected the crucifix in which was preserved a morsel of the true cross, they have beaten the monks, they have driven them out with stones, and having taken one of them, they have treated him in an infamous manner." (1)

Until the stimulus given by the crusades was felt, subinfeudation went on uninterruptedly; the Capetians were as unable to stem the current as the Carlovingians before them, so that, under Philip I., the royal domain had become almost as much dismembered as the kingdom of Lothaire a century earlier. Consolidation began after the council of Clermont, and Suger's *Life of Louis the Fat* is the story of the last years of the partisan warfare between the crown and the petty nobility which had been going on since the time of Hugh Capet.

During this long period the kings had fought a losing battle, and without the material resources of the Church would have been overpowered. Even as it was they failed to hold their own, and yet the wealth of the clergy was relatively enormous. The single abbey of Saint Denis was said to have controlled ten thousand men, and though this may be an exaggeration, the corporation was organized on a gigantic scale.

Between the eleventh and thirteenth centuries it held in France alone three cities, upwards of seventy-four villages, twenty-nine manors attached to these possessions, over a hundred parishes, and a great many chapels bringing in valuable rentals, beside numerous vineyards, mills and fields, with fifteen forests of the first class. (2)

Suger's description of the country at the beginning of the twelfth century is highly dramatic. Every strong position, like a hill or a forest, was a baron's hold, from whence he rode to plunder and torment the people. One of the most terrible of these robbers was Hugh du Puiset, a man whom the Abbot of Saint Denis calls a ruffian, the issue of a long line of ruffians. To the churchman, Hugh was the incarnation of evil. He oppressed the clergy, and though hated by all, few dared oppose him. At last he attacked Adèle, Countess of Chartres, daughter of William the Conqueror, who went with her son Tybalt to seek redress from the king. Louis did not relish the campaign, and the monk described how the lady taunted him with the defeat his father had suffered from the father of Hugh, who pursued him to Orleans, captured a hundred of his knights, and cast his bishops into dungeons.

Afterward, an assembly was held at Melun to consider the situation, and there a concourse of prelates, clerks, and monks "threw themselves at the king's feet and implored him, to his great embarrassment, to repress this most greedy robber Hugh, who, more rapacious than a wolf, devoured their lands." (3)

Certainly the priests had cause for alarm, for the venerable Archbishop of Chartres, who was present, had been captured, loaded with irons, and long left to languish in prison.

Three times this baron was defeated, but even when a prisoner, his family connection was so powerful he was permitted to escape. At last he died like a wolf, fighting to the last, having impaled the Seneschal of France on his spear.

Even singly, such men were almost a match for both Church and Crown; but when joined in a league, especially if allied to one of the great feudatories, such as the Duke of Normandy, they felt sure of victory. One day, when Eudes, Count of Corbeil, to join this very Hugh, he put aside his armour-bearer who was attending him, and said to his wife:

"Pray, noble countess, bring the glittering sword to the noble count, since he who takes it from you as a count, shall to-day return it as a king." (4)

The immediate effect of the crusades was to carry numbers of these petty princes to Palestine, where they were often killed or ruined. As their power of resistance weakened, the crown gained, and Louis the Fat reconquered the domain. His active life began in 1097, the year of the invasion of Palestine, and his absorption of the lordship of Montlhéri is a good illustration of his success.

The family of Rochefort-Montlhéri owned several of the strongest donjons near Paris, and was divided into two branches, the one represented by Guy Trousseau, Lord of Montlhéri, the other by Guy the Red, Lord of Rochefort. Guy Trousseau's father was named Milo, and all three went to Syria, where Milo was killed, and his son disgraced himself. Suger spoke of him with extreme disdain:—

"Guy Trousseau, son of Milo of Montlhéri, a restless man and a disturber of the kingdom, returned home from a pilgrimage to the Holy Sepulchre, broken down by the anxiety of a long journey and by the vexation of many troubles. And... [being] panic stricken at Antioch at the approach of Corboran, and escaping down from a wall [he]... abandoned the army of God and fled destitute of everything." (5)

Returning a ruined man, he married his daughter to the illegitimate son of Philip, a half-brother of Louis, a child of twelve; and as his guardians, the king and prince got possession of the castle. This castle was almost at the gates of Paris, and a standing menace to the communications of the kingdom: therefore their delight was great. "They rejoiced as though they had taken a straw from their eyes, or as though they had burst the barrier which imprisoned them." (6) And the old king said to his son: "Guard well the tower, Louis, which has aged me with chagrin, and through whose treachery and wicked fraud I have never known peace and quiet."(7)

Yet the destruction of the local nobility in Syria was the least important part of the social revolution wrought by the crusades, for though the power of the barons might have thus been temporarily broken, they could never have been reduced to impotence unless wealth had grown equal to organizing an overwhelming attack. The accumulation of wealth followed the opening of the Eastern trade, and its first effect was to cause the incorporation of the communes.

Prior to 1095 but one town is known to have been chartered, Saint Quentin, the capital of Vermandois, about 1080,(8) but after the opening of the Syrian ports the whole complexion of society changed. Noyon was chartered in 1108, Laon in 1111, Amiens in 1113, and then free boroughs sprang up on every side.

For want of the mariner's compass, commerce could not pass north by the Straits of Gibraltar. Merchandise had therefore to go by land, and exchanges between the north and south of Europe centred in the County of Champagne, whose fairs became the great market of the thirteenth century.

The earliest dated document relating to these fairs is a deed drawn in 1114 by Hugh, Count of Troyes, by which he conveyed certain revenues derived from them to the Abbey of Montier-en-Der. Fifty years later, such mentions had grown frequent, and by the year 1200 the fairs had attained their full development.(9)

Weaving had been an industry in Flanders under the Romans, and in the time of Charlemagne the cloth of the Low Countries had been famous; but in the twelfth century the manufacture spread into the adjoining provinces of France, and woollen became the most valuable European export. The fleeces were brought chiefly from England, the weaving was done on the Continent, and one of the sources of the Florentine wealth was the dressing and dyeing of these fabrics to prepare them for the Asiatic market.

For mutual defence, the industrial towns of the north formed a league called the Hanse of London, because London was the seat of the chief countinghouse. This league at first included only seventeen cities, with Ypres and Bruges at the head, but the association afterward increased to fifty or sixty, stretching as far west as Le Mans, as far south as the Burgundian frontier, and as far east as Liège. Exclusive of the royal domain, which was well consolidated under Philip Augustus, the French portion of this region substantially comprised the counties of Blois, Vermandois, Anjou, Champagne, and the Duchy of Normandy. This district, which has ever since formed the core of France, became centralized at Paris between the beginning of the reign of Philip Augustus in 1180 and the reign of Philip the Fair a century later, and there can be little doubt that this centralization was the effect of the accumulation of capital, which created a permanent police.

The merchants of all the cities of the league bound themselves to trade exclusively at the fairs of Champagne, and, to prosper, the first obstacle they had to overcome was the difficulty and cost of transportation. Not only were the roads unsafe, because of the strength of the castles in which the predatory nobility lived, but the multiplicity of jurisdictions added to taxes. As late as the end of the thirteenth century, a convention was made between fifteen of the more important Italian cities, such as Florence, Genoa, Venice, and Milan, and Otho of Burgundy, by which, in consideration of protection upon the roads, tolls were to be paid at Gevry, Dôlé, Augerans, Salins, Chalamont, and Pontarlier. When six imposts were levied for crossing a single duchy, the cost of importing the cheaper goods must have been prohibitory.

The Italian caravans reached Champagne ordinarily by two routes: one by some Alpine pass to Geneva, and then through Burgundy; the other by water to Marseilles or Aigues-Mortes, up the Rhone to Lyons, and north, substantially as before. The towns of Provins, Troyes, Bar-sur-Aube, and Lagny-sur-Marne lie about midway between

Bruges and Ypres on the one side, and Lyons and Geneva on the other, and it was at these cities that exchanges centralized, until the introduction of the mariner's compass caused traffic to go by the ocean, and made Antwerp the monied metropolis.

The market was, in reality, open continuously, for six fairs were held, each six weeks long, and the trade was so lucrative that places which, in 1100, had been petty villages, in 1200 had wealth enough to build those magnificent cathedrals which are still wonders of the world.

The communal movement had nothing about it necessarily either liberal or democratic. The incorporated borough was merely an instrument of trade, and at a certain moment became practically independent, because for a short period traders organized locally, before they could amalgamate into centralized communities with a revenue sufficient to pay a police capable of coercing individuals.

What the merchant wanted was protection for trade, and, provided he had it, the form in which it came was immaterial. Where the feudal government was strong, communes did not exist: Paris never had a charter. Conversely, where the government was weak, communes grew up, because traders combined for mutual protection, and therefore the communes reached perfection in ecclesiastical capitals.

As a whole, the secular nobility rather favoured the incorporated towns, because they could sell to them their services as policemen, and could join with them in plundering the Church; (10) on their side the tradesmen were always ready to commute personal military service into a tax, and thus both sides benefited. To the Church, on the contrary, the rise of the mercantile class was pure loss, not only because it caused their vassals to seek better protection than ecclesiastics could give, but because the propagation of the materialistic mind bred heresy. The clergy had no police to sell, and the townsmen had, therefore, either to do the work themselves or hire a secular noble. In the one case they became substantially independent; in the other they transferred their allegiance to a stranger. In any event, a new fief was carved out of an ecclesiastical lordship, and such accessions steadily built up the royal domain.

From the outset, the sacred class seems to have been conscious of its danger, and some of the most ferocious wars of the Middle Ages were those waged upon ecclesiastical serfs who tried to organize for self-defence. In one of his books Luchaire has told, at length, the story of the massacre of the peasantry of the Laonnais by a soldier whom the chapter of Laon elected bishop for the purpose,(11) and this was but a single case out of hundreds. Hardly a bishop or an abbot lived at peace with his vassals, and, as the clergy were the natural prey of the secular nobility, the barons often sided with the populace, and used the burghers as an excuse for private war. A speech made by one of the Counts of Nevers, during a rising of the inhabitants of Vézelay, gives a good idea of the intrigues which kept the prelates in perpetual misery.

"O very illustrious men, celebrated for great wisdom, valiant by your strength and rich by the riches you have acquired by your own merit, I am deeply afflicted at the miserable condition to which you are reduced. Apparently the possessors of much, in reality you are masters of nothing; and more than this, you do not enjoy any portion of your natural liberty.... If I think on these things I am greatly astonished, and ask myself what has become of, or rather to what depth of cowardice has fallen within you, that vigour formerly so renowned, when you put to death your Lord, the abbot Artaud."

The count then dwelt upon the harshness of the living abbot, and ended thus:—

"Separate from this man, and bind yourselves to me by a mutual agreement: if you consent, I engage myself to free you from all exactions, from all illegal rentals, and to defend you from the evils which are ready to fall upon you." (12)

Wherever developed, the mercantile mind had always the same characteristic: it was unimaginative, and, being unimaginative, it doubted the utility of magic. Accordingly, all commercial communities have rebelled against paying for miracles, and it was the spread of a scepticism already well developed in the thirteenth century among the manufacturing towns, which caused the Reformation of the sixteenth. At Saint-Riquier the monks carried the relics of Saint Vigor each year in procession. In 1264 the burghers took a dead cat and put it in a shrine, while in another casket they placed a horse-bone, to do service as the arm of Saint Vigor. When the procession reached a certain spot, the reliquaries were set down, and a mock fight began between two mummers. Then the bearers cried out, "Old Saint Riquier, you shall go no further unless you reconcile these enemies," whereupon the combatants fell into each other's arms, and all cried out that Saint Riquier had wrought a miracle.

Afterward they built a chapel and oratory, with an altar draped with cloth of gold, and deposited the dead cat and the horse-bone; and simple pilgrims, ignorant of the sacrilege, stopped to worship the relics, the mayor and council aiding and abetting the crime, "to the detriment of the whole Church universal" (13)

The clergy retaliated with frightful ferocity. As heresy followed in the wake of trade, the Inquisition followed in the wake of heresy, and the beginning of the thirteenth century witnessed simultaneously the prosperity of the mercantile class and the organization of the Holy Office.

Jacques de Vitry breathed the ecclesiastical spirit. One of the most famous preachers of his age, he rose from a simple monk to be Cardinal-bishop of Tusculum, legate in France, and Patriarch of Jerusalem. He led a crusade against the Albigenses, was present at the siege of Damietta, and died at Rome in 1240. His sermons burn with his hatred of the bourgeoisie: "That detestable race of men... hurrying to meet its fate, which none or few could escape," all of whom "were making haste toward hell....

But above all other evils of these Babylonish cities, there is one which is the worst, for hardly is there a community to be found in which there are not abettors, receivers, defenders of, or believers in, heretics." (14)

The basis of the secular society of the early Middle Ages was individual physical force. Every layman, noble or serf, owed military service, and when a borough was incorporated, it took its place in the feudal hierarchy, like any other vassal. With the spread of the mercantile type, however, a change began—the transmutation of physical force into money—and this process went on until individual strength or courage ceased to have importance.

As soldiers the burgesses never excelled; citizen troops have seldom been formidable, and those of the communes rarely withstood the first onset of the enemy. The tradesmen themselves recognized their own limitations, and in 1317 the deputies of the cities met at Paris and requested the government to undertake the administration of the local militia.

Though unwarlike, the townsmen were wealthy, and, in the reign of Philip Augustus, the same cause which led to the consolidation of the kingdom, brought about, as Luchaire has pointed out, "a radical modification of the military and financial organization of the monarchy;" the substitution by the privileged corporations of money payments for personal service. (15)

Thus, from the time when the economic type had multiplied sufficiently to hire a police, the strength of the State came to depend on its revenue, and financiers grew to be the controlling element of civilization. Before the crusades, the high offices of the kingdom of France, such as the office of the seneschal, were not only held by nobles, but tended to become hereditary in certain warlike families. After the rise of the Eastern trade the royal council was captured by the bourgeoisie. Jacques Cœur is a striking specimen of the class which ruled in the fifteenth century. Of this class the lawyers were the spokesmen, and men like Flotte and

Nogaret, the chancellors of Philip the Fair, expressed the notion of centralization as perfectly as the jurists of ancient Rome. No one has understood the movement better than Luchaire. He has pointed out, in his work on French institutions, that from the beginning of the reign of Saint Louis (1226) the Privy Council steadily gained in consequence.(16) The permanent civil service, of which it was the core, served as a school for judges, clerks, seneschals, and all judicial and executive officers. At first the administration retained a strong clerical tinge, probably because a generation elapsed before laymen could be equally well trained for the work, but after the accession of Philip the Fair, toward the end of the century, the laymen decisively predominated, and when they predominated, the plunder of the Church began.

Abstract justice is, of course, impossible. Law is merely the expression of the will of the strongest for the time being, and therefore laws have no fixity, but shift from generation to generation. When the imagination is vivid and police weak, emotional or ecclesiastical law prevails. As competition sharpens, and the movement of society accelerates, religious ritual is supplanted by civil codes for the enforcement of contracts and the protection of the creditor class.

The more society consolidates the more legislation is controlled by the wealthy, and at length the representatives of the monied class acquire that absolute power once wielded by the Roman proconsul, and now exercised by the modern magistrate.

"The two great figures of Saint Louis and of Philip the Fair which dominate the third period are profoundly unlike. But considering the facts as a whole... [they] have but moderately influenced the direction of the communal development. With the bailiffs and Parliament the monarchical machine is in possession of its essential works; it operates and will stop no more. In vain the king shall essay to arrest its march, or to direct it in another course: the innumerable army of agents of the crown does not cease for a moment to destroy rival jurisdictions, to suppress embarrassing powers, to replace everywhere private jurisdictions by the single authority of the sovereign. "To the infinite diversity of local liberties its will is to substitute regularity of institutions; political and administrative centralization." (17)

As Luchaire has elsewhere observed, the current everwhere "substituted, in the paths of administration, justice, and finance, the lay and burgher for the ecclesiastical and noble element." In other words, the economic type steadily gained ground, and the process went on until the Revolution. Saint Simon never forgave Louis XIV. for surrounding himself with men of mean birth, dependent on his will.

"The Duke of Beauvilliers was the single example in the whole course of his reign, as has been remarked in speaking of this duke, the only nobleman who was admitted into his council between the death of Cardinal Mazarin and his own; that is to say, during fifty-four years." (18)

From the middle of the twelfth to the middle of the thirteenth century was an interval of almost unparalleled commercial prosperity—a prosperity which is sufficiently proved by the sumptuous quality of the architecture of the time. Unquestionably the most magnificent buildings of modern Europe date from this period, and this prosperity was not limited to any country, but extended from Cairo to London. Such an expansion of trade would have been impossible without a corresponding expansion of the currency, and as no new mines were discovered, recourse was had to paper. By the year 1200 bills of exchange had been introduced,(19) and in order to give the bill of exchange its greatest circulating power, a system of banking was created which operated as a universal clearing house, and by means of which these bills were balanced against each other.

In the thirteenth century, Florence, Genoa, and Venice were the chief monied centres. In these cities the purchase and sale of commercial paper was, at the outset, monopolized by a body of money-changers, who, in Venice at least, seem to have been controlled by the council of merchants, and who probably were not always in the best credit. At all events, they were required in 1318 to make a deposit of £3,000 as security for their customers, and afterward the amount was increased.(20) Possibly some such system of deposits may have originally formed the capital of the Bank of Venice, but everything relating to the organization of the mediæval banks is obscure. All that seems certain is, that business was conducted by establishments of this character long before the date of any records which now remain. Amidst the multiplicity of mediæval jurisdictions, not only did the currency become involved in inextricable confusion, but it generally was debased through abrasion and clipping. Before clearings could be conveniently made, therefore, a coinage of recognized value had to be provided, and this the banks undertook to supply by their system of deposits. They received coin fresh from the mints, for which they gave credits, and these credits or notes were negotiable, and were always to be bought in the market. The deposits themselves were seldom withdrawn, as they bore a premium over common currency, which they lost when put in circulation, and they were accordingly only transferred on the books of the corporations, to correspond with the sales of the notes which represented them. Thus merchants from all parts of Europe and the Levant could draw on Venice or Genoa, and have their balances settled by transfers of deposits at the banks, without the intervention of coin. A calculation has been made that, by this means, the effective power of the currency was multiplied tenfold. Of all these institutions, the corporations of Genoa and Venice were the most famous. The Bank of Saint George, at Genoa, was formally organized in 1407, but it undoubtedly had conducted business from the beginning of the twelfth century;(21) next to nothing is known of the development at Venice. Probably, however, Florence was more purely a monied centre than either

Venice or Genoa, and no money-lenders of the Middle Ages ever equalled the great Florentine banking families. Most of the important commercial centres came to have institutions of the kind.

The introduction of credit had the same effect as a large addition to the stock of bullion, and, as gold and silver grew more plentiful, their relative value fell, and a general reform of the currency took place. Venice began the movement with the grosso, it spread through Italy and into France, and the coin of Saint Louis was long considered as perfect money.

With the expansion of the currency went a rise in prices, all producers grew rich, and, for more than two generations, the strain of competition was so relaxed that the different classes of the population preyed upon each other less savagely than they are wont to do in less happy times.

Meanwhile no considerable additions were made to the volume of the precious metals, and, as the bulk of commerce swelled, the capacity of the new system of credit became exhausted, and contraction set in. The first symptom of disorder seems to have been a rise in the purchasing power of both the precious metals, but particularly of gold, which rose in its ratio to silver from about one to nine and a half, to one to twelve.(22) At the same time the value of commodities, even when measured in silver, appears to have fallen sharply.(23) The consequence of this fall was a corresponding addition to the burden of debt, and a very general insolvency. The communes had been large borrowers, and their straits were deplorable. Luchaire has described their condition as shown "in the municipal accounts addressed by the communes to the government." (24) Everywhere there was a deficit, almost everywhere ruin. Amiens, Soissons, Roye, Saint Quentin, and Rouen were all in difficulty with their loans, but Noyon was perhaps the worst of all. In 1278 Noyon owed 16,000 pounds which it was unable to pay. After a suspension for fourteen years the king issued an ordinance regulating liquidation; a part of the claims had to be cancelled, and the balance collected by a levy on private property. The bankruptcy was complete.

The royal government, equally hardly pressed, was unable to meet its obligations in the standard coin, and resorted to debasement. Under Saint Louis the mark of silver yielded but 2 pounds 15 sous 6 pence; in 1306 the same weight of metal was cut into 8 pounds 10 sous. The pressure upon the population was terrible, and led to terrible results—the beginning of the spoliation of the emotionalists.

Perhaps the combination of the two great forces of the age, of the soldier and the monk, was the supreme effort of the emotional mind. What a hold the dazzling dream of omnipotence, through the possession of the Sepulchre, had upon the twelfth century, can be measured by the gifts showered upon the crusading orders, for they represented a prodigious sacrifice.

At Paris the Temple had a capital city over against the capital of the king. Within a walled enclosure of sixty thousand square metres, stood the conventual buildings and a gigantic donjon of such perfect masonry that it never needed other repairs than the patching of its roof. Beyond the walls the domain extended to the Seine, a property which, even in 1300, had an almost incalculable value.

On every Eastern battle-field, and at every assault and siege, the knights had fought with that fiery courage which has made their name a proverb down to the present day. In 1265, at Safed, three hundred had been butchered upon the ramparts in cold blood, rather than renounce their faith. At Acre, whose loss sealed the fate of Palestine, they held the keep at all odds until the donjon fell, burying Christians and Moslems in a common grave. But skill and valour avail nothing against nature. Step by step the Templars had been driven back, until Tortosa surrendered in 1291. Then the Holy Land was closed, the enthusiasm which had generated the order had passed away, and, meanwhile, economic competition had bred a new race at home, to which monks were a predestined prey.

In 1285, as the Latin kingdom in Syria was tottering towards its fall, Philip the Fair was crowned. Subtle, sceptical, treacherous, and cruel, few kings have left behind them a more sombre memory, yet he was the incarnation of the economic spirit in its conflict with the Church. Nine years later Benedetto Gaetani was elected pope: a man as completely the creation of the social revolution of the thirteenth century as Philip himself. Trained at Bologna and Paris, a jurist rather than a priest, his faith in dogma was so scanty that his belief in the immortality of the soul has been questioned. A thorough worldling, greedy, ambitious, and unscrupulous, he was suspected of having murdered his predecessor, Celestin V.

When Boniface came to the throne, the Church is supposed to have owned about one-third of the soil of Europe, and on this property the governments had no means of enforcing regular taxation. Toward the close of the thirteenth century the fall of prices increased the weight of debt, while it diminished the power of the population to pay. On the other hand, as the system of administration became more complex, the cost of government augmented, and at last the burden became more than the laity could endure. Both England and France had a permanent deficit, and Edward and Philip alike turned toward the clergy as the only source of supply. Both kings met with opposition, but the explosion came in France, where Clairvaux, the most intractable of convents, appealed to Rome.

Boniface had been elected by a coalition ' between the Colonna and the Orsini factions, but after his coronation he turned upon the Colonnas, who, in revenge, plundered his treasure. A struggle followed, which ended fatally to the pope; but at first he had the advantage, sacked their city of Praeneste, and forced them to fly to France. On the brink of this war, Boniface was in no condition to rouse so dangerous an adversary as Philip, and, in answer to Clairvaux's appeal, he confined himself to excommunicating the prince who should tax the priest and the priest who should pay the impost.

Nevertheless, the issue had to be met. The Church had weakened as terror of the unknown had waned, and could no longer defend its wealth, which was destined to pass more and more completely into the hands of the laity.

Philip continued his aggressions, and, when peace had been established in Italy, the rupture came. Not realizing his impotence, and exasperated at the royal policy, Boniface sent Bernard de Saisset, Bishop of Pamiers, to Paris as his ambassador. Bernard had recently been consecrated in defiance of Philip, and they were bitter enemies. He was soon dismissed from court, but he continued his provocations, calling the king a false coiner and a blockhead, and when he returned to Pamiers he plotted an insurrection. He was arrested and prosecuted by the Chancellor Flotte, but when delivered to the Archbishop of Narbonne for degradation, action was suspended to await the sanction of Rome. Then Flotte was sent to Italy to demand the surrender "of the child of perdition," that Philip might make of him "an excellent sacrifice to God." The mission necessarily failed, for it was a struggle for supremacy, and the issue was well summed up in the final words of the stormy interview which brought it to a close. "My power, the spiritual power," cried Boniface, "embraces and encloses the temporal." "True," retorted Flotte, "but yours is verbal, the king's is real."

An ecclesiastical council was convoked for October, 1302, and Philip was summoned to appear before the greatest prelates of Christendom. But, not waiting the meeting of this august assembly, Boniface, on December 5, 1301, launched his famous bull, "Ausculta, fili," which was his declaration of war. (25)

Listen, my son: do not persuade yourself that you have no superior, and are not in subjection to the head of the ecclesiastical hierarchy: he who says this is mad, he who sustains it is an infidel. You devour the revenues of the vacant bishoprics, you pillage churches. I do not speak now of the alterations in the coinage, and of the other complaints which arise on all sides, and which cry to us against you, but not to make myself accountable to God for your soul, I summon you to appear before me, and in case of your refusal shall render judgment in your absence. (26)

A century before, the barons of France had abandoned Philip Augustus, through fear of the incantations of Innocent, but, in the third generation of the commercial type, such fears had been discarded. In April, 1302, the estates of the realm sustained the "little one-eyed heretic," as Boniface called Flotte, in burning the papal bull, and in answering the admonitions of the pope with mockery.

"Philip, by the grace of God king of the French, to Boniface, who calls himself sovereign pontiff, little greeting or none. Let your very great foolishness know that we are subject to no one for the temporalty; that the collation to the vacant churches and prebends belongs to us by royal right; that their fruits are ours; that collations which have been made, or are to be made by us, are valid for the past and for the future, and that we will manfully protect their possessors against all comers. Those who think otherwise we hold fools or madmen." (27)

The accepted theory long was that the bourgeoisie were neutral in this quarrel; that they were an insignificant factor in the state, and obeyed passively because they were without the power to oppose. In reality, consolidation had already gone so far that money had become the prevailing form of force in the kingdom of France; therefore the monied class was on the whole the strongest class, and Flotte was their mouthpiece. They accepted the papers drawn by the chancellor, because the chancellor was their representative. (28)

In July, 1302, Philip met with the defeat of Courtray, and the tone of the ecclesiastical council, convened in October, shows that the clergy thought his power broken. A priest relies upon the miracle, and, if defied, he must either conquer by supernatural aid, or submit to secular coercion.

Boniface boldly faced the issue, and planted himself by Hildebrand. In his bull, Unam Sanctam, he defined his claim to the implicit obedience of laymen.

"We are provided, under his authority, with two swords, the temporal and the spiritual;... both, therefore, are in the power of the Church; to wit, the spiritual and the material sword:... the one is to be used by the priest, the other by kings and soldiers; sed ad nutum et patientiam sacerdotis." (29)

A sentence of excommunication had also been prepared and sent to France, which was to have been followed by deposition; but when it arrived, Philip convened an assembly of prelates and barons at the Louvre, and presented an indictment against Boniface, probably without a parallel in modern history. The pope was accused of every crime. He was an infidel, a denier of the immortality of the soul, a scoffer at the eucharist, a murderer, and a sorcerer. He was guilty of unnatural crimes and of robbery. (30)

The bearer of the bull was arrested, the property of the bishops who had attended the council sequestered, and Philip prepared to seize Boniface in his own palace. Boniface, too, felt the decisive hour at hand. He tried to reconcile himself with his enemies, drew the bull of deposition, and prepared to affix it to the church door at Anagni on September 8, 1303. Before the day came he was a prisoner, and face to face with death.

Flotte had been killed at Courtray, and had been succeeded by the redoubtable Nogaret, whose grandfather was believed to have been burned as a heretic. With Nogaret Philip joined Sciarra Colonna, the bloodiest of the Italian nobles, and sent them together to Italy to deal with his foe. Boniface had made war upon the Colonnas, and Sciarra had been hunted like a wild beast. Flying disguised, he had been taken by pirates, and had preferred to toil four years as a galley-slave, rather than run the risk of ecclesiastical mercy by surrendering himself to the vicar of Christ. At last Philip heard of his misfortunes, bought him, and, at the crisis, let him slip like a mad dog at the old man's throat. Nogaret and Colonna succeeded in corrupting the governor of Anagni, and entered the town at dead of night; but the pope's nephews had time to barricade the streets, and it was not until the church, which communicated with the papal apartments, had been fired, that the palace was forced. There, it was said, they found the proud old priest sitting upon his throne, with his crown upon his head, and men whispered that, as he sat there, Colonna struck him in the face with his gauntlet.

Probably the story was false, but it reflected truly enough the spirit of the pope's captors. He himself believed them capable of poisoning him, for from Saturday night till Monday morning he lay without food or drink, and when liberated was exhausted. Boniface was eighty-six, and the shock killed him. He was taken to Rome, and died there of fever, according to the rumour, blaspheming, and gnawing his hands in frenzy. (31)

The death of Boniface was decisive. Benedict XI., who succeeded him, did not attempt to prolong the contest; but peace without surrender was impossible. The economic classes held the emotionalists by the throat, and strangled them till they disgorged.

Vainly Benedict revoked the acts of his predecessor. Philip demanded that Boniface should be branded as a heretic, and sent Nogaret to Rome as his ambassador. The insult was more than the priesthood could yet endure. Summoning his courage, Benedict excommunicated Nogaret, Colonna, and thirteen others, whom he had seen break into the palace at Anagni. Within a month he was dead. Poison was whispered, and, for the first time since the monks captured the papacy, the hierarchy was paralyzed by fear. No complaint was made, or pursuit of the criminal attempted; the consistory met, but failed to unite on a successor.

According to the legend, when the cardinals were unable to agree, the faction opposed to Philip consented to name three candidates, from whom the king should select the pope. The prelate he chose was Bertrand de Goth, Archbishop of Bordeaux. Boniface had been his patron, but Philip, who knew men, knew that this man had his price. The tale goes that the king visited the bishop at an abbey near Saint-Jean-d'Angély, and began the conversation as follows: "My lord Archbishop, I have that in my hand will make you pope if I like, and it is for that I am come." Bertrand fell on his knees, and the king imposed five conditions, reserving a sixth, to exact thereafter. The last condition was the condemnation of the Templars. (32)

Doubtless the picturesque old tale is as false in detail as it is true in spirit. Probably no such interview took place, and yet there seems little doubt that Clement owed his election to Philip, and gave pledges which bound him from the day of his coronation. Certainly he surrendered all liberty of action, for he established himself at Avignon, whence the battlements of Ville-Neuve can still be seen, built by Philip to overawe the town. Within an hour he could have filled the streets with his mercenaries. The victory was complete. The Church was prostrate, and spoliation began.

Clement was crowned in 1305, and after two years of slavery he began to find his compact heavy upon him. He yielded up the patronage, he consented to the taxation of the clergy, and he ordered the grandmasters of the crusading orders to return to Europe, all at Philip's bidding. But when he was commanded to condemn Boniface as a heretic, he recoiled in terror. Indeed, to have rejected Boniface as an impostor, and a false pope, would have precipitated chaos. His bishops and cardinals would have been set aside, Clement's own election would have been invalidated; none could foresee where the disorganization would end. To gain time, Clement pleaded for a general council, which the king morosely conceded, but only on the condition that the excommunications against his agents, even against Nogaret, should be withdrawn. Clement assented, for he was practically a prisoner at Poitiers, a council at Vienne was agreed to, and the Crown seized the Templars without opposition from the Church.

Criticism has long ago dispelled the mystery which once shrouded this bloody process. No historian now suggests that the knights were really guilty of the fantastic enormities charged against them, and which they confessed under torture. Scepticism doubtless was rife among them, as it was among the cardinals, but there is nothing to show that the worst differed materially from the population about them, and the superb fortitude with which they perished, demonstrates that lack of religious enthusiasm was not the crime for which they died.

When Philip conceived the idea of first murdering and then plundering the crusaders, is uncertain. Some have thought it was in 1306, while sheltered in the Temple, when, he having suddenly raised his debased money to the standard of Saint Louis, the mob destroyed the house of his master of the mint.

Probably it was much earlier, and was but the necessary result of the sharpening of economic competition, which began with the accelerated movement accompanying the crusades.

After Clement's election, several years elapsed before the scheme ripened. Nothing could be done until one or both of the grand-masters had been enticed to France with their treasure. Under pretence of preparing for a new crusade this was finally accomplished, and, in 1306, Jacques de Molay, a chivalrous Burgundian gentleman, journeyed unsuspectingly to Paris, taking with him his chief officers and one hundred and fifty thousand florins in gold, beside silver "enough to load ten mules."

Philip first borrowed all the money de Molay would lend, and then, at one sudden swoop, arrested in a single night all the Templars in France. On October 13, 1307, the seizure was made, and Philip's organization was so perfect, and his agents so reliable, that the plan was executed with precision.

The object of the government was plunder, but before the goods of the order could be confiscated, legal conviction of some crime was necessary, which would entail forfeiture. Heresy was the only accusation adapted to the purpose; accordingly Philip determined to convict the knights of heresy, and the best evidence was confession. To extort confession the Inquisition had to be set in motion by the pope, and thus it came to pass that, in order to convey to the laymen the property of ecclesiastics, Christ's soldiers were tormented to death by his own vicar.

In vain, in the midst of the work, Clement, in agonies of remorse, revoked the commissions of the inquisitors. Philip jeered when the cardinals delivered the message, saying "that God hated the luke-warm" and the torture went on as before. When he had extorted what he needed, he set out for Poitiers; Clement fled, but was arrested and brought back a prisoner. Then his resolution gave way, and he abandoned the knights to their fate, reserving only the grandmaster and a few high officials for himself. Still, though he forsook the individuals, he could not be terrified into condemning the order in its corporate capacity, and the final process was referred to the approaching council. Meanwhile, a commission, presided over by the Archbishop of Narbonne, proceeded with the trial of the knights.

For three years these miserable wretches languished in their dungeons, and the imagination recoils from picturing their torments. Finally Philip felt that an end must be made, and in March, 1310, 546 of the survivors were taken from their prisons and made to choose delegates, for their exasperation was so deep that the government feared to let them appear before the court in a body.

The precaution availed little, for the knights who conducted the common defence proved themselves as proud and bold in this last extremity of human misery, as they had ever been upon the day of battle. They denied the charges brought against them, they taunted their judges with the lies told them to induce them to confess, and they showed how life and liberty had been promised them, under the royal seal, if they would admit the allegations of the government. Then they told the story of those who had been steadfast to the end.

"It is not astonishing that some have bore false witness, but that any have told the truth, considering the sorrows and suffering, the threats and insults, they daily endure.... What is surprising is that faith should be given to those who have testified untruly to save their bodies, rather than to those who have died in their tortures in such numbers, like martyrs of Christ, in defence of the truth, or who solely for conscience sake, have suffered and still daily suffer in their prisons, so many torments, trials, calamities, and miseries, for this cause." (33)

The witnesses called confirmed their statements. Bernard Peleti, when examined, was asked if he had been put to the torture. He replied that for three months previous to his confession to the Bishop of Paris, he had lain with his hands so tightly bound behind his back that the blood started from his finger nails. He had beside been put in a pit. Then he broke out: "If I am tortured I shall deny all I have said now, and shall say all they want me to say. If the time be short, I can bear to be beheaded, or to die by boiling water, or by fire, for the honour of the order; but I can no longer withstand the torments which, for more than two years, I have endured in prison." (34)

"I have been tortured three times," said Humbert de Podio. "I was confined thirty-six weeks in a tower, on bread and water, quia non confitebatur quae volebant." (35) Bernard de Vado showed two bones which had dropped from his heels after roasting his feet. (36)

Such testimony was disregarded, for condemnation was necessary as a preliminary to confiscation. The suppression of the Temple was the first step in that long spoliation of the Church which has continued to the present day, and which has been agonizing to the victims in proportion to their power of resistance. The fourteenth century was still an age of faith, and the monks died hard.

Philip grasped the situation with the intuition of genius, and provided himself with an instrument fit for the task before him. He forced Clement to raise Philip de Marigni to the See of Sens, and Marigni was a man who shrank from nothing.

When made archbishop, he convoked a provincial council at Paris, and condemned, as relapsed heretics, the knights who had repudiated their confessions. Fifty-nine of these knights belonged to his own diocese. He had them brought to a fenced enclosure in a field near the Abbey of Saint Antoine, and there offered them pardon if they would recant. Then they were chained to stakes, and slowly burned to ashes from the feet upward. Not one flinched, but amidst shrieks of anguish, when half consumed, they protested their innocence, and died imploring mercy of Christ and of the Virgin.(37)

Devotion so superb might have fired the imagination of even such a craven as Clement, but Philip was equal to the emergency. He had caused scores of witnesses to be examined to prove that Boniface was a murderer, a sorcerer, a debauchee, and a heretic. Suddenly he offered to drop the prosecution, and to restore the Temple lands to the Church, if the order might be abolished and the process closed. Clement yielded. In October, 1311, the council met at Vienne. The winter was spent in intimidation and bribery; the second meeting was not held until the following April, and then the decree of suppression was published. By this decree the corporation was dissolved, but certain of the higher officers still lived, and in an evil moment Clement bethought him of their fate. In December, 1313, he appointed a commission to try them. They were brought before a lofty scaffold at the portal of the Cathedral of Paris, and there made to reiterate the avowals which had been wrung from them in their dungeons. Then they were sentenced to perpetual imprisonment. But at this supreme moment, when it seemed that all was over, de Molay, the grand-master, and the Master of Normandy, broke into a furious defence. The commissioners adjourned in a panic, but Philip, thirsting for blood, sprang upon his prey.

He gave his orders to his own officers, without consulting any prelate. On March 18, 1314, as night fell, the two crusaders were taken from the provost, who acted as their gaoler, and carried to a little island in the Seine, on which a statue of Henry of Navarre now stands. There they were burned together, without a trial and without a sentence. They watched the building of their funeral pile with "hearts so firm and resolute, and persisted with such constancy in their denials to the end, and suffered death with such composure, that they left the witnesses of their execution in admiration and stupor." (38)

An ancient legend told how de Molay, as he stood upon his blazing fagots, summoned Clement to meet him before God's judgment-seat in forty days, and Philip within a year. Neither survived the interval. Philip had promised to restore the goods of the Temple to the Church, but the plunder, for which this tremendous deed was done, was not surrendered tamely to the vanquished after their defeat. The gold and silver, and all that could be stolen, disappeared. The land was in the end ceded to the Hospital, but so wasted that, for a century, no revenue whatever accrued from what had been one of the finest conventual estates in Europe. (39)

Such was the opening of that social revolution which, when it reached its height, was called the Reformation.

Footnotes

(1) *Bibl. de l'École des Chartes*, 3d series, ii. 353.

(2) *Histoire del'Abbaye de Saint Denis*, D'Ayzac, i. 361-9.

(3) *Vie de Louis le Gros*, Suger, ed. Molinier, 61, 62.

(4) *Vie de Louis le Gros*, Suger, ed. Molinier, 70.

(5) *Ibid.*, 18.

(6) Suger, ed. Molinier, 18.

(7) *Ibid.*

(8) *Études sur les origines de la commune de Saint Quentin*, Giry, 9.

(9) See *Études sur les Faires de Champagne*, Bourquelot, 72, 74; and generally on this subject.

(10) *Les Communes Françaises*, Luchaire, 221-225.

(11) *Les Communes Françaises*, Luchaire, 85.

(12) *Les Communes Françaises*, Luchaire, 233-234.

(13) *Les Communes Françaises*, Luchaire, 260.

(14) *Documents sur les Relations de la Royauté avec les Villes de France*, Giry, 59, 61.

(15) *Les Communes Françaises*, Luchaire, 189.

(16) *Manuel des Institutions Françaises*, Luchaire, 535.

(17) *Les Communes Françaises*, Luchaire, 283.

(18) *Mémoires du Duc de Saint-Simon*, ed. 1874, xii. 19.

(19) *Le Commerce de Marseille au Moyen Age*, Blancard, 3.

(20) *La Libertà delle Banche a Venezia*, Lattes, 26.

(21) *Les Grandes Compagnies de Commerce*, Bonnassieux, 23.

(22) *La Rapport entre l'or et l'argent au Temps de Saint Louis*, Marchéville, 22, 33.

(23) *Ibid.*, 42.

(24) *Les Communes Françaises*, 200, 201.

(25) The documents relating to the controversy are printed in the *Histoire du Différend*, Dupuy.

(26) Dupuy, 48.

(27) *Ibid.*, 44.

(28) See letters of Beauvais and Laon, of 1303, *Documents*, Giry, 160.

(29) Dupuy, 55.

(30) Dupuy, 351. Articles presented June, 1303.

(31) See *Cronica di Villani*, viii. 63.

(32) *Cronica di Villani*, viii. 80. Also *Ann. Eccl.*, Baronius, year 1305.

(33) *Documents Inédits sur l'Histoire de France, Procès des Templiers*, Michelet, i. 166.

(34) *Procès des Templiers*, Michelet, i. 37.

(35) *Ibid.*, 264.

(36) *Ibid.*, 75.

(37) *Cronica di Villani*, viii. 92.

(38) *Continuatio Chronici Guilelmi de Nangiaco*, mcccxiii.

(39) *La Maison du Temple*, Curzon, 200, 204.

Chapter VII: The English Reformation

MANY writers have pointed out the relation between commerce and scepticism in the Middle Ages, and, among others, Thorold Rogers has a passage in his *History of Agriculture and Prices* so interesting that it should be read entire:—

"The general spread of Lollardy, about which all the theologians of the age complain, was at once the cause and the effect of progressive opulence. It cannot be by accident that all the wealthiest parts of Europe, one district only excepted, and that for very sufficient reasons, were suspected during the Middle Ages of theological nonconformity. Before the campaigns of Simon de Montfort, in the first half of the thirteenth century, Provence was the garden and workshop of Europe. The sturdiest advocates of the Reformation were the burghers of the Low Countries.... In England the strength of the Lollard party was, from the days of Wiklif to the days of Cranmer, in Norfolk [the principal manufacturing county]; and I have no doubt that... the presence of students from this district must have told on the theological bias of Cambridge University, which came out markedly at the epoch of the Reformation....

"English Lollardy was, like its direct descendant Puritanism, sour and opinionative, but it was also moral and thrifty. They who denounced the lazy and luxurious life of the monks, the worldliness and greed of the prelates, and the gross and shallow artifices of the popular religion, were pretty sure to inculcate parsimony and saving. By voluntarily and sturdily cutting themselves off from the circumstance of the old faith, they were certain, like the Quakers of more than two centuries later, to become comparatively wealthy. They had nothing to spare for monk or priest...." (1)

The Lollards were of the modern economic type, and discarded the miracle because the miracle was costly and yielded an uncertain return. Yet the mediæval cult was based upon the miracle, and many of the payments due for the supernatural services of the ecclesiastics were obligatory; beside, gifts as an atonement for sin were a drain on savings, and the economist instinctively sought cheaper methods of propitiation.

In an age as unscientific as the sixteenth century, the conviction of the immutability of natural laws was not strong enough to admit of the abrogation of religious formulas. The monied class, therefore, proceeded step by step, and its first experiment was to suppress all fees to middle-men, whether priests or saints, by becoming their own intercessors with the Deity.

As Dr. Witherspoon has observed, "fear of wrath from the avenger of blood" made men "fly to the city of refuge";(2) but, as the tradesman replaced the enthusiast, a dogma was evolved by which mental anguish, which cost nothing, was substituted for the offering which was effective in proportion to its money value. This dogma was "Justification by Faith," the corner-stone of Protestantism.

Far from requiring an outlay from the elect, "Justification by Faith" discouraged it. The act consisted in "a deep humiliation of mind, confession of guilt and wretchedness... and acceptance of pardon and peace through Christ Jesus, which they have neither contributed to the procuring, nor can contribute to the continuance of, by their own merit." (3)

Yet the substitution of a mental condition for a money payment, led to consequences more far-reaching than the suppression of certain clerical revenues, for it involved the rejection of the sacred tradition which had not only sustained relic worship, but which had made the Church the channel of communication between Christians and the invisible world.

That ancient channel once closed, Protestants had to open another, and this led to the deification of the Bible, which, before the Reformation, had been supposed to derive its authority from that divine illumination which had enabled the priesthood to infallibly declare the canon of the sacred books. Calvin saw the weak spot in the position of the reformers, and faced it boldly. He maintained the Scripture to be "self-authenticated, carrying with it its own evidence, and ought not to be made the subject of demonstration and arguments from reason," and that it should obtain "the same complete credit and authority with believers... as if they heard the very words pronounced by God himself." (4)

Thus for the innumerable costly fetishes of the imaginative age were substituted certain writings, which could be consulted without a fee. The expedient was evidently the device of a mercantile community, and the saving to those who accepted it enormous, but it disintegrated Christendom, and made an organized priesthood impossible. When each individual might pry into the sacred mysteries at his pleasure, the authority of the clergy was annihilated. Men of the priestly type among the reformers saw the danger and tried to save themselves. The thesis which the early evangelical divines maintained was the unity of truth. The Scriptures were true: therefore if the whole body of Christians searched aright they could not fail to draw truth from them, and this truth must be the creed of the universal Church. Zwingli thus explained the doctrine:—

"Whoever hears the holy scriptures read aloud in church, judges what he hears. Nevertheless what is heard is not itself the Word through which we believe. For if we believed through the simple hearing or reading of the Word, all would be believers. On the contrary, we see that many hear and see and do not believe. Hence it is clear that we believe only through the word which the Heavenly Father speaks in our hearts, by which he enlightens us so that we see, and draws us so that we follow.... For God is not a God of strife and quarrel, but of unity and peace. Where there is true faith, there the Holy Spirit is present; but where the Holy Spirit is, there is certainly effort for unity and peace.... Therefore there is no danger of confusion in the Church since, if the congregation is assembled through

God, he is in the midst of them, and all who have faith strive after unity and peace."(5)

The inference the clergy sought to draw was, that though all could read the Bible, only the enlightened could interpret it, and that they alone were the enlightened. Hence Calvin's pretensions equalled Hildebrand's:—

"This is the extent of the power with which the pastors of the Church, by whatever name they may be distinguished, ought to be invested; that by the word of God they may venture to do all things with confidence; may constrain all the strength, glory, wisdom, and pride of the world to obey and submit to his majesty; supported by his power, may govern all mankind, from the highest to the lowest; may build up the house of Christ, and subvert the house of Satan; may feed the sheep, and drive away the wolves; may instruct and exhort the docile; may reprove, rebuke, and restrain the rebellious and obstinate; may bind and loose; may discharge their lightnings and thunders, if necessary; but all in the Word of God." (6)

In certain regions, poor and remote from the centres of commerce, these pretensions were respected. In Geneva, Scotland, and New England, men like Calvin, Knox, and Cotton maintained themselves until economic competition did its work: then they passed away. Nowhere has faith withstood the rise of the mercantile class. As a whole the Reformation was eminently an economic phenomenon, and is best studied in England, which, after the Reformation, grew to be the centre of the world's exchanges.

From the beginning of modern history, commerce and scepticism have gone hand in hand. The Eastern trade began to revive after the reopening of the valley of the Danube, about 1000, and perhaps, in that very year, Berenger, the first great modern heretic, was born. By 1050 he had been condemned and made to recant, but with the growth of the Fairs of Champagne his heresy grew, and in 1215, just in the flush of the communal development, the Church found it necessary to define the dogma of transubstantiation, and declare it an article of faith. A generation later came the burning of schismatics; in 1252, by his bull "Ad extirpanda," Innocent IV. organized the Inquisition, and the next year Grossetête, Bishop of Lincoln, died, with whom the organized opposition of the English to the ancient costly ritual may be said to have opened.

In Great Britain the agitation for reform appears to have been practical from the outset. There was no impatience with dogmas simply because they were incomprehensible: the Trinity and the Double Procession were always accepted. Formulas of faith were resisted because they involved a payment of money, and foremost among these were masses and penances. Another grievance was the papal patronage, and, as early as the fourteenth century, Parliament passed the statutes of provisors and præemunire to prevent the withdrawal of money from the realm.

The rise of the Lollards was an organized movement to resist ecclesiastical exactions, and to confiscate ecclesiastical property; and, if 1345 be taken as the opening of Wickliffe's active life, the agitation for the seizure of monastic estates started just a generation after Philip's attack on the Temple in France. There was at least this difference in the industrial condition of the two nations, and probably much more.

Wickliffe was rather a politician than a theologian, and his preaching a diatribe against the extravagance of the Church. In one of his Saints' Days sermons he explained the waste of relic worship as shrewdly as a modern man of business:—

"It would be to the benefit of the Church, and to the honour of the saints, if the costly ornaments so foolishly lavished upon their graves were divided among the poor, I am well aware, however, that the man who would sharply and fully expose this error would be held for a manifest heretic by the image worshippers and the greedy people who make gain of such graves; for in the adoration of the eucharist, and such worshipping of dead bodies and images, the Church is seduced by an adulterous generation." (7)

The laity paid the priesthood fees because of their supernatural powers, and the possession of these powers was chiefly demonstrated by the miracle of the mass. Wickliffe, with a leader's eye, saw where the enemy was vulnerable, and the last years of his life were passed in his fierce controversy with the mendicants upon transubstantiation. Even at that early day he presented the issue with incomparable clearness: "And thou, then, that art an earthly man, by what reason mayst thou say that thou makest thy maker?" (8)

The deduction from such premises was inexorable. The mass had to be condemned as fetish worship, and with it went the adoration of relics.

"Indeed, many nominal Christians are worse than pagans; for it is not so bad that a man should honour as God, for the rest of the day, the first thing he sees in the morning, as that regularly that accident should be really his God, which he sees in the mass in the hands of the priest in the consecrated wafer." (9)

Wickliffe died December 30, 1384, and ten years later the Lollards had determined to resist all payments for magic. They presented their platform to Parliament in 1395, summed up in their Book of Conclusions. Some of these "conclusions" are remarkably interesting:—

5th.—"That the exorcisms and hallowings, consecrations and blessings, over the wine, bread, wax, water, oil, salt, incense, the altar-stone, and about the church-walls, over the vestment, chalice, mitre, cross, and pilgrim-staves, are the very practices of necromancy, rather than of sacred divinity.

....

7th.—"We mightily affirm... that spiritual prayers made in the church for the souls of the dead... is a false foundation of alms, whereupon all the houses of alms in England are falsely founded.

8th.—"That pilgrimages, prayers, and oblations made unto blind crosses or roods, or to deaf images made either of wood or stone, are very near of kin unto idolatry."(10)

When Lord Cobham, the head of the Lollard party, was tried for heresy in 1413, Archbishop Arundel put him four test questions. First, whether he believed, after the sacramental words had been spoken, any material bread or wine remained in the sacrament; fourth, whether he believed relic worship meritorious.

His answers did not give satisfaction, and they roasted him in chains, in Saint Giles's Fields, in 1418.

A hundred years of high commercial activity followed Cobham's death. The discovery of America, and of the sea passage to India, changed the channels of commerce throughout the world, human movement was accelerated, gunpowder made the attack overwhelming; centralization took a prodigious stride, scepticism kept pace with centralization, and in 1510 Erasmus wrote thus, and yet remained in the orthodox communion:—

"Moreover savoureth it not of the same saulce [folly] (trow ye) when everie countrey chalengeth a severall sainct for theyr patrone, assignyng further to each sainct a peculiar cure and office, with also sundrie ways of worshipping; as this sainct helpeth for the tooth-ache, that socoureth in childbyrth; she restoreth stolene goods; an other aydeth shipmen in tempests; an other taketh charge of husbandmens hoggs; and so of the rest; far too long were it to reherse all. Then some saincts there be, that are generally sued for many thynges; amongst whom chiefly is the virgin Mother of God, in whom vulgar folke have an especiall confidence, yea almost more than in her Sonne." (11)

When Erasmus wrote, the Reformation was at hand, but the attack on Church property had begun in England full two centuries before, comtemporaneously with Philip's onslaught on the Temple. All over Europe the fourteenth century was a period of financial distress; in France the communes became bankrupt and the coinage deteriorated, and in England the debasement of the currency began in 1299, and kept pace with the rise of Lollardy. In 1299 the silver penny weighed 22½ grains; Edward I. reduced it to 22¼ grains; Edward III. to 18 grains; Henry IV. to 15 grains; and Henry VI., during his restoration in 1470, to 12 grains.

As the stringency increased, the attack on the clergy gained in ferocity. Edward I. not only taxed the priesthood, but seized the revenues of the alien priories; of these there might have been one hundred and fifty within the realm, and what he took from them he spent on his army.

Edward II. and Edward III. followed the precedent, and during the last reign, when the penny dropped four grains, these revenues were sequestered no less than twenty-three years. Under Henry IV. the penny lost three grains, and what remained of the income of these houses was permanently applied to defraying the expenses of the court. Henry V. dissolved them, and vested their estates in the crown.

In the reign of Henry IV., when the penny was on the point of losing three grains of its silver, the tone of Parliament was similar to that of the parliaments of the Reformation. On one occasion the king asked for a subsidy, and the Speaker suggested that without burdening the laity he might "supply his occasions by seizing on the revenues of the clergy"; (12) and in 1410 Lord Cobham anticipated the Parliament of 1536 by introducing a bill for the confiscation of conventual revenues to the amount of 322,000 marks, a sum which he averred represented the income of certain corporations whose names he appended in a schedule. (13)

Year by year, as society consolidated, the economic type was propagated; and, as the pressure of a contracting currency stimulated these men to action, the demand for cheap religion grew fiercer. London, the monied centre, waxed hotter and hotter, and a single passage from the *Supplicacyon for Beggers* shows how bitter the denunciations of the system of paying for miracles became:—

"Whate money pull they yn by probates of testamentes, priuy tithes, and by mennes offeringes to theyre pilgrimages, and at theyre first masses? Euery man and childe that is buried, must pay sumwhat for masses and diriges to be song for him, or elles they will accuse the dedes frendes and executours of heresie. whate money get they by mortuaries, by hearing of confessions... by halowing of churches, altares, superaltares, chapelles, and bells, by cursing of men and absoluing theim agein for money?" (14)

One of the ballads of Cromwell's time ridiculed, in this manner, all the chief pilgrimages of the kingdom:—

"Ronnying hyther and thyther,
We cannot tell whither,
In offryng candels and pence
To stones and stockes,
And to olde rotten blockes.
That came, we know not from whense.

"To Walsyngham a gaddyng,
To Canterbury a maddyng,
As men distraught of mynde;
With fewe clothes on our backes,
But an image of waxe.
For the lame and for the blynde.

"Yet offer what ye wolde,
Were it otes, syluer, or golde
Pyn, poynt, brooche, or rynge,
The churche were as then,

Such charitable men,
That they would refuse nothyng." (15)

But the war was not waged with words alone. At the comparatively early date of 1393, London had grown so unruly that Richard assumed the government of the city himself. First he appointed Sir Edward Darlington warden, but Sir Edward proving too lenient, he replaced him with Sir Baldwin Radington. Foxe, very frankly, explained why:—

"For the Londoners at that time were notoriously known to be favourers of Wickliffs side, as partly before this is to be seen, and in the story of Saint Alban's more plainly doth appear, where the author of the said history, writing upon the fifteenth year of King Richard's reign, reporteth in these words of the Londoners, that they were 'not right believers in God, nor in the traditions of their forefathers; sustainers of the Lollards, depravers of religious men, withholders of tithes, and impoverishers of the common people.'

"... The king, incensed not a litle with the complaint of the bishops, conceived eftsoons, against the mayor and sheriffs, and against the whole city of London, a great stomach; insomuch, that the mayor and both the sheriffs were sent for, and removed from their office." (16)

By the opening of the sixteenth century a priest could hardly collect his dues without danger; the Bishop of London indeed roundly declared to the government that justice could not be had from the courts.

In 1514 the infant child of a merchant tailor named Hun died, and the parson of the parish sued the father for a bearing sheet, which he claimed as a mortuary. Hun contested the case, and got out a writ of præmunire against the priest, which so alarmed the clergy that the chancellor of the diocese accused him of heresy, and confined him in the Lollard's tower of Saint Paul's.

In due time the usual articles were exhibited against the defendant, charging that he had disputed the lawfulness of tithes, and had said they were ordained "only by the covetousness of priests"; also that he possessed divers of "Wickliff's damnable works," and more to the same effect.

Upon these articles Fitzjames, Bishop of London, examined Hun on December 2, and after the examination recommitted him. On the morning of the 4th, a boy sent with his breakfast found him hanging to a beam in his cell. The clergy said suicide, but the populace cried murder, and the coroner's jury found a verdict against Dr. Horsey, the chancellor. The situation then became grave, and Fitzjames wrote to Wolsey a remarkable letter, which showed not only high passion, but serious alarm:—

"In most humble wise I beseech you, that I may have the king's gracious favour... for assured am I, if my chancellor be tried by any twelve men in London, they be so maliciously set, 'in favorem hæreticæ pravitatis,' that they will cast and condemn any clerk, though he were as innocent as Abel." (17)

The evidence is conclusive that, from the outset, industry bred heretics; agriculture, believers. Thorold Rogers has explained that the east of England, from Kent to the Wash and on to Yorkshire, was the richest part of the kingdom, (18) and Mr. Blunt, in his *Reformation of the Church of England*, has published an analysis of the martyrdoms under Mary. He has shown that out of 277 victims, 234 came from the district to the east of a line drawn from Boston to Portsmouth. West of this line Oxford had most burnings; but, by the reign of Mary, manufactures had spread so far inland that the industries of Oxfordshire were only surpassed by those of Middlesex.(19) In Wickliffe's time Norwich stood next to London, and Norwich was infested with Lollards, many of whom were executed there.

On the other hand, but two executions are recorded in the six agricultural counties north of the Humber—counties which were the poorest and the farthest removed from the lines of trade. Thus the eastern counties were the hot-bed of Puritanism. There, Kett's rebellion broke out under Edward VI.; there, Cromwell recruited his Ironsides, and throughout this region, before the beginning of the Reformation, assaults on relics were most frequent and violent. One of the most famous of these relics was the rood of Dovercourt. Dovercourt is part of Harwich, on the Essex coast; Dedham lies ten miles inland, on the border of Suffolk; and the description given by Foxe of the burning of the image of Dovercourt, is an example of what went on throughout the southeast just before the time of the divorce:—

"In the same year of our Lord 1532, there was an idol named the Rood of Dovercourt, whereunto was much and great resort of people: for at that time there was great rumour blown abroad amongst the ignorant sort, that the power of the idol of Dovercourt was so great, that no man had power to shut the church-door where he stood; and therefore they let the church-door, both night and day, continually stand open, for the more credit unto their blind rumour. This once being conceived in the heads of the vulgar sort, seemed a great marvel unto many men; but to many again, whom God had blessed with his spirit, it was greatly suspected, especially unto these, whose names here follow: as Robert King of Dedham, Robert Debnam of Eastbergholt, Nicholas Marsh of Dedham, and Robert Gardner of Dedham, whose consciences were sore burdened to see the honour and power of the almighty living God so to be blasphemed by such an idol. Wherefore they were moved by the Spirit of God, to travel out of Dedham in a wondrous goodly night, both hard frost and fair moonshine, although the night before, and the night after, were exceeding foul and rainy. It was from the town of Dedham, to the place where the filthy Rood stood, ten miles. Notwithstanding, they were so willing in that their enterprise, that they went these ten miles without pain, and found the church door open, according to the blind talk of the ignorant people: for there durst no unfaithful body shut it. This happened well for their purpose, for they found the idol, which had as much power to keep the door shut, as to keep it open; and for proof thereof, they took the idol from his shrine, and carried him quarter of a mile from the place where he stood, without any resistance of the said idol. Whereupon they struck fire with a flint-stone, and suddenly set him on fire, who burned out so brim, that he lighted them homeward one good mile of the ten.

"This done, there went a great talk abroad that they should have great riches in that place; but it was very untrue; for it was not their thought or enterprise, as they themselves afterwards confessed, for there was nothing taken away but his coat, his shoes, and the tapers. The tapers did help to burn him, the shoes they had again, and the coat one Sir Thomas Rose did burn; but they had neither penny, halfpenny, gold, groat, nor jewel.

"Notwithstanding, three of them were afterwards indicted of felony, and hanged in chains within half a year, or thereabout.

....

"The same year, and the year before, there were many images cast down and destroyed in many places: as the image of the crucifix in the highway by Coggeshall, the image of Saint Petronal in the church of Great Horksleigh, the image of Saint Christopher by Sudbury, and another image of Saint Petronal in a chapel of Ipswich." (20)

England's economic supremacy is recent, and has resulted from the change in the seat of exchanges which followed the discovery of America and the sea-route to India; long before Columbus, however, the introduction of the mariner's compass had altered the paths commerce followed between the north and south of Europe during the crusades.

The necessity of travel by land built up the Fairs of Champagne; they declined when safe ocean navigation had cheapened marine freights. Then Antwerp and Bruges superseded Provins and the towns of Central France, and rapidly grew to be the distributing points for Eastern merchandise for Germany, the Baltic, and England. In 1317 the Venetians organized a direct packet service with

Flanders, and finally, the discoveries of Vasco-da-Gama, at the end of the fifteenth century, threw Italy completely out of the line of the Asiatic trade.

British industries seem to have sympathized with these changes, for weaving first assumed some importance under Edward I., although English cloth long remained inferior to continental. The next advance was contemporaneous with the discovery of the Cape of Good Hope. On July 8, 1497, Vasco-da-Gama sailed for Calicut, and in the previous year Henry VII. negotiated the "Magnus Intercursus," by which treaty the Merchant Adventurers succeeded for the first time in establishing themselves advantageously in Antwerp. Thenceforward England began to play a part in the industrial competition of Europe, but even then her progress was painfully slow. The accumulations of capital were small, and increased but moderately, and a full century later, when the Dutch easily raised £600,000 for their East India Company, only £72,000 were subscribed in London for the English venture.

Throughout the Middle Ages, while exchanges centred in North Italy, Great Britain hung on the outskirts of the commercial system of the world, and even at the beginning of the reign of Henry VIII. she could not compare, either in wealth, refinement, or organization, with such a kingdom as France.

The crown had not been the prize of the strongest in a struggle among equals, but had fallen to a soldier of a superior race, under whom no great nobility ever grew up. No baron in England corresponded with such princes as the dukes of Normandy and Burgundy, the counts of Champagne and Toulouse. Fortifications were on a puny scale; no strongholds like Pierrefonds or Vitré, Coucy or Carcassonne existed, and the Tower of London itself was insignificant beside the Chateau Gaillard, which Coeur-de-Lion planted on the Seine.

The population was scanty, and increased little. When Henry VIII. came to the throne in 1509, London may have had forty or fifty thousand inhabitants, York eleven thousand, Bristol nine or ten thousand, and Norwich six thousand.(21) Paris at that time probably contained between three and four hundred thousand, and Milan and Ghent two hundred and fifty thousand each.

But although England was not a monied centre during the Middle Ages, and perhaps for that very reason, she felt with acuteness the financial pressure of the fourteenth and fifteenth centuries. She had little gold and silver, and gold and silver rose in relative value; she had few manufactures, and manufactures were comparatively prosperous; her wealth lay in her agricultural interests, and farm products were, for the most part, severely pinched.

Commenting on the prices between the end of the thirteenth century and the middle of the sixteenth, Mr. Rogers has observed:—

"Again, upon several articles of the first importance, there is a marked decline in the price from the average of 1261-1400 to that of 1401-1540. This would have been more conspicuous, if I had in my earlier volumes compared all prices from 1261 to 1350 with those of 1351-1400. But even over the whole range, every kind of grain, except wheat and peas, is dearer in the thirteenth and fourteenth centuries than it is in the first hundred and forty years of the present period [1401-1582]; and had I taken the average price of wheat during the last fifty years of the fourteenth century, it would have been (6s. 1½d.) dearer than the average of 1401-1540 (5s. 11¾d.), heightened as this is by the dearness of the last thirteen years." (22)

The tables published by Mr. Rogers make it possible to form some idea of the strain to which the population of Great Britain was exposed, during the two hundred and fifty years which intervened between the crisis at the close of the thirteenth century, and the discovery of the mines of Potosi in 1545, which flooded the world with silver. Throughout this long interval an expanding commerce unceasingly enlarged the demand for currency, while no adequate additions were made to the stock of the precious metals; the consequence was that their relative value rose, while the value of commodities declined, and this process had a tendency to debase the coinage.

The latter part of the Middle Ages was a time of rapid centralization, when the cost of administration grew from year to year; but in proportion as the necessities of the government increased, the power of the people to pay taxes diminished, because the products which they sold brought less of the standard coin. To meet the deficit the same weight of metal had to be cut into more pieces, and thus by a continued inflation of the currency, general bankruptcy was averted. The various stages of pressure are pretty clearly marked by the records of the Mint.

Apparently the stringency which began in France about the end of the reign of Saint Louis, or somewhat later, did not affect England immediately, for prices do not seem to have reached their maximum until after 1290, and Edward I. only reduced the penny, in 1299, from 22.5 grains of silver to 22.25 grains. Thenceforward the decline, though spasmodic, on the whole tended to increase in severity from generation to generation. The long French wars, and the Black Death, produced a profound effect upon the domestic economy of the kingdom under Edward III.; and the Black Death, especially, seems to have had the unusual result of raising prices at a time of commercial collapse. This rise probably was due to the dearth of labour, for half the population of Europe is said to have perished, and, at all events, the crops often could not be reaped through lack of hands. More than a generation elapsed before normal conditions returned.

Immediately before the French war the penny lost two grains, and between 1346 and 1351, during the Black Death, it lost two grains and a quarter more, a depreciation of four grains and a half in fifty years; then for half a century an equilibrium was maintained. Under Henry IV. there was a sharp decline of three grains, equal to an inflation of seventeen per cent, and by 1470, under Henry VI., the penny fell to twelve grains. Then a period of stability followed, which lasted until just before the Reformation, when a crisis unparalleled in severity began, a crisis which probably was the proximate cause of the confiscation of the conventual estates.

In 1526 the penny suddenly lost a grain and a half, or about twelve and a half per cent, and then, when further reductions of weight would have made the piece too flimsy, the government resorted to adulteration. In 1542, a ten-grain penny was coined with one part in five of alloy; in 1544, the alloy had risen to one-half, and in 1543, two-thirds of the coin was base metal—a depreciation of more than seventy per cent in twenty years.

Meanwhile, though prices had fluctuated, the trend had been downward, and downward so strongly that it had not been fully counteracted by the reductions of bullion in the money. Rogers thought lath-nails perhaps the best gauge of prices, and in commenting on the years which preceded the Reformation, he remarked:—

"From 1461 to 1540, the average [of lath-nails] is very little higher than it was from 1261 to 1350, illustrating anew that significant decline in prices which characterizes the economical history of England during the eighty years 1461-1540."(23)

Although wheat rose more than other grains, and is therefore an unfavourable standard of comparison, wheat yields substantially the same result. During the last forty years of the thirteenth century, the average price of the quarter was 5s. 10¾d., and for the last decade, 6s. 1d. For the first forty years of the sixteenth century the average was 6s. l0d. The penny of 1526, however, contained only about forty-seven per cent of the bullion of the penny of 1299. "The most remarkable fact in connection with the issue of base money by Henry VIII. is the singular identity of the average price of grain, especially wheat, during the first 140 years of my present period, with the last 140 of my first two volumes." (24)

After a full examination of his tables, Rogers concluded that the great rise which made the prosperity of Elizabeth's reign did not begin until some "year between 1545 and 1549." (25) This corresponds precisely with the discovery of Potosi in 1545, and that the advance was due to the new silver, and not to the debasement of the coinage, seems demonstrated by the fact that no fall took place when the currency was restored by Elizabeth, but, on the contrary, the upward movement continued until well into the next century.

Some idea may be formed from these figures of the contraction which prevailed during the years of the Reformation. In 1544, toward the close of Henry's reign, the penny held five grains of pure silver as against about 20.8 grains in 1299, and yet its purchasing power had not greatly varied. Bullion must therefore have had about four times the relative value in 1544 that it had two hundred and fifty years earlier, and, if the extremely debased issues of 1545 and later be taken as the measure, its value was much higher.

Had Potosi been discovered a generation earlier, the whole course of English development might have been modified, for it is not impossible that, without the aid of falling prices, the rising capitalistic class might have lacked the power to confiscate the monastic estates. As it was, the pressure continued until the catastrophe occurred, relic worship was swept away, the property of the nation was redistributed, and an impulsion was given to large farming which led to the rapid eviction of the yeomanry. As the yeomen were driven from their land, they roamed over the world, colonizing and conquering, from the Mississippi to the Ganges; building up, in the course of two hundred and fifty years, a centralization greater than that of Rome, and more absolute than that of Constantinople.

Changes so vast in the forms of competition necessarily changed the complexion of society. Men who had flourished in an age of decentralization and of imagination passed away, and were replaced by a new aristocracy.

The soldier and the priest were overpowered; and, from the Reformation downward, the monied type possessed the world.

Thomas Cromwell, Earl of Essex, was the ideal of this type, and he was accordingly the Englishman who rose highest during the convulsion of the Reformation. He was a perfect commercial adventurer, and Chapuys, the ambassador of Charles V. at London, thus described his origin to his master:—

"Cromwell is the son of a poor farrier, who lived in a little village a league and a half from here, and is buried in the parish graveyard. His uncle, father of the cousin whom he has already made rich, was cook of the late Archbishop of Canterbury. Cromwell was ill-behaved when young, and after an imprisonment was forced to leave the country. He went to Flanders, Rome, and elsewhere in Italy. When he returned he married the daughter of a shearman, and served in his house; he then became a solicitor."(26)

The trouble which drove him abroad seems to have been with his father, and he probably started on his travels about 1504. He led a dissolute and vagabond life, served as a mercenary in Italy, "was wild and youthful,... as he himself was wont ofttimes to declare unto Cranmer, Archbishop of Canterbury; showing what a ruffian he was in his young days,.. also what a great doer he was with Geffery Chambers in publishing and setting forth the pardons of Boston everywhere in churches as he went." (27)

These "pardons" were indulgences he succeeded in obtaining from the pope for the town of Boston, which he peddled about the country as he went. He served as a clerk in the counting house of the Merchant Adventurers at Antwerp, and also appears to have filled some such position with a Venetian merchant. On his return to England in 1513, he married and set up a fulling-mill; he also became an attorney and a usurer, dwelling by Fenchurch, in London.

In 1523, having been elected to Parliament, Cromwell was a most prosperous man. At this time he entered Wolsey's service, and made himself of use in suppressing convents to supply endowments for the cardinal's colleges at Oxford and Ipswich. When Wolsey fell, he ingratiated himself with Henry, and thenceforward rose rapidly. He became chancellor of the exchequer, master of the rolls, secretary of state, vicar general, a Knight of the Garter, and Earl of Essex. At once the head of Church and State, probably no English subject has ever been so powerful.

Both he and Cranmer succeeded through flexibility and adroitness. He suggested to Henry to accomplish his ends by robbing the convents, and Mr. Brewer, an excellent authority, thought him notoriously venal from the outset.

His executive and business capacity was unrivalled. He had the instinct for money, and provided he made it, he scrupled not about the means. In the *State Papers* there is an amusing account of the treatment he put up with, when at the pinnacle of greatness:—

"And as for my Lord Prevye Sealle, I wold not be in his case for all that ever he hatha, for the King beknaveth him twice a weke, and some-tyme knocke him well about thee pate; and yet when he hathe bene well pomeld aboute the hedde, and shaken up, as it were a dogge, he will come out into the great chambre, shaking of the bushe with as mery a countenance as thoughe he mought rule all the roste." (28)

Though good-natured where his interests were not involved, he appears to have been callous to the sight of pain, and not only attended to the racking of important witnesses, but went in state to see Father Forest roasted in chains for denying the royal supremacy, which he was labouring to establish. His behaviour to Lambert, whom he sent to the fire for confessing his own principles, astonished even those who knew him well. How he became a Protestant is uncertain; Foxe thought, by reading Erasmus's translation of the New Testament. More probably he was sceptical because he was of the economic type. At all events, he hated Rome, and Foxe said that in 1538 he was "the chief friend of the gospellers."

In that same year Lambert was tried for heresy regarding transubstantiation, and it was then Cromwell sentenced him to be burned alive. Characteristically, he is said to have invited him to breakfast on the morning of the execution, and to have then begged his pardon for what he had done.

Pole described a conversation he had with Essex about the duty of ministers to kings. Pole thought their first obligation was to consider their masters' honour, and insisted on the divergence between honour and expediency. Such notions seemed fantastic to Cromwell, who told Pole that a prudent politician would study a prince's inclinations and act accordingly. He then offered Pole a manuscript of Machiavelli's *Prince*. Such a temperament differed, not so much in degree as in kind, from that of Godfrey de Bouillon or Saint Louis, Bayard or the Black Prince. It was subtler, more acquisitive, more tenacious of life, and men and women of the breed of Cromwell rose rapidly to be the owners of England during the sixteenth century. Social standards changed. Even in semi-barbarous ages a lofty courtesy had always been deemed befitting the great. Saint Anselm and Héloïse, Saladin and Cœur-de-Lion have remained ideals for centuries, because they represented a phase of civilization; and Froissart has described how the Black Prince entertained his prisoners after Poitiers:—

"The prince himself served the king's table, as well as the others, with every mark of humility, and would not sit down at it, in spite of all his entreaties for him so to do, saying that 'he was not worthy of such an honour, nor did it appertain to him to seat himself at the table of so great a king, or of so valiant a man as he had shown himself by his actions that day.'" (29)

One hundred and fifty years of progress had eliminated chivalry. Manners were coarse and morals loose at the court of Henry VIII. Foreign ambassadors spoke with little respect of the society they saw. Chapuys permitted himself to sneer at Lady Jane Seymour, who afterward became queen, because he seems to have thought the ladies of the court venal:—

"I leave you to judge whether, being English, and having frequented the court, 'si elle ne tiendroit pas à conscience de navoir pourveu et prévenu de savoir que cest de faire nopces.'" (30)

The scandals of the Boleyn family are too well known to need notice,(31) and it would be futile to accumulate examples of the absence of female virtue when the fact is notorious. The rising nobility resembled Cromwell more or less feebly. The mercenary quality was the salient characteristic of the favoured class. Thomas Boleyn, Earl of Wiltshire, made his fortune through his own shrewdness and the beauty of his daughters. Mary, the younger, was an early mistress of Henry; Anne, the elder and the astuter, was his wife. Boleyn's title and his fortune came through this connection. Boleyn was a specimen of a class; in him the instinct of self-preservation was highly developed. When his daughter Anne, and his son Lord Rochford, were tried at the Tower for incest, the evidence was so flimsy that ten to one was bet in the court-room on acquittal. At this supreme moment, the attitude of the father was thus described by Chapuys, who had good sources of information:—

"On the 15th the said concubine and her brother were condemned of treason by all the principal lords of England, and the Duke of Norfolk [her uncle] pronounced sentence. I am told the Earl of Wiltshire was quite as ready to assist at the judgment as he had done at the condemnation of the other four." (32)

The grandfather of Thomas Boleyn had been an alderman of London and a rich tradesman; his son had been knighted, and had retired from business, and Wiltshire himself, though a younger son and with but fifty pounds a year when married, raised himself by his wits, and the use of his children, to be a wealthy earl.

The history of the Cecil family is not dissimilar. David, the first of the name who emerged from obscurity, gained a certain favour under Henry VIII.; his son Richard, a most capable manager, obtained a fair share of the monastic plunder, was groom of the robes, constable of Warwick Castle, and died rich. His son was the great Lord Burleigh, in regard to whom perhaps it may be best to quote an impartial authority. Macaulay described him as possessed of "a cool temper, a sound judgment, great powers of application, and a constant eye to the main chance.... He never deserted his friends till it was very inconvenient to stand by them, was an excellent Protestant when it was not very advantageous to be a Papist, recommended a tolerant policy to his mistress as strongly as he could recommend it without hazarding her favour, never put to the rack any person from whom it did not seem probable that useful information might be derived, and was so moderate in his desires that he left only three hundred distinct landed estates, though he might, as his honest servant assures us, have left much more, 'if he would have taken money out of the exchequer for his own use, as many treasurers have done.'" (33)

The Howards, though of an earlier time, were of the same temperament. The founder was a lawyer, who sat on the bench of the Common Pleas under Edward I., and who, therefore, did not earn his knighthood on a stricken field, as the Black Prince won his spurs at Crécy. After his death his descendants made little stir for a century, but they married advantageously, accumulated money, and, in the fifteenth century, one Robert Howard married a daughter of Thomas Mowbray, Duke of Norfolk. This he hardly would have done had he not been a man of substance, since he seems not to have been a man of war. The alliance made the fortune of the family. It also appears to have added some martial instinct to the stock, for Richard III. gave John Howard the title of the Mowbrays, and this John was afterwards killed at Bosworth. His son commanded at Flodden, and his grandson was the great spoiler of the convents under Henry VIII., who also suppressed the northern rebellion.

Thomas Howard, the minister of Henry VIII., was one of the most interesting characters of his generation. He was naturally a strong Conservative; Chapuys never doubted that "the change in matters of religion [was] not to his mind": in 1534 he even went so far as to tell the French ambassador that he would not consent to a change, and this speech having been repeated to the king, occasioned his momentary disgrace.(34) At one time Lord Darcy, the head of the reactionary party, counted on his support against Cromwell, though he warned Chapuys not to trust him implicitly, because of "his inconstancy." (35) Yet, under a certain appearance of vacillation, he hid a profound and subtle appreciation of the society which environed him; this "inconstancy" made his high fortune. He had a sure instinct, which taught him at the critical moment where his interests lay, and he never was deceived. Henry distrusted him, but could not do without him, and paid high for his support. Howard, on his side, was keenly distressed when he found he had gone too far; and when the northern insurrection broke out, and he was offered the command of the royal forces, the Bishop of Carlisle, with whom he dined, said he had never seen the duke "so happy as he was to-day." (36)

Once in the field against his friends, there were no lengths to which Thomas Howard would not go. He never wearied of boasting of his lies and of his cruelty; he wrote to assure Henry he would spare no pains to entrap them, and would esteem no promise he made to the rebels, "for surely I shall observe no part thereof, for any respect of that other might call mine honor dystayned." (37)

As Cromwell behaved toward Lambert, so he behaved toward the Carthusians. Though they were men in whose religion he probably believed as sincerely as he believed anything, and in whose cause he had professed himself ready to take up arms, when they were sent to the stake he attended the execution as a spectacle, and watched them expire in torments, without a pang. Men gifted like Howard were successful in the Reformation, and Norfolk made a colossal fortune out of his politics. The price of his service was thirteen convents, and his son Surrey had two; of what he made in other ways no record remains.

Such was the new aristocracy; but the bulk of the old baronage was differently bred, and those who were of the antiquated type were doomed to pass away.

The publication of the *State Papers* leaves no doubt that the ancient feudal gentry, both titled and untitled, as a body, opposed the reform. Many of the most considerable of these were compromised in the Pilgrimage of Grace in 1536, among whom was Thomas Lord Darcy. If a mediæval baron still lived in the middle of the sixteenth century, that man was Darcy. Since the Conqueror granted the Norman de Areci thirty lordships in Lincolnshire, his ancestors had been soldiers, and at his home in the north his retainers formed an army as of old. Born in 1467, at twenty-five he bound himself by indenture to serve Henry VII. beyond the sea, at the head of a thousand men, and more than forty years afterward he promised Chapuys that he would march against London with a force eight thousand strong, if the emperor would attack Henry VIII. All his life long he had fought upon the borders. He had been captain of Berwick, warden of the east and middle marches, and in 1511 he had volunteered to lead a British contingent against the Moors. He was a Knight of the Garter, a member of the Privy Council, and when the insurrection broke out, he commanded at Pontefract Castle, the strongest position in Yorkshire.

A survival of the past, he retained the ideas of Crecy and Poitiers, and these brought him to the block. While negotiations were pending, Norfolk seems to have wanted to save him, though possibly he may have been actuated by a more sinister purpose. At all events he certainly wrote suggesting to Darcy to make his peace by ensnaring Aske, the rebel leader, and giving him up to the government. To Norfolk this seemed a perfectly legitimate transaction. By such methods he rose to eminence. To Darcy it seemed dishonour, and he died for it. Instead of doing as he was bid, he reproached Norfolk for deeming him capable of treachery:—

"Where your lordship advises me to take Aske, quick or dead, as you think I may do by policy, and so gain the king's favour; alays my good lord yt ever ye being a man of so much honour and gret experyence shold advice or chuss mee a man to be of eny such sortt or facion to betray or dissav eny liffyng man, French man, Scott, yea, or a Turke; of my faith, to gett and wyn to me and myn heyres fowr of the best dukes landdes in Fraunce, or to be kyng there, I wold nott do it to no liffyng person." (38)

Darcy averred that he surrendered Pontefract to the rebels because the government neglected to relieve him, and although doubtless he always sympathized with the rising, he promptly wrote to London when the outbreak began, to warn Henry not only of the weakness of his fortress, but of the power of the enemy. (39) When the royal herald visited the castle to treat with the insurgents, he found Darcy, Sir Robert Constable, Aske, and others, who told him they were on a pilgrimage to London to have all the "vile blood put from" the Privy Council, "and noble blood set up again," and to make restitution for the wrongs done the Church. (40)

This Aske was he whom Darcy refused to betray, but instead he offered to do all he could "as a true knight and subject" to pacify the country, and he did help to persuade the rebels to disperse on Henry's promise of a redress of grievances. In the moment of peril both Darcy and Aske were pardoned and cajoled, but the rising monied type were not the men to let the soldiers escape them, once they held them disarmed. Even while Henry was plotting the destruction of those to whom he had pledged his word, Norfolk wrote from the north to Cromwell: "I have by policy brought him [Aske] to desire me to yeve him licence to ride to London, and have promised to write a letter... which... I pray you take of the like sort as you did the other I wrote for Sir Thomas Percy. If neither of them both come never in this country again I think neither true nor honest men woll be sorry thereof, nor in likewise for my Lord Darcy nor Sir Robert Constable."(41) Percy and Constable, Aske and Darcy, all perished on the scaffold.

Darcy and his like recognized that a new world had risen about them, in which they had no place. During his imprisonment in London, before his execution, he was examined by Cromwell, and thus, almost with his dying words, addressed the man who was the incarnation of the force that killed him:—

"Cromwell, it is thou that art the very original and chief causer of all this rebellion and mischief, and art likewise causer of the apprehension of us that be noble men and dost daily earnestly travail to bring us to our end and to strike off our heads, and I trust that or thou die, though thou wouldst procure all the noblemen's heads within the realm to be stricken off, yet shall there one head remain that shall strike off thy head."(42)

Footnotes

(1) *A History of Agriculture and Prices*, J. E. Thorold Rogers, iv. 72.

(2) *On Justification*, Works, i. 60.

(3) *On Justification*, Works, i. 51.

(4) *Institutes*, I. vii. 1 and 5.

(5) *Zwinglis Theologie*, August Baur, 319, 320.

(6) *Institutes*, IV. viii. 9.

(7) *John Wicliffe and his English Precursors*, Lechler, Eng. trans., 302.

(8) Lechler, 349, note 1.

(9) Lechler, 348, note. Extract from *De Eucharistia*.

(10) *Acts and Monuments*, iii. 204, 205.

(11) *The Praise of Folie*, 1541. Englished by Sir Thomas Challoner.

(12) *Parl. Hist.*, Cobbett, i. 295.

(13) *Ibid.*, 310.

(14) *A Supplicacyon for Beggers*, 2. Early Eng. Text Soc.

(15) *Acts and Monuments*, v. 404.

(16) *Ibid.*, iii. 218.

(17) *Acts and Monuments*, iv. 196.

(18) *Agriculture and Prices*, iv. 18.

(19) *Reformation of the Church of England*, Blunt, ii. 222.

(20) *Acts and Monuments*, iv. 706.

(21) *Industrial and Commercial History of England*, Rogers, 48.

(22) *Agriculture and Prices*, iv. 715.

(23) *Agriculture and Prices*, iv. 454.

(24) *Ibid.*, iv. 200. For the average prices of grain see tables in vol. i. 245, and iv. 292.

(25) *Agriculture and Prices*, iv. 734.

(26) Chapuys to Granville, *Cal.* ix. No. 862. The State Papers edited by Messrs. Brewer and Gairdner are referred to by the word "Cal."

(27) *Acts and Monuments*, v. 365.

(28) *State Papers*, ii. 552.

(29) *Chronicles*, 1, clxvii.

(30) Chapuys to Perrenot, *Cal.* x. No. 901.

(31) See *Anne Boleyn*, Friedmann, i. 43, and elsewhere.

(32) *Cal.* X. No. 908.

(33) *Burleigh and his Times*, Essays.

(34) *Cal.* vii. No. 296.

(35) *Ibid.*, xi. No. 576, Chapuys to Charles.

(36) *Ibid.*, xi. No. 576.

(37) *Ibid.*, xi. No. 864.

(38) *Cal.* xi. No. 1045.

(39) *Cal.* xi. No. 729.

(40) *Ibid.* xi. No. 826.

(41) *Ibid.*, xii. pt. i. No. 698.

(42) *Cal.* xii. pt. i. No. 976.

Chapter VIII: The Suppression of the Convents

AT the apex of the new society stood Henry VIII., who, like Philip the Fair, had many of the qualities which make a great religious reformer in an economic age. In reaching an estimate of his nature, however, the opinions of Englishmen are of no great value, since they are usually distorted by prejudice. The best observers were the foreign ministers at his court, whose business was to collect information for their governments. At a time when there were no newspapers, these agents had to be accurate, and their despatches are trustworthy.

Charles de Marillac was born in 1510. He belonged to an old family, and had an unblemished reputation. He had no leaning against Protestants, for he was disgraced by the Guise party. He was thirty when in London as ambassador of Francis I. After having been a year in England, he wrote:—

"This prince seems to me subject among other vices to three, which certainly in a king may be called pests, of which the first is, that he is so avaricious and covetous, that all the riches of the world would not be sufficient to satisfy and content his ambition.... From this proceeds the second evil and pest, which is distrust and fear... wherefore he ceaselessly embrews his hands in blood, feeling in his mind doubt of those about him, wishing to live without suspicion, which every day augments.... And in part from these two evils proceeds the last pest, which is levity and inconstancy; and partly also from the temper of the nation, by which they have perverted the rights of religion, of marriage, of honesty and honour, as if they were wax, the which alloy can change itself into whatever forms they wish." (1)

Cruelty was one of Henry's most salient traits, and was, perhaps, the faculty by which he succeeded in imposing himself most strongly upon his contemporaries. He not only murdered his wives, his ministers, and his friends, but he pursued those who opposed him with a vindictiveness which appalled them. He was ingenious in devising torments.

Friar Forrest, whose crime was the denial of the royal supremacy, he caused to be slowly roasted over a rood which he had fetched from Wales on purpose. They "hanged [him] in Smithfield in chains, upon a gallows quick, by the middle and arm-holes, and fire was made under him, and so was he consumed and burned to death." (2) Henry relished the idea of the show so much, that Chapuys thought him disappointed at not being able to attend with his whole court.

His way of dealing with the Carthusians was equally characteristic. The Carthusians were in the Church what Darcy was in the State: men of the old imaginative type, of austere life and ascetic habits, in whom still glowed the fiery enthusiasm of Hildebrand. They could not accept Henry as God's vicegerent upon earth. The three priors— Houghton, Webster, and Lawrence—"were ripped up in each other's presence, their arms torn off, their hearts cut out and rubbed in their mouths and faces." (3)

Three more were chained upright to posts, where they stood for fourteen days, "without the possibility of stirring for any purpose whatever, held fast by iron collars on their necks, arms, and thighs." (4) Then they were hanged and disembowelled.

In 1537, ten were still resolute. They were chained in Newgate like the others, where, according to Stowe, nine "died... with stink and miserably smothered." The tenth, who survived, was hanged.

Had Henry been hampered, like Darcy, with scruples about honour, truth, or conscience, he too might have been undone. His power lay in his capacity for doing what was needful for success. He enticed Aske to London, and when he held him, slew him. He pardoned Darcy, and then sent him to Tower Hill.

Lacking force to crush the rebels, Norfolk, in the royal name, pacified the people with pardon and promises of redress. They dispersed, thinking themselves safe. Henry ignored his pledges, risings followed; but when the country had been tranquillized and his army was again in peaceful possession, he thus instructed the Duke:—

"Our pleasure is, that,... you shal, in any wise, cause suche dredfull execution to be doon upon a good nombre of thinhabitauntes of every towne, village, and hamlet, that have offended in this rebellion, as well by the hanging of them uppe in trees, as by the quartering of them, and the setting of their heddes and quarters in every towne, greate and small, and in al suche other places, as they may be a ferefull spectacle to all other herafter, that wold practise any like mater; whiche We requyre you to doo, without pitie or respecte, according to our former letters; remembring that it shal be moche better, that these traitours shulde perishe in their wilfull, unkynde, and traitorous folyes, thenne that so slendre punishment shuld be doon upon them, as the dredde thereof shuld not be a warning to others." (5)

Norfolk was after Henry's pattern. The rebels were his friends—men with whom he had pledged himself to act shortly before. But he had chosen his side, he had made his bargain, and he earned his pay. He was never weary of boasting of his cruelty toward the defenceless yeomanry:—

"They shall be put to death in every town where they dwelt.... As many as chains of iron can be made for in this town and in the country shall be hanged in them; the rest in ropes. Iron is marvellous scarce."

He tried his prisoners by court martial, for he dared not trust the juries. Many of the farmers declared they had been forced to join in the insurrection through threats of violence, and these might have been acquitted. "They say I came out for fear of my life, or for fear of burning my houses and destroying of my wife and children." (6) But where Henry and Norfolk were concerned there were no acquittals.

In the same way Henry destroyed his ministers when he had done with them. Though Cromwell was sagacious, he was less crafty than Henry. Just before his fall the king made him Earl of Essex, and he lived in such complete ignorance of his fate that his disgrace fell like a thunderbolt. Marillac has described how one day, in the council chamber, Cromwell was arrested without warning, and "moved with indignation, he plucked his hat from his head and threw it wrathfully upon the ground, saying to Norfolk and to the rest of the council assembled, that this was his reward for his services to the king... adding that since he was so treated, he renounced all hope, and all he asked of the king his master....was not to let him languish..."

The Duke of Norfolk, having reproached him with all the villainies done by him, tore from him the Order of Saint George, which he wore about his neck; and the Admiral, to show himself as much his enemy in adversity as he had been believed to be his friend in prosperity, undid his garter. (7)

From one point of view, Henry's vanity was a weakness, for it laid him open to attack, and the diplomatic correspondence is filled with sneers like this of Castillon's: "Il n'oublye jamais sa grandeur et se taist de celle des autres." (8) Probably nothing in English civilization has ever equalled the adulation he exacted from his courtiers, and especially from his bishops; yet even this vanity was a source of strength, for it made him insensible to ridicule which would have unnerved Saint Louis.

On very scanty evidence, he caused his wife to be arraigned for incest, and during the trial appeared in public so gaily dressed, and after her conviction danced before the Court in such open delight, that Chapuys himself was surprised:—

"There are still two English gentlemen detained on her account, and it is suspected that there will be many more, because the king has said he believed that more than 100 had to do with her. You never saw prince or man who made greater show of his horns, or bore them more pleasantly." (9)

His manners, like those of Cromwell and Norfolk, lacked the courtesy which distinguished men, even of his own generation, like Sir Thomas More. He was gluttonous and self-indulgent, and, toward the end of his life, so bloated as to be helpless. His habits were well understood at Court, and suitors tried to approach him in the afternoon, when he was tipsy. Marillac thought his gormandising would kill him:—

"There has been little doubt about the king, not so much for the fever as for the trouble with the leg which he has had, which trouble seizes him very often because he is very gross, and marvellously excessive in eating and drinking, so that you often find him of a different purpose and opinion in the morning from what you do after dinner." (10)

On May 14th, 1538, Castillon wrote:—

"Furthermore, the king has had one of the fistulas on his legs closed, and since ten or twelve days the humors, which have no vent, have taken to stifling him, so much so, that he has been some of the time speechless, the face all black, and in great danger." (11)

The most marked characteristic of the feudal aristocracy had been personal courage; but as centralization advanced and a paid police removed the necessity of self-defence, bravery ceased to be essential to success; Henry apparently was not courageous—certainly was not courageous in regard to disease. When most infatuated with Anne Boleyn, she fell ill of the sweating sickness; he fled at once, and wrote from a distance to beg her to fear nothing, as few or no women... have died of it."(12) Marillac declared roundly that, in such matters, the king was "the most timid person one could know." (13)

On the other hand, he was habitually so overbearing as to be brutal to the weak. Lambert was a poor sectary, of whom he determined to make an example. He therefore prepared a solemn function, at which he presided, assisted by the bishops and the other dignitaries of the realm. The accused, when brought before this tribunal, apparently showed some confusion, and Foxe has left a striking description of how Henry tried to heighten this terror. Henry was dressed "all in white," probably emblematic of the purity of the head of the Church, and his "look, his cruel countenance, and his brows bent unto severity, did not a little augment this terror, plainly declaring a mind full of indignation far unworthy such a prince, especially in such a matter, and against so humble and obedient a subject." (14)

Gifted with such qualities, Henry could not have failed to be a great religious reformer at the opening of a great economic age. More than five hundred years before, when society hung on the brink of dissolution, the Church sustained centralization by electing Hugh Capet king of France. A century later the armed pilgrimages to Palestine had accelerated the social movement, and consolidation again began. Generation by generation the rapidity of movement had increased, communication had been re-established between the East and West, the mariner's compass and gunpowder had been introduced into Europe, the attack had mastered the defence, and as the forms of competition slowly changed, capital accumulated, until, at the beginning of the sixteenth century, wealth reached the point where it could lay the foundation of the paid police—the crowning triumph of the monied class.

The Reformation was the victory of this class over the archaic type of man, and with the Reformation the old imaginative civilization passed away; but with all its power the monied intellect has certain weaknesses, and neither in ancient Rome nor modern England have capitalists been soldiers. The Tudor aristocracy was not a martial caste. Lacking physical force, this new nobility feared the ancient farming population whom they slowly exterminated; and they feared them with reason, for from among the yeomanry Cromwell drew his Ironsides. Therefore one of the chief pre-occupations of the Tudor nobility was to devise means to hold this dangerous element in check, and as it could not organize an army, it utilized the Church. The landowners had other purposes for the priesthood than simply to rob it; they had also to enslave it, and Henry's title to greatness lies in his having attained both ends.

He not only plundered as no other man has plundered, but he succeeded in assuming the functions of God's high priest, and becoming Christ's vicar upon earth. Upon this point there can be no difference of opinion; not only are the formularies of the Church of England clear, but Anglicans themselves admit it. Macaulay was of Henry's communion; Macaulay is an historian whose opinion on such a point commands respect, and Macaulay has summed up the position of Henry VIII. as the head of the capitalistic hierarchy in these words:—

"What Henry and his favourite counsellors meant, at one time, by the supremacy, was certainly nothing less than the whole power of the keys. The king was to be the Pope of his kingdom, the vicar of God, the expositor of Catholic verity, the channel of sacramental graces. He arrogated to himself the right of deciding dogmatically what was orthodox doctrine and what was heresy, of drawing up and imposing confessions of faith, and of giving religious instruction to his people.

"He proclaimed that all jurisdiction, spiritual as well as temporal, was derived from him alone, and that it was in his power to confer episcopal authority, and to take it away....

"According to this system, as expounded by Cranmer, the king was the spiritual as well as the temporal chief of the nation. In both capacities his Highness must have lieutenants. As he appointed civil officers to keep his seal, to collect his revenues, and to dispense justice in his name, so he appointed divines of various ranks to preach the gospel, and to administer the sacraments. It was unnecessary that there should be any imposition of hands. The king—such was the opinion of Cranmer given in the plainest words—might, in virtue of authority derived from God, make a priest; and the priest so made needed no ordination whatever." (15)

Under the Tudors commerce and industry were yet in their infancy. Great Britain still remained substantially agricultural, and capital primarily sought investment in land. The enclosure of the commons and the confiscations of the monastic estates together formed a gigantic real estate speculation, with which faith had little to do, and which was possible only because force began to express itself through another type of intellect than that which had been able to defend its property during an imaginative age.

The commercial conmmunity always demanded cheap religion. Under Henry they inclined toward Zwingli, under Elizabeth toward Calvin, under Charles they were Presbyterian; the gentry, on the contrary, were by nature conservative, and favoured orthodoxy as far as their interest in church plunder permitted them. Henry and Norfolk stood at the head of this class; Norfolk's conversion to Protestantism has been explained by Chapuys, and Henry remained a bigot to his death.

"Shortly before he died, when about to communicate, as he always did, under one kind, he rose up from his chair, and fell on his knees to adore the Body of our Lord. The Zwinglians who were present said that his majesty, by reason of his bodily weakness, might make his communion sitting in his chair. The king's answer was, 'If I could throw myself down, not only on the ground, but under the ground, I should not then think that I gave honour enough to the most Holy Sacrament.'"(16)

As to Norfolk, Chapuys has left his opinion in very plain words:—

"He [Norfolk] has a good deal changed his tune, for it was he alone [in] the Court who showed himself the best of Catholics, and who favoured most the authority of the pope; but he must act in this way not to lose his remaining influence, which apparently does not extend much further than Cromwell wishes."(17)

To attain their end, the rising class, at whose head these two men stood, had to doubly despoil the Church in whose dogmas they believed. They confiscated her lands to enrich themselves, and they suppressed her revenues to buy the support of the traders. Finally, their lack of physical force suggested to them the expedient of seizing on the ecclesiastical organization and filling it with their servants, who should teach the people the religious duty of submission to an authority which distrusted an appeal to arms.

As Henry and Norfolk represented the landed magnates, so Cromwell represented the mercantile community; and when the alliance between these two monied interests had been perfected by the appointment of Cromwell as Secretary of State, some time previous to April, 1534, events moved with precision and rapidity. They crowned Anne Boleyn on June 1st, 1533; in July the breach between the king and pope was made irreparable; in November, 1534, Parliament declared Henry "Supreme Head" of the Church; and in the following winter the whole administration, both civil and ecclesiastical, was concentrated in Cromwell's hands. He acted with astonishing energy.

In the autumn of 1535 he set on foot a visitation preparatory to the dissolution of the convents, and Parliament passed the bill for suppression the next February. Cromwell also, as Vicar General, presided over the convocation of Canterbury, which made the first reformation of faith. This convocation met in June, 1536, only shortly before the Pilgrimage of Grace, and, under the fear of violence, Henry and the Conservatives were reduced to silence. The evangelical influence for the moment held control, and the "Ten Articles," the foundation of the "Thirty-nine Articles," together with the "Institution of a Christian Man" which were produced, were a great departure from orthodoxy.

In the fourth article, the dogma of the "Supper" was made broad enough to include Lutherans, and in the sixth, image worship was condemned. On the other hand, "Justification by Faith" began to assume the importance it must always hold in all really Protestant confessions. In one of his homilies Cranmer, at a later time, showed the comparative futility of good works:—

"A man must needs be nourished by good works; but first he must have faith. He that doeth good deeds, yet without faith, he hath no life. I can show a man that by faith without works lived, and came to heaven; but without faith never man had life." (18)

"Never had the Jews, in their most blindness, so many pilgrimages unto images... as hath been used in our time.... Keeping in divers places, as it were marts or markets of merits; being full of their holy relics, images, shrines, and works of overflowing abundance ready to be sold.... Holy cowls, holy girdles, holy pardons, beads, holy shoes, holy rules, and all full of holiness.... Which were so esteemed and abused to the great prejudice of God's glory and commandments, that they were made most high and most holy things, whereby to attain to the everlasting life, or remission of sin." (19)

The anti-sacerdotal movement under Henry VIII. culminated in 1536 and 1537, when the country rebelled, and the land-owners were in need of help from the towns. As long as the latter felt uncertain of their grip on Church lands, the radical mercantile interest was permitted to mould doctrine; but when Norfolk had triumphed in the north, and Aske and Darcy had been executed, a reaction set in. In December, 1538, Lambert was burned for denying transubstantiation, and in 1539 the chapter in the statute book which followed that providing for the suppression of the mitred abbeys, re-established auricular confession, communion in one kind, private masses, and, in a word, strict orthodoxy, saving in the single tenet of the royal supremacy. To have conceded that would have endangered property. Twelve months later the landed magnates felt strong enough to discard the tradesmen; the alliance which had carried through the Reformation was dissolved, and Cromwell was beheaded.

Never did pope enforce the worship of the miracle more savagely than did Henry. By the act of the "Six Articles," the denial of the miracle of the mass was punished by burning and forfeiture of goods without the privilege of abjuration. Purity of faith could not have been the ideal of reformers.

Until quite recently, Protestants have accepted the tradition that the convents of England were suppressed by the revolt of a people outraged by the disclosure of abominations perpetrated under the shelter of monasticism. Within a few years the publication of the British archives has thrown a new and sombre light upon the Reformation. They seem to prove beyond a doubt that as Philip dealt with the Templars, so did Henry deal with all the religious orders of his realm.

In 1533 Henry's position was desperate. He confronted not only the pope and the emperor, but all that remained of the old feudal society, and all that survived of the decaying imaginative age. Nothing could resist this combination save the rising power of centralized capital, and Henry therefore had to become the mouthpiece of the men who gave expression to this force.

He needed money, and money in abundance, and Cromwell rose to a practical dictatorship because he was fittest to provide it. On all that relates to Essex, Foxe is an undoubted authority, and Foxe did not hesitate to attribute to Cromwell Henry's policy at this crisis.

"For so it pleased Almighty God, by means of the said Lord Cromwell, to induce the king to suppress first the chantries, then the friars' houses and small monasteries, till, at length, all the abbeys in England, both great and less, were utterly overthrown and plucked up by the roots....

"Of how great laud and praise this man was worthy, and what courage and stoutness was in him, it may hereby evidently appear unto all men, that he alone, through the singular dexterity of his wit and counsel, brought to pass that, which, even unto this day no prince or king, throughout all Europe, dare or can bring to pass. For whereas Britannia alone, of all other nations, is and hath been, of her own proper nature, most superstitious; this Cromwell, being born of a common or base stock, through a divine method or policy of wit and reason received, suffered, deluded, brake off, and repressed, all the policies, trains, malice, and hatred of friars, monks, religious men, and priests, of which sort there was a great rabble in England." (20)

Cromwell's strength lay in his superiority to those scruples of truth and honour which hamper feebler men. He did what circumstances demanded. His object, like Philip's, was to blacken his victims that he might destroy them, and to gather the evidence he used instruments adapted to the work. To have used others would have demonstrated himself unfit. Mr. Gairdner has remarked in his preface to the tenth volume of the *Calendar*: "We have no reason indeed to think highly of the character of Cromwell's visitors." (21) This opinion of Mr. Gairdner is supported by all the evidence extant. Thomas Legh, one of the commissioners, not only always took bribes, but, having been appointed master of Sherburn Hospital, administered it "to the utter disinheritance, decay and destruction of the ancient and godly foundation of the same house." (22) Henry probably thought him dishonest, since he had his accounts investigated. Even Legh's colleague, Ap Rice, though venal himself, and in great fear of being murdered for his treachery, denounced him in set terms to Cromwell:-

"And surely he asketh no less for every election than £20 as of duty, which in my opinion is too much, and above any duty that was ever taken heretofore. Also in his visitations he refuseth many times his reward, though it be competent, for that they offer him so little and maketh them to send after him such rewards as may please him, for surely religious men were never afraid so much of Dr. Allen as they be of him, he useth such rough fashion with them." (23)

The next day, however, Ap Rice, in alarm lest his frankness might lead to his assassination, wrote to beg his master to be cautious:—

"Forasmuch as the said Mr. Doctor is of such acquaintance and familiarity with many rufflers and serving men,... I, having commonly no great assistance when I go abroad, might take perchance irrevocable harm of him or his ere I were aware. Please keep secret what I have said." (24)

Ap Rice himself had been in difficulty, and had been exposed by Legh, for he admitted being "so abashed" at the accusation he could make no defence. He had also certainly done something which put him in the power of Cromwell, for he wrote: "I know from my own experience how deadly it is for any man to incur your displeasure,... which I would not wish for my greatest enemy." (25)

The testimony of such witnesses would be of doubtful value, even had they expressed themselves freely; but the government only tolerated one form of report. A good example of the discipline enforced is to be found in Layton's correspondence. He incautiously praised the abbot of Glastonbury, and was reprimanded by Cromwell, for he wrote to excuse himself:—

"Whereas I understand by Mr. Pollard you much marvel why I would so greatly praise... the abbot of Glaston.... So that my excessive and indiscrete praise... must needs now redound to my great folly and untruth, and cannot... but much diminish my credit towards his majesty, and even so to your lordship.... And although they be all false, feigned, flattering hypocritical knaves, as undoubtedly there is none other of that sort. I must therefore now at this my necessity, most humbly beseech your lordship to pardon me for that my folly then committed,... and of your goodness to mitigate the king's highness majesty in the premisses." (26)

The charges made by the visitors are of a kind notoriously difficult to prove, even with ample time, and with trained investigators. Cromwell's examination was carried on by men of small worth and in hot haste; no opportunity was given for more than a cursory inspection of the premises and the inmates:—

"This day we leave Bath for Kensam, where we shall make an end by Tuesday, and then go on toward Maiden Bradley, within two miles of which is a charterhouse called Wittame, and Bruton Abbey seven miles, and Glastonbury seven miles.... If you tarry with the king eight days we shall dispatch all the houses above named." (27)

The visitation began in August, 1535, and ended in February, 1536. During these six months four or five men often travelling together undertook to examine one hundred and fifty-five houses scattered all over England. "To judge by the proportion in Yorkshire," says Mr. Gairdner, "the visitors examined only about four out of ten." (28) So far as can be ascertained, the evidence upon which the reports were based was generally of the flimsiest kind, either the scandal of some discontented monk or nun, or the tattle of servants. There was a striking instance of this at a nunnery at Chicksand, where Layton accused two nuns of incontinence, although "the two prioresses would not confess this, neither the parties, nor any of the nuns, but one old beldame." (29)

When nothing could be elicited, the accused were deemed in a conspiracy. At Newark the house seemed well ordered, and nothing questionable appeared on the surface, therefore Layton charged the monks with being "confederyde," but he added that he would object various horrible crimes against them, "which I have learnt from others. What I shall find I cannot tell." (30)

Where silence was taken as confession, the nuns especially fared ill. Very generally they were too frightened or too disgusted to answer. Even if such evidence were uncontradicted, no great weight could attach to it, but it happens that there is much on the other side. Not to speak of the episcopal visitations, which were carried on as part of the discipline of the Church, Henry's own government subsequently appointed boards of commissioners composed of country gentlemen, and these boards, which made examinations at leisure in five counties, formed conclusions generally favourable to the ecclesiastics. Two examples will suffice to show the discrepancy between the views of the men whom Cromwell did and did not control. At Geradon in Leicestershire, Cromwell's board reported a convent of White Cistercians, which contained five monks addicted to sodomy with ten boys.(31) The second board described the same corporation as "of good conversation, and God's service well maintained." (32)

At Grace Dieu two nuns were charged with incontinence.(33) The country gentlemen found there only fifteen White Nuns of Saint Austin, "of good and virtuous conversation and living." (34)

No one familiar with the development of police during the later middle ages could have much doubt that, on the whole, the discipline of the convents would correspond pretty accurately with the prevailing tone of society, and that although asceticism and enthusiasm might have declined since the twelfth century, subordination to authority would have increased with the advance of centralization. Rebellious monks, like those who tried to murder Abelard, would certainly have been rarer at the time of the Reformation than at the opening of the Crusades.

The crime of the English monks, like the crime of the Templars, was defenceless wealth; and, like the Templars, they fared hardly in proportion to their devotion and their courage. The flexible and the corrupt, who betrayed their trust, received pensions or promotion; the Carthusians, against whose stern enthusiasm torments were powerless, perished as their predecessors had perished in the field of Saint Antoine.

The attack of Cromwell's hirelings resembled the onlaught of an invading army. The convents fared like conquered towns; the shrines were stripped and the booty heaped on carts, as at the sack of Constantinople. Churches were desecrated, windows broken, the roofs stripped of lead, the bells melted, the walls sold for quarries. Europe overflowed with vestments and altar ornaments, while the libraries were destroyed. Toward the end of 1539 Legh reached Durham, and the purification of the sanctuary of Saint Cuthbert may be taken as an example of the universal spoliation.

"After the spoil of his ornaments and jewels, coming nearer to his sacred body, thinking to have found nothing but dust and bones, and finding the chest that he did lie in, very strongly bound with iron, then the gold-smith did take a great forge-hammer of a smith, and did break the said chest open.

"And when they had opened the chest, they found him lying whole, uncorrupt, with his face bare and his beard as it had been a fortnight's growth, and all his vestments upon him as he was accustomed to say mass withall, and his meet wand of gold lying beside him.

"Then when the goldsmith did perceive that he had broken one of his legs, when he did break open the chest, he was very sorry for it and did cry, 'Alas, I have broken one of his legs.'

"Then Dr. Henley [one of the commissioners], hearing him say so, did call upon him, and did bid him cast down his bones." (35)

By the statute of 1536, only those convents were suppressed which were worth less than £200 a year, or which, within twelve months after the passage of the Act, should be granted to the king by the abbot. This legislation spared the mitred abbeys, and as long as any conventual property remained undivided, the land-owners kept

Cromwell in office, not feeling, perhaps, quite sure of their capacity to succeed alone.

In 1539 it had proved impossible to force the three great abbots of Glastonbury, Reading, and Colchester into a surrender to the crown, and accordingly Cromwell devised an act to vest in Henry such conventual lands as should be forfeited through attainder. Then he indicted the abbots for treason, and thus sought to bring the estates they represented constructively within the statute. The fate of Abbot Whiting, whom Layton incautiously praised, will do for all. He was eighty when he died, and his martyrdom is unusually interesting, as it laid the fortune of the great house of Bedford, one of the most splendid of modern dukedoms.

The commissioners came unexpectedly, and found the old monk at a grange at Sharpham, about a mile from Glastonbury. On September 19th they apprehended him, searched his apartment, and finding nothing likely to be of service, sent him up to London for Cromwell to deal with, though he was "very weak and sickly." Cromwell lodged him in the Tower, and examined him, apparently in a purely perfunctory fashion, for the government had decided on its policy. The Secretary of State simply jotted down a memorandum to see "that the evidence be well sorted and the indictments well drawn," and left the details of the murder to John Russell, a man thoroughly to be trusted. Cromwell's only anxiety was about the indictments, and he had "the king's learned counsel" with him "all day" discussing the matter. Finally they decided between them that it would be better to proceed at Glaston, and Whiting was sent to Somersetshire, to be dealt with by the progenitor of a long line of opulent Whig landlords.

In superintending the trial, Russell showed an energy and judgment which won its reward. On the 14th of November, when the invalid reached Wells, he wrote that he had provided for him "as worshipful a jury as was ever charged here these many years. And there was never seen in these parts so great appearance as were here at this present time, and never better willing to serve the king."(36) Russell wasted no time. He arranged for the trial one day and the execution the next. "The Abbot of Glastonbury was arraigned, and the next day put to execution with two other of his monks, for the robbing of Glastonbury church." (37)

He had the old man bound on a hurdle and dragged to the top of Tor Hill, "but... he would confess no more gold nor silver, nor any other thing more than he did before your Lordship in the Tower.... And thereupon took his death very patiently and his head and body bestowed in like manner as I certified your Lordship in my last letter." (38) "One quarter standeth at Wells, another at Bath and at Ilchester and Bridgewater the rest. And his head upon the abbey gate at Glaston." (39)

On the 17th of the following April, Henry created Cromwell Earl of Essex, preparatory to slaughtering him. Within two months the new earl was arrested by his bitterest enemy, the Duke of Norfolk, the chief of the landed interest; on the 28th of July he lost his head on Tower Hill, and his colossal fortune fed the men who had divided the body of Whiting.

Footnotes

(1) *Marillac au Connetable*, Kaulek, 211.

(2) *Acts and Memorials.* v. 180.

(3) *Cal.* viii. No. 726.

(4) *Sander*, Lewis' trans., 119.

(5) *State Papers*, i. 538.

(6) *Cal.* xii. pt. i. No. 498.

(7) Kaulek, 193, 194.

(8) Kaulek, 82.

(9) *Cal.*, x. No. 909.

(10) Kaulek, 274; *Sander*, Lewis, 162, and note 2.

(11) Kaulek, 50.

(12) *Lettres de Henri VIII a Anne Boleyn*, Crapelet, Lettre 3.

(13) Kaulek, 199.

(14) *Acts and Memorials* v. 229.

(15) *History of England*, i. chap. 1.

(16) *Rise and Growth of the Anglican Schism*, Sander, trans. by Lewis, 161.

(17) Chapuys to Charles, *Cal.* vi. No. 1510, date Dec, 1533.

(18) *The Homilies*, Corrie, 49.

(19) *Ibid.*, 56, 58.

(20) *Acts and Monuments*, v. 368, 369.

(21) *Cal.*, x. No. 43.

(22) See citations to the original authorities in *Henry VIII. and the* English Monasteries, *Gasquet, i. 454, and note.*

(23) *Cal.* ix. No. 622. In the *Calendar* the letter is condensed. The extract is given in full in Gasquet, i. 261, 262.

(24) *Ibid.*, No. 630. In full in Gasquet, i. 263.

(25) *Ibid.*, No. 630.

(26) *Henry VIII. and the English Monasteries*, i. 439.

(27) *Cal.* ix. No. 42.

(28) *Cal.* x. pref. xlv. note.

(29) *Ibid.*, ix. No. 1005.

(30) *Ibid.*, ix. No. 1005.

(31) *Cal.* x. No. 364.

(32) *Ibid.*, No. 1191.

(33) *Ibid.*, No. 364.

(34) *Ibid.*, No. 1191.

(35) *Rites of Durham*, Surtees Soc., 86.

(36) Wright, 260.

(37) Ellis, 1st Series, ii. 99.

(38) Wright, 261, 262.

(39) Ellis, 1st Series, ii. 99.

Chapter IX: The Eviction of the Yeomen

LIKE primitive Rome, England, during the Middle Ages, had an unusually homogeneous population of farmers, who made a remarkable infantry. Not that the cavalry was defective; on the contrary, from top to bottom of society, every man was a soldier, and the aristocracy had excellent fighting qualities. Many of the kings, like Cœur-de-Lion, Edward III., and Henry V., ranked among the ablest commanders of their day; the Black Prince has always been a hero of chivalry; and earls and barons could be named by the score who were famous in the Hundred Years' War.

Yet, although the English knights were a martial body, there is nothing to show that, on the whole, they surpassed the French. The English infantry won Crécy and Poitiers, and this infantry, which was long the terror of Europe, was recruited from among the small farmers who flourished in Great Britain until they were exterminated by the advance of civilization.

As long as the individual could at all withstand the attack of the centralized mass of society, England remained a hot-bed for breeding this species of man. A mediæval king had no means of collecting a regular revenue by taxation; he was only the chief of the free-men, and his estates were supposed to suffice for his expenditure. The revenue the land yielded consisted of men, not money, and to obtain men, the sovereign granted his domains to his nearest friends, who, in their turn, cut their manors into as many farms as possible, and each farmer paid his rent with his body.

A baron's strength lay in the band of spears which followed his banner, and therefore he subdivided his acres as much as possible, having no great need of money. Himself a farmer, he cultivated enough of his fief to supply his wants, to provide his table, and to furnish his castle, but, beyond this, all he kept to himself was loss. Under such a system money contracts played a small part, and economic competition was unknown.

The tenants were free-men, whose estates passed from father to son by a fixed tenure; no one could underbid them with their landlord, and no capitalist could ruin them by depressing wages, for the serfs formed the basis of society, and these serfs were likewise land-owners. In theory, the villains may have held at will; but in fact they were probably the descendants, or at least the representatives, of the *coloni* of the Empire, and a base tenure could be proved by the roll of the manorial court. Thus even the weakest were protected by custom, and there was no competition in the labour market.

The manor was the social unit, and, as the country was sparsely settled, waste spaces divided the manors from each other, and these wastes came to be considered as commons appurtenant to the domain in which the tenants of the manor had vested rights. The extent of these rights varied from generation to generation, but substantially they amounted to a privilege of pasture, fuel, or the like; aids which, though unimportant to large property owners, were vital when the margin of income was narrow.

During the old imaginative age, before centralization gathered headway, little inducement existed to pilfer these domains, since there was room in plenty, and the population increased slowly, if at all. The moment the form of competition changed, these conditions were reversed. Precisely when a money rent became a more potent force than armed men, may be hard to determine, but certainly that time had come when Henry VIII. mounted the throne, for then capitalistic farming was on the increase, and speculation in real estate already caused sharp distress. At that time the establishment of a police had destroyed the value of the retainer, and competitive rents had generally supplanted military tenures. Instead of tending to subdivide, as in an age of decentralization, land consolidated in the hands of the economically strong, and capitalists systematically enlarged their estates by enclosing the commons, and depriving the yeomen of their immemorial rights.

The sixteenth-century landlords were a type quite distinct from the ancient feudal gentry. As a class they were gifted with the economic, and not with the martial instinct, and they throve on competition. Their strength lay in their power of absorbing the property of their weaker neighbours under the protection of an overpowering police.

Everything tended to accelerate consolidation, especially the rise in the value of money. While, even with the debasement of the coin, the price of cereals did not advance, the growth of manufactures had caused wool to double in value. "We need not therefore be surprised at finding that the temptation to sheep-farming was almost irresistible, and that statute after statute failed to arrest the tendency." (1) The conversion of arable land into pasture led, of course, to wholesale eviction, and by 1515 the suffering had become so acute that details were given in acts of Parliament. Places where two hundred persons had lived, by growing com and grain, were left desolate, the houses had decayed, and the churches fallen into ruin.(2) The language of these statutes proves that the descriptions of contemporaries were not exaggerated.

"For I myselfe know many townes and villages sore decayed, for yt where as in times past there wer in some town an hundred householdes there remain not now thirty; in some fifty, ther are not now ten; yea (which is more to be lamented) I knowe townes so wholly decayed, that there is neyther sticke nor stone standyng as they use to say.

"Where many men had good lyuinges, and maynteined hospitality, able at times to helpe the kyng in his warres, and to susteyne other charges, able also to helpe their pore neighboures, and vertuously to bring up theyr children in Godly letters and good scyences, nowe sheepe and conies deuoure altogether, no man inhabiting the aforesayed places. Those beastes which were created of God for the nouryshment of man doe nowe deuoure man.... And the cause of all thys wretchednesse and beggery in the common weale are the gredy Gentylmen, whyche are shepemongers and grasyars. Whyle they study for their owne priuate commoditie, the common weale is lyke to decay. Since they began to be shepe maysters and feders of cattell, we neyther had vyttayle nor cloth of any reasonable pryce. No meniayle, for these forstallars of the market, as they use to saye, haue gotten all thynges so into theyr handes, that the poore man muste eyther bye it at their pryce, or else miserably starue for hongar, and wretchedly dye for colde." (3)

The reduction of the acreage in tillage must have lessened the crop of the cereals, and accounts for their slight rise in value during the second quarter of the sixteenth century. Nevertheless this rise gave the farmer no relief, as, under competition, rents advanced faster than prices, and in the generation which reformed the Church, the misery of yeomen had become extreme. In 1549 Latimer preached a sermon, which contains a passage often quoted, but always interesting:—

"Furthermore, if the king's honour, as some men say, standeth in the great multitude of people; then these graziers, inclosers, and rent-rearers, are hinderers of the king's honour. For where as have been a great many householders and inhabitants, there is now but a shepherd and his dog....

"My father was yeoman, and had no lands of his own, only he had a farm of three or four pound by year at the uttermost, and hereupon he tilled so much as kept half a dozen men. He had walk for a hundred sheep; and my mother milked thirty kine. He was able, and did find the king a harness, with himself and his horse, while he came to the place that he should receive the king's wages. I can remember that I buckled his harness when he went unto Blackheath field. He kept me to school, or else I had not been able to have preached before the king's majesty now.

"He married my sisters with five pound, or twenty nobles apiece; so that he brought them up in godliness and fear of

God. He kept hospitality for his poor neighbours, and some alms he gave to the poor. And all this he did of the said farm, where he that now hath it payeth sixteen pound by year, or more, and is not able to do anything for his prince, for himself, nor for his children, or give a cup of drink to the poor."(4)

The small proprietor suffered doubly: he had to meet the competition of large estates, and to endure the curtailment of his resources through the enclosure of the commons. The effect was to pauperize the yeomanry and lesser gentry, and before the Reformation the homeless poor had so multiplied that, in 1530, Parliament passed the first of a series of vagrant acts.(5) At the outset the remedy applied was comparatively mild, for able-bodied mendicants were only to be whipped until they were bloody, returned to their domicile, and there whipped until they put themselves to labour. As no labour was supplied, the legislation failed, and in 1537 the emptying of the convents brought matters to a climax. Meanwhile Parliament tried the experiment of killing off the unemployed; by the second act vagrants were first mutilated and then hanged as felons.(6)

In 1547, when Edward VI. was crowned, the great crisis had reached its height. The silver of Potosi had not yet brought relief, the currency was in chaos, labour was disorganized, and the nation seethed with the discontent which broke out two years later in rebellion. The land-owners held absolute power, and before they yielded to the burden of feeding the starving, they seriously addressed themselves to the task of extermination. The preamble of the third act stated that, in spite of the "great travel" and "godly statutes" of Parliament, pauperism had not diminished, therefore any vagrant brought before two justices was to be adjudged the slave of his captor for two years. He might be compelled to work by beating, chaining, or otherwise, be fed on bread and water, or refuse meat, and confined by a ring of iron about his neck, arms or legs. For his first attempt at escape, his slavery became perpetual, for his second, he was hanged.(7)

Even as late as 1591, in the midst of the great expansion which brought prosperity to all Europe, and when the monks and nuns, cast adrift by the suppression of the convents, must have mostly died, beggars so swarmed that at the funeral of the Earl of Shrewsbury "there were by the report of such as served the dole unto them, the number of 8000. And they thought that there were almost as many more that could not be served, through their unruliness. Yea, the press was so great that divers were slain and many hurt. And further it is reported of credible persons, that well estimated the number of all the said beggars, that they thought there were about 20,000." It was conjectured "that all the said poor people were abiding and dwelling within thirty miles' compass of Sheffield."(8)

In 1549, just as the tide turned, insurrection blazed out all over England. In the west a pitched battle was fought between the peasantry and foreign mercenaries, and Exeter was relieved only after a long siege. In Norfolk the yeomen, led by one Kett, controlled a large district for a considerable time. They arrested the unpopular landlords, threw open the commons they had appropriated, and ransacked the manor houses to pay indemnities to evicted farmers. When attacked, they fought stubbornly, and stormed Norwich twice.

Strype described "these mutineers" as "certain poor men that sought to have their commons again, by force and power taken from them; and that a regulation be made according to law of arable lands turned into pasture."(9)

Cranmer understood the situation perfectly, and though a consummate courtier, and himself a creation of the capitalistic revolution, spoke in this way of his patrons:—

"And they complain much of rich men and gentlemen, saying, that they take the commons from the poor, that they raise the prices of all manner of things, that they rule the poverty, and oppress them at their pleasure....
"And although here I seem only to speak against these unlawful assemblers, yet I cannot allow those, but I must

needs threaten everlasting damnation unto them, whether they be gentlemen or whatsoever they be, which never cease to purchase and join house to house, and land to land, as though they alone ought to possess and inhabit the earth." (10)

Revolt against the pressure of this unrestricted economic competition took the form of Puritanism, of resistance to the religious organization controlled by capital, and even in Cranmer's time, the attitude of the descendants of the men who formed the line at Poitiers and Crécy was so ominous that Anglican bishops took alarm.

"It is reported that there be many among these unlawful assemblies that pretend knowledge of the gospel, and will needs be called gospellers.... But now I will go further to speak somewhat of the great hatred which divers of these seditious persons do bear against the gentlemen; which hatred in many is so outrageous, that they desire nothing more than the spoil, ruin, and destruction of them that be rich and wealthy."(11)

Somerset, who owed his elevation to the accident of being the brother of Jane Seymour, proved unequal to the crisis of 1449, and was supplanted by John Dudley, now better remembered as Duke of Northumberland. Dudley was the strongest member of the new aristocracy. His father, Edmund Dudley, had been the celebrated lawyer who rose to eminence as the extortioner of Henry VII., and whom Henry VIII. executed, as an act of popularity, on his accession. John, beside inheriting his father's financial ability, had a certain aptitude for war, and undoubted courage; accordingly he rose rapidly. He and Cromwell understood each other; he flattered Cromwell, and Cromwell lent him money.(12) Strype has intimated that Dudley had strong motives for resisting the restoration of the commons.(13)

In 1547 he was created Earl of Warwick, and in 1549 suppressed Kett's rebellion. This military success brought him to the head of the State; he thrust Somerset aside and took the title of Duke of Northumberland. His son was equally distinguished. He became the favourite of Queen Elizabeth, who created him Earl of Leicester; but, though an expert courtier, he was one of the most incompetent generals whom even the Tudor landed aristocracy ever put in the field.

The disturbances of the reign of Edward VI. did not ripen into revolution, probably because of the relief given by rising prices after 1550; but, though they fell short of actual civil war, they were sufficiently formidable to terrify the aristocracy into abandoning their policy of killing off the surplus population. In 1552 the first statute was passed (14) looking toward the systematic relief of paupers. Small farmers prospered greatly after 1660, for prices rose strongly, very much more strongly than rents; nor was it until after the beginning of the seventeenth century, when rents again began to advance, that the yeomanry once more grew restive. Cromwell raised his Ironsides from among the great-grandchildren of the men who stormed Norwich with Kett.

"I had a very worthy friend then; and he was a very noble person, and I know his memory is very grateful to all,—Mr. John Hampden. At my first going out into this engagement, I saw our men were beaten at every hand. I did indeed; and desired him that he would make some additions to my Lord Essex's army, of some new regiments; and I told him I would be serviceable to him in bringing

such men in as I thought had a spirit that would do something in the work. This is very true that I tell you; God knows I lie not 'Your troops,' said I, 'are most of them old decayed serving-men, and tapsters, and such kind of fellows; and,' said I, 'their troops are gentlemen's sons, younger sons and persons of quality: do you think that the spirits of such base and mean fellows will ever be able to encounter gentlemen, that have honour and courage and resolution in them?... Truly I did tell him; 'You must get men of a spirit:... a spirit that is likely to go on as far as gentlemen will go;—or else you will be beaten still....'

"He was a wise and worthy person; and he did think that I talked a good notion, but an impracticable one. Truly I told him I could do somewhat in it,... and truly I must needs say this to you,... I raised such men as had the fear of God before them, as made some conscience of what they did; and from that day forward, I must say to you, they were never beaten, and wherever they were engaged against the enemy, they beat continually."(15)

Thus, by degrees, the pressure of intensifying centralization split the old homogeneous population of England into classes, graduated according to their economic capacity. Those without the necessary instinct sank into agricultural day labourers, whose lot, on the whole, has probably been somewhat worse than that of ordinary slaves. The gifted, like the Howards, the Dudleys, the Cecils, and the Boleyns, rose to be rich nobles and masters of the State. Between the two accumulated a mass of bold and needy adventurers, who were destined finally not only to dominate England, but to shape the destinies of the world.

One section of these, the shrewder and less venturesome, gravitated to the towns, and grew rich as merchants, like the founder of the Osborn family, whose descendant became Duke of Leeds; or like the celebrated Josiah Child, who, in the reign of William III., controlled the whole eastern trade of the kingdom. The less astute and the more martial took to the sea, and as slavers, pirates, and conquerors, built up England's colonial empire, and established her maritime supremacy. Of this class were Drake and Blake, Hawkins, Raleigh, and Clive.

For several hundred years after the Norman conquest, Englishmen showed little taste for the ocean, probably because sufficient outlet for their energies existed on land. In the Middle Ages the commerce of the island was mostly engrossed by the Merchants of the Steelyard, an offshoot of the Hanseatic league; while the great explorers of the fifteenth and early sixteenth centuries were usually Italians or Portuguese; men like Columbus, Vespucius, Vasco-da-

Gama, or Magellan. This state of things lasted, however, only until economic competition began to ruin the small farmers, and then the hardiest and boldest race of Europe were cast adrift, and forced to seek their fortunes in strange lands.

For the soldier or the adventurer, there was no opening in England after the battle of Flodden. A peaceful and inert bourgeoisie more and more supplanted the ancient martial baronage; their representatives shrank from campaigns like those of Richard I., the Edwards, and Henry V., and therefore, for the evicted farmer, there was nothing but the far-off continents of America and Asia, and to these he directed his steps.

The lives of the admirals tell the tale on every page. Drake's history is now known. His family belonged to the lesser Devon gentry, but fallen so low that his father gladly apprenticed him as ship's boy on a channel coaster, a life of almost intolerable hardship. From this humble beginning he fought his way, by dint of courage and genius, to be one of England's three greatest seamen; and Blake and Nelson, the other two, were of the same blood.

Sir Humphrey Gilbert was of the same west country stock as Drake; Frobisher was a poor Yorkshire man, and Sir Walter Raleigh came from a ruined house. No less than five knightly branches of Raleigh's family once throve together in the western counties; but disaster came with the Tudors, and Walter's father fell into trouble through his Puritanism. Walter himself early had to face the world, and carved out his fortune with his sword. He served in France in the religious wars; afterward, perhaps, in Flanders; then, through Gilbert, he obtained a commission in Ireland, but finally drifted to Elizabeth's court, where he took to buccaneering, and conceived the idea of colonizing America.

A profound gulf separated these adventurers from the landed capitalists, for they were of an extreme martial type; a type hated and feared by the nobility. With the exception of the years of the Commonwealth, the landlords controlled England from the Reformation to the Revolution of 1688, a period of one hundred and fifty years, and, during that long interval, there is little risk in asserting that the aristocracy did not produce a single soldier or sailor of more than average capacity. The difference between the royal and the parliamentary armies was as great as though they had been recruited from different races. Charles had not a single officer of merit, while it is doubtful if any force has ever been better led than the troops organized by Cromwell.

Men like Drake, Blake, and Cromwell were among the most terrible warriors of the world, and they were distrusted and feared by an oligarchy which felt instinctively its inferiority in arms. Therefore, in Elizabeth's reign, politicians like the Cecils took care that the great seamen should have no voice in public affairs. And though these men defeated the Armada, and though England owed more to them than to all the rest of her population put together, not one reached the peerage, or was treated with confidence and esteem. Drake's fate shows what awaited them. Like all his class, Drake was hot for war with Spain, and from time to time he was unchained, when fighting could not be averted; but his policy was rejected, his operations more nearly resembled those of a pirate than of an admiral, and when he died, he died in something like disgrace.

The aristocracy even made the false position in which they placed their sailors a source of profit, for they forced them to buy pardon for their victories by surrendering the treasure they had won with their blood. Fortescue actually had to interfere to defend Raleigh and Hawkins from Elizabeth's rapacity. In 1592 Borough sailed in command of a squadron fitted out by the two latter, with some contribution from the queen and the city of London. Borough captured the carack, the Madre-de-Dios, whose pepper alone Burleigh estimated at £102,000. The cargo proved worth £141,000, and of this Elizabeth's share according to the rule of distribution in use, amounted to one-tenth, or £14,000. She demanded £80,000 and allowed Raleigh and Hawkins, who had spent £34,000, only £36,000. Raleigh bitterly contrasted the difference made between himself a soldier, and peer, or a London speculator. "I was the cause that all this came to the Queen, and that the King of Spaine spent 300,000[li] the last yere.... I that adventured all my estate, lose of my principall.... I tooke all the care and paines;... they only sate still... for which double is given to them, and less then mine own to me." (16)

Raleigh was so brave he could not comprehend that his talent was his peril. He fancied his capacity for war would bring him fame and fortune, and it led him to the block. While Elizabeth lived, the admiration of the woman for the hero probably saved him, but he never even entered the Privy Council, and of real power he had none. The sovereign the oligarchy chose was James, and James imprisoned and then slew him. Nor was Raleigh's fate peculiar, for through timidity, the Cavaliers conceived an almost equal hate of many soldiers. They dug up the bones of Cromwell, they tried to murder William III., and they dragged down Marlborough in the midst of victory. Such were the new classes into which economic competition divided the people of England during the sixteenth century, and the Reformation was only one among many of the effects of this profound social revolution.

In the first fifty-three years of the sixteenth century, England passed through two distinct phases of ecclesiastical reform; the earlier, under Henry, when the conventual property was appropriated by the rising aristocracy; the later, under Edward, when portions of the secular endowments were also seized. Each period of spoliation was accompanied by innovations in doctrine, and each was followed by a reaction, the final one, under Mary, taking the form of reconciliation with Rome. Viewed in connection with the insurrections, the whole movement can hardly be distinguished from an armed conquest of the imaginative by the economic section of society; a conquest which produced a most curious and interesting development of a new clerical type.

During the Middle Ages, the hierarchy had been a body of miracle-workers, independent of, and at first superior to, the State. This great corporation had subsisted upon its own resources, and had generally been controlled by men of the ecstatic temperament, of whom Saint Anselm is, perhaps, the most perfect example. After the conquest at the Reformation, these conditions changed. Having lost its independence, the priesthood lapsed into an adjunct of the civil power; it then became reorganized upon an economic basis, and gradually turned into a salaried class, paid to inculcate obedience to the representative of an oligarchy which controlled the national revenue. Perhaps, in all modern history, there is no more striking example of the rapid and complete manner in which, under favourable circumstances, one type can supersede another, than the thoroughness with which the economic displaced the emotional temperament, in the Anglican Church, during the Tudor dynasty. The mental processes of the new pastors did not differ so much in degree as in kind from those of the old.

Although the spoliations of Edward are less well remembered than those of his father, they were hardly less drastic. They began with the estates of the chantries and guilds, and rapidly extended to all sorts of property. In the Middle Ages, one of the chief sources of revenue of the sacred class had been their prayers for souls in purgatory, and all large churches contained chapels, many of them richly endowed, for the perpetual celebration of masses for the dead; in England and Wales more than a thousand such chapels existed, whose revenues were often very valuable. These were the chantries, which vanished with the imaginative age which created them, and the guilds shared the same fate.

Before economic competition had divided men into classes according to their financial capacity, all craftsmen possessed capital, as all agriculturists held land. The guild established the craftsman's social status; as a member of a trade corporation he was governed by regulations fixing the number of hands he might employ, the amount of goods he might produce, and the quality of his workmanship; on the other hand, the guild regulated the market, and ensured a demand. Tradesmen, perhaps, did not easily grow rich, but they as seldom became poor.

With centralization life changed. Competition sifted the strong from the weak; the former waxed wealthy, and hired hands at wages, the latter lost all but the ability to labour; and, when the corporate body of producers had thus disintegrated, nothing stood between the common property and the men who controlled the engine of the law. By the 1 Edward VI., c. 14, all the possessions of the schools, colleges, and guilds of England, except the colleges of Oxford and Cambridge and the guilds of London, were conveyed to the king, and the distribution thus begun extended far and wide, and has been forcibly described by Mr. Blunt:—

"They tore off the lead from the roofs, and wrenched out the brasses from the floors. The books they despoiled of their costly covers, and then sold them for waste paper. The gold and silver plate they melted down with copper and lead, to make a coinage so shamefully debased as was never known before or since in England. The vestments of altars and priests they turned into table-covers, carpets, and hangings, when not very costly; and when worth more money than usual, they sold them to foreigners, not caring who used them for 'superstitious' purposes, but caring to make the best 'bargains' they could of their spoil. Even the very surplices and altar linen would fetch something, and that too was seized by their covetous hands." (17)

These "covetous hands" were the privy councillors. Henry had not intended that any member of the board should have precedence, but the king's body was not cold before Edward Seymour began an intrigue to make himself protector. To consolidate a party behind him, he opened his administration by distributing all the spoil he could lay hands on; and Mr. Froude estimated that "on a computation most favourable to the council, estates worth... in modern currency about five millions" of pounds, were "appropriated—I suppose I must not say stolen—and divided among themselves." (18) At the head of this council stood Cranmer, who took his share without scruple. Probably Froude's estimate is far too low; for though Seymour, as Duke of Somerset, had, like Henry, to meet imperative claims which drained his purse, he yet built Somerset House, the most sumptuous palace of London.

Seymour was put to death by Dudley when he rose to power by his military success in Norfolk. Dudley as well as Cromwell was fitted for the emergency in which he lived; bold, able, unscrupulous and energetic, his party hated but followed him, because without him they saw no way to seize the property they coveted. He too, like Cromwell, allied himself with the evangelical clergy, and under Edward the orthodoxy of the "Six Articles" gave way to the doctrine of Geneva. Even in 1548 Calvin had been able to write to Somerset, thanking God that, through his wisdom, the "pure truth" was preached; (19) but when Dudley administered the government as Duke of Northumberland, bishops did not hesitate to teach that the dogma of the "carnal presence" in the sacrament "maintaineth that beastly kind of cruelty of the 'Anthropophagi,' that is, the devourers of man's flesh: for it is a more cruel thing to devour a quick man, than to slay him." (20)

Dudley resembled Henry and Norfolk in being naturally conservative, for he died a Catholic; but with them all, money was the supreme object, and as they lacked the physical force to plunder alone, they were obliged to conciliate the Radicals. These were represented by Knox, and to Knox the duke paid assiduous court. The Scotchman began preaching in Berwick in 1549, but the government soon brought him to London, and in 1551 made him a royal chaplain, and, as chaplain, he was called upon to approve the Forty-two Articles of 1552. This he could do conscientiously, as they contained the dogmas of election and predestination, original sin, and justification by faith, beside a denial of "the reall and bodilie presence... of Christes fleshe, and bloude, in the Sacramente of the Lordes Supper."

Dudley tried hard to buy Knox, and offered him the See of Rochester; but the duke excited the deepest distrust and dislike in the preacher, who called him "that wretched and miserable Northumberland." He rejected the preferment, and indeed, from the beginning, bad blood seems to have lain between the Calvinists and the court. Writing at the beginning of 1554, Knox expressed his opinion of the reforming aristocracy in emphatic language, beginning with Somerset, "who became so cold in hearing Godis Word, that the year befoir his last apprehensioun, he wald ga visit his masonis, and wald not dainyie himself to ga frome his gallerie to his hall for heiring of a sermone." (21) Afterward matters grew worse, for "the haill Counsaile had said, Thay wald heir no mo of thair sermonis: thay wer but indifferent fellowis; (yea, and sum of thame eschameit not to call thame pratting knaves.)" (22)

Finally, just before Edward's death the open rupture came. Knox had a supreme contempt and antipathy for the Lord Treasurer, Paulet, Marquis of Winchester, whom he called a "crafty fox." During Edward's life, jeered Knox, "who was moste bolde to crye, Bastarde, bastarde, incestuous bastarde, Mary shall never rule over us," and now that Mary is on the throne it is to her Paulet "crouches and kneeleth."(23) In the last sermon he preached before the king he let loose his tongue, and probably he would have quitted the court, even had the reign continued. In this sermon Dudley was Ahithophel, Paulet, Shebna:—

"I made this affirmacion, That commonlye it was sene, that the most godly princes hadde officers and chief counseilours moste ungodlye, conjured enemies to

Goddes true religion, and traitours to their princes.... Was David, sayd I, and Ezechias, princes of great and godly giftes and experience, abused by crafty counsailers and dissemblyng hypocrites? What wonder is it then, that a yonge and innocent Kinge be deceived by craftye, covetouse, wycked, and ungodly counselours? I am greatly afrayd, that Achitophel be counsailer, that Judas beare the purse, and that Sobna be scribe, comptroller, and treasurer. This, and somwhat more I spake that daye, not in a corner (as many yet can wytnesse) but even before those whome my conscience judged worthy of accusation." (24)

Knox understood the relation which men of his stamp bore to Anglicanism. In 1549 much land yet remained to be divided, therefore he and his like were flattered and cajoled until Paulet and his friends should be strong enough to discard them. Faith, in the hands of the monied oligarchy, became an instrument of police, and, from the Reformation downward, revelation has been expounded in England by statute. Hence men of the imaginative type, who could not accept their creed with their stipend, were at any moment in danger of being adjudged heretics, and suffering the extreme penalty of insubordination.

Docility to lay dictation has always been the test by which the Anglican clergy have been sifted from Catholics and Puritans. To the imaginative mind a faith must spring from a revelation, and a revelation must be infallible and unchangeable. Truth must be single. Catholics believed their revelation to be continuous, delivered through the mouth of an illuminated priesthood, speaking in its corporate capacity. Puritans held that theirs had been made once for all, and was contained in a book. But both Catholics and Puritans were clear that divine truth was immutable, and that the universal Church could not err. To minds of this type, statutes regulating the appearance of God's body in the elements were not only impious but absurd, and men of the priestly temperament, whether

Catholic or Puritan, have faced death in its most appalling forms, rather than bow down before them.

Here Fisher and Knox, Bellarmine and Calvin, agreed. Rather than accept the royal supremacy, the flower of the English priesthood sought poverty and exile, the scaffold and the stake. For this, the aged Fisher hastened to the block on Tower Hill; for this, Forest dangled over the embers of the smouldering rood; for this, the Carthusians rotted in their noisome dens. Nor were Puritans a whit behind Catholics in asserting the sacerdotal dignity; "Erant enim blasphemi qui vocarent eum [Henricum VIII.] summum caput ecclesiae sub Christo," wrote Calvin, and on this ground the Nonconformists fought the established Church, from Elizabeth's accession downward.

The writings of Martin Marprelate only restated an issue which had been raised by Hildebrand five hundred years before; for the advance of centralization had reproduced in England something of the same conditions which prevailed at Constantinople when it became a centre of exchanges. Wherever civilization has reached the point at which energy expresses itself through money, faith must be subordinate to the representative of wealth. Stephen Gardiner understood the conditions under which he lived, and accepted his servitude in consideration of the great See of Winchester. With striking acuteness he cited Justinian as a precedent for Henry:—

"Then, Sir, who did ever disallow Justinian's fact, that made laws concerning the glorious Trinity, and the Catholic faith, of bishops, of men, of the clergy, of heretics, and others, such like?" (25)

From the day of the breach with Rome, the British priesthood sank into wage-earners, and those of the ancient clergy who remained in the Anglican hierarchy after the Reformation, acquiesced in their position, as appeared in all their writings, but in none, perhaps, more strikingly than in the Formularies of Faith of Henry VIII., where the episcopal bench submitted their views of orthodoxy to the revision of the secular power:—

"And albeit, most dread and benign sovereign lord, we do affirm by our learnings with one assent, that the said treatise is in all points so concordant and agreeable to holy scripture, as we trust your majesty shall receive the same as a thing most sincerely and purely handled, to the glory of God, your grace's honour, the unity of your people, the which things your highness, we may well see and perceive, doth chiefly in the same desire: yet we do most humbly submit it to the most excellent wisdom and exact judgment of your majesty, to be recognised, overseen, and corrected, if your grace shall find any word or sentence in it meet to be changed, qualified, or further expounded, for the plain setting forth of your highness's most virtuous desire and purpose in that behalf. Whereunto we shall in that case conform ourselves, as to our most bounden duties to God and to your highness appertaineth."

Signed by "your highness' most humble subjects and daily beadsmen, Thomas Cantuarien" and all the bishops. (26)

A Church thus lying at the mercy of the temporal power, became a chattel in the hands of the class which controlled the revenue, and, from the Reformation to the revolution of 1688, this class consisted of a comparatively few great landed families, forming a narrow oligarchy which guided the Crown. In the Middle Ages, a king had drawn his army from his own domain. Cœur-de-Lion had his own means of attack and defence like any other baron, only on a larger scale. Henry VIII., on the contrary, stood alone and helpless. As centralization advanced, the cost of administration grew, until regular taxation had become necessary, and yet taxes could only be levied by Parliament. The king could hardly pay a body-guard, and such military force as existed within the realm obeyed the landlords. Had it not been for a few opulent nobles, like Norfolk and Shrewsbury, the Pilgrims of Grace might have marched to London and plucked Henry from his throne, as easily as William afterward plucked James. These landlords, together with the London tradesmen, carried Henry through the crisis of 1536, and thereafter he lay in their hands. His impotence appeared in every act of his reign. He ran the risk and paid the price, while others fattened on the plunder. The Howards, the Cecils, the Russells, the Dudleys, divided the Church spoil among themselves, and wrung from the Crown its last penny, so that Henry lived in debt, and Edward faced insolvency.

Deeply as Mary abhorred sacrilege, she dared not ask for restitution to the abbeys. Such a step would probably have caused her overthrow, while Elizabeth never attempted opposition, but obeyed Cecil, the incarnation of the spirit of the oligarchy. The men who formed this oligarchy were of totally different type from anything which flourished in England in the imaginative age. Unwarlike, for their insular position made it possible for them to survive without the martial quality, they always shrank from arms. Nor were they numerous enough, or strong enough, to overawe the nation even in quiet times. Accordingly they generally lay inert, and only from necessity allied themselves with some more turbulent faction.

The Tudor aristocracy were rich, phlegmatic, and unimaginative men, in whom the other faculties were subordinated to acquisition, and they treated their religion as a financial investment. Strictly speaking, the Church of England never had a faith, but vibrated between the orthodoxy of the "Six Articles," and the Calvinism of the "Lambeth Articles," according to the exigencies of real estate. Within a single generation, the relation Christ's flesh and blood bore to the bread and wine was changed five times by royal proclamation or act of Parliament.

But if creeds were alike to the new economic aristocracy, it well understood the value of the pulpit as a branch of the police of the kingdom, and from the outset it used the clergy as part of the secular administration. On this point Cranmer was exlicit. Elizabeth probably represented the landed gentry more perfectly than any other sovereign, and she told her bishops plainly that she cared little for doctrine, but wanted clerks to keep order. She remarked that she had seen it said:—

"that hir Protestants themselves misliked hir, and in deede so they doe (quoth she) for I have heard that some of them of late have said, that I was of no religion, neither hot nor cold, but such a one, as one day would give God the vomit.... After this she wished the bishops to look unto private Conventicles, and now (quoth she) I miss my Lord of London who looketh no better unto the Citty where every merchant must have his schoolemaster and nightly conventicles." (28)

Elizabeth ruled her clergy with a rod of iron. No priest was allowed to marry without the approbation of two justices of the peace, beside the bishop, nor the head of a college without the leave of the visitor. When the Dean of St. Paul's offended the queen in his sermon, she told him "to retire from that ungodly digression and return to his text," and Grindall was suspended for disobedience to her orders.

In Grindall's primacy, monthly prayer meetings, called "prophesyings," came into fashion among the clergy. For some reason these meetings gave the government offence, and Grindall was directed to put a stop to them. Attacked thus, in the priests' dearest rights, the archbishop refused. Without more ado the old prelate was suspended, nor was he pardoned until he made submission five years later.

The correspondence of the Elizabethan bishops is filled with accounts of their thraldom. Pilkington, among others, complained that "We are under authority, and cannot make any innovation without the sanction of the queen... and the only alternative now allowed us is, whether we will bear with these things or disturb the peace of the Church. (29)

Even ecclesiastical property continued to be seized, where it could be taken safely; and the story of Ely House, although it has been denied, is authentic in spirit. From the beginning of the Reformation the London palaces of the bishops had been a tempting prize. Henry took York House for himself, Raleigh had a lease of Durham House, and, about 1565, Sir Christopher Hatton, whose relations with the queen were hardly equivocal, undertook to force Bishop Cox to convey him Ely House. The bishop resisted. Hatton applied to the queen, and she is said to have cut the matter short thus:—

"Proud prelate: I understand you are backward in complying with your agreement, but I would have you know that I who made you what you are can unmake you, and if you do not forthwith fulfil your engagement, by God, I will immediately unfrock you. ELIZABETH."

Had the great landlords been either stronger, so as to have controlled the House of Commons, or more military, so as to have suppressed it, English ecclesiastical development would have been different. As it was, a knot of ruling families, gorged with plunder, lay between the Catholics and the more fortunate of the evicted yeomen, who had made money by trade, and who hated and competed with them. Puritans as well as Catholics sought to unsettle titles to Church lands:—

"It is wonderfull to see how dispitefully they write of this matter. They call us church robbers, devourers of holly things, cormorantes, etc. affirminge that by the lawe of god, things once consecrated to god for the service of this churche, belong unto him for ever.... ·ffor my owne pte I have some imppriations, etc. & I thanke god I keepe them wth a good conscience, and many wold be ondone. The law appveth us." (30)

Thus beset, the landed capitalists struggled hard to maintain themselves, and, as their best defence, they organized a body of priests to preach and teach the divine right of primogeniture, which became the distinctive dogma of this national church. Such at least was the opinion of the non-jurors, who have always ranked among the most orthodox of the Anglican clergy, and who certainly were all who had the constancy to suffer for their faith. John Lake, Bishop of Chichester, suspended in 1689 for not swearing allegiance to William and Mary, on his death-bed made the following statement:—

"That whereas I was baptized into the religion of the Church of England, and sucked it in with my milk, I have constantly adhered to it through the whole course of my life, and now, if so be the will of God, shall dye in it; and I had resolved through God's grace assisting me to have dyed so, though at a stake.

"And whereas that religion of the Church of England taught me the doctrine of non-resistance and passive obedience, which I have accordingly inculcated upon others, and which I took to be the distinguishing character of the Church of England, I adhere no less firmly and steadfastly to that, and in consequence of it, have incurred a suspension from the exercise of my office and expected a deprivation." (31)

In the twelfth century, the sovereign drew his supernatural quality from his consecration by the priesthood; in the seventeenth century, money had already come to represent a force so predominant that the process had become reversed, and the priesthood attributed its prerogative to speak in the name of the Deity, to the interposition of the king. This was the substance of the Reformation in England. Cranmer taught that God committed to Christian princes "the whole cure of all their subjects, as well concerning the administration of God's word... as... of things political"; therefore bishops, parsons, and vicars were ministers of the temporal ruler, to whom he confided the ecclesiastical office, as he confided the enforcement of order to a chief of police. (32) As a part of the secular administration, the main function of the Reformed priesthood was to preach obedience to their patrons; and the doctrine they evolved has been thus summed up by Macaulay:—

"It was gravely maintained that the Supreme Being regarded hereditary monarchy, as opposed to other forms of government, with peculiar favour; that the rule of succession in order of primogeniture was a divine institution, anterior to the Christian, and even to the Mosaic dispensation; that no human power... could deprive a legitimate prince of his rights; that the authority of such a prince was necessarily always despotic...." (33)

In no other department of public affairs did the landed gentry show particular energy or ability. Their army was ineffective, their navy unequal to its work, their finances indifferently handled, but down to the time of their overthrow, in 1688, they were eminently successful in ecclesiastical organization. They chose their instruments with precision, and an oligarchy has seldom been more adroitly served. Macaulay was a practical politician, and Macaulay rated the clergy as the chief political power under Charles II:—

"At every important conjuncture, invectives against the Whigs and exhortations to obey the Lord's anointed resounded at once from many thousands of pulpits; and the effect was formidable indeed. Of all the causes which, after the dissolution of the Oxford Parliament, produced the violent reaction against the exclusionists, the most potent seems to have been the oratory of the country clergy." (34)

For country squires a wage-earning clergy was safe, and although Macaulay's famous passage describing their fear of an army has met with contradiction, it probably is true:—

"In their minds a standing army was inseparably associated with the Rump, with the Protector, with the spoliation of the Church, with the purgation of the Universities, with the abolition of the peerage, with the murder of the King, with the sullen reign of the Saints, with cant and asceticism, with fines and sequestrations, with the insults which Major Generals, sprung from the dregs of the people, had offered to the oldest and most honourable families of the kingdom. There was, moreover, scarcely a baronet or a squire in the parliament who did not owe part of his importance in his own county to his rank in the militia. If that national force were set aside, the gentry of England must lose much of their dignity and influence." (35)

The work to be done by the Tudor hierarchy was mercenary, not imaginative; therefore pastors had to be chosen who could be trusted to labour faithfully for wages. Perhaps no equally large and intelligent body of men has ever been more skilfully selected. The Anglican priests, as a body, have uniformly been true to the hand which fed them, without regard to the principles they were required to preach. A remarkable instance of their docility, where loss of income was the penalty for disobedience, was furnished at the accession of William and Mary. Divine right was, of course, the most sacred of Anglican dogmas, and yet, when the clergy were commanded to take the oath of allegiance to him whom they held to be an usurper, as Macaulay has observed, "some of the strongest motives which can influence the human mind, had prevailed. Above twenty-nine thirtieths of the profession submitted to the law."(36) Moreover, the landlords had the economic instinct, bargaining accordingly, and Elizabeth bluntly told her bishops that they must get her sober, respectable preachers, but men who should be cheap.

"Then spake my Lord Treasurer.... Her Maty hath declared unto you a marvellous great fault, in that you make in this time of light so many lewd and unlearned ministers.... It is the Bishop of Litchfield... that I mean, who made LXX. ministers in one day for money, some taylors, some shoemakers, and other craftsmen, I am sure the greatest part of them not worthy to keep horses. Then said the Bp. of Rochester, that may be so, for I know one that made 7 in one day, I would every man might beare his own burthen, some of us have the greatest wrong that can be offred.... But my Lord, if you would have none but learned preachers to be admitted into the ministery, you must provide better livings for them....

"To have learned ministers in every parish is in my judgmᵗ impossible (quoth my Ld. of Canterbury) being 13,000 parishes in Ingland, I know not how this realm should yield so many learned preachers.

"Jesus (quoth the Queen) 13,000 it is not to be looked for, I thinke the time hath been, there hath not been 4.

preachers in a diocesse, my meaning is not you should make choice of learned ministers only for they are not to be found, but of honest, sober, and wise men, and such as can reade the scriptures and homilies well unto the people." (37)

The Anglican clergy under the Tudors and the Stuarts were not so much priests, in the sense of the twelfth century, as hired political retainers. Macaulay's celebrated description is too well known to need full quotation: "for one who made the figure of a gentleman, ten were mere menial servants.... The coarse and ignorant squire" could hire a "young Levite" for his board, a small garret, and ten pounds a year. This clergyman "might not only be the most patient of butts and of listeners, might not only be always ready in fine weather for bowls, and in rainy weather for shovelboard, but might also save the expense of a gardener, or of a groom. Sometimes the reverend man nailed up the apricots; and sometimes he curried the coach horses. (38)

Yet, as Macaulay has also pointed out, the hierarchy was divided into two sections, the ordinary labourers and the managers. The latter were indispensable to the aristocracy, since without them their machine could hardly have been kept in motion, and these were men of talent who demanded and received good wages. Probably for this reason a large revenue was reserved for the higher secular clergy, and from the outset the policy proved successful. Many of the ablest organizers and astutest politicians of England, during the sixteenth and seventeenth centuries, sat on the episcopal bench, and two of the most typical, as well as the ablest Anglicans who ever lived, were the two eminent bishops who led the opposing wings of the Church when it was reformed by Henry VIII.: Stephen Gardiner and Thomas Cranmer.

Gardiner was the son of a clothworker of Bury Saint Edmunds, and was born about 1483. At Cambridge he made himself the best civil lawyer of the kingdom, and on meeting Wolsey, so strongly impressed him with his talent that the cardinal advanced him rapidly, and in January 1529 sent him to negotiate for the divorce at Rome. Nobody doubts that to the end of his life Gardiner remained a sincere Catholic, but above all else he was a great Anglican. Becoming secretary to the king in June, 1529, as Wolsey was tottering to his fall, he laboured to bring the University of Cambridge to the royal side, and he also devoted himself to Anne until he obtained the See of Winchester, when his efforts for the divorce slackened. He even went so far as to assure Clement that he had repented, and meant to quit the court, but notwithstanding he "bore up the laps" of Anne's robe at her coronation.

In 1535 the ways parted, a decision could not be deferred, he renounced Rome and preached his sermon "de vera Obedientia," in which he recognized in Henry the supremacy of a Byzantine emperor. The pang this act cost him lasted till he died, and he told the papal nuncio "he made this book under compulsion, not having the strength to suffer death patiently, which was ready for him." (39) Indeed, when dying, his apostacy seems to have been his last thought, for in his closing hours, as the story of the passion was read to him he exclaimed, "Negavi cum Petro, exivi cum Petro, sed nondum flevi cum Petro." All his life long his enemies accused him of dissimulation and hypocrisy for acts like these, but it was precisely this quality which raised him to eminence. Had he not been purchasable, he could hardly have survived as an Anglican bishop; an enthusiast like Fisher would have ended on Tower Hill.

Perhaps more fully than any other prelate of his time, Gardiner represented the faction of Henry and Norfolk; he was as orthodox as he could be and yet prosper. He hated Cromwell and all "gospellers," and he loved power and splendour and office. Fisher, with the temperament of Saint Anselm, shivering in his squalid house, clad in his shirt of hair, and sleeping on his pallet of straw, might indeed "humbly thank the king's majesty" who rid him of "all this worldly business," but men who rose to eminence in the reformed church were made of different stuff, and Gardiner's ruling passion never burned more fiercely than as he neared his death. Though in excruciating torments from disease, he clung to office to the last. Noailles, the French ambassador, at a last interview, found him "livid with jaundice and bursting with dropsy: but for two hours he held discourse with me calmly and graciously, without a sign of discomposure; and at parting he must needs take my arm and walk through three saloons, on purpose to show himself to the people, because they said that he was dead." (40)

Gardiner was a man born to be a great prelate under a monied oligarchy, but, gifted as he surely was, he must yield in glory to that wonderful arch-bishop who stamped the impress of his mind so deeply on the sect he loved, and whom most Anglicans would probably call, with Canon Dixon, the first clergyman of his age. Cranmer was so supremely fitted to meet the requirements of the economic revolution in which he lived, that he rose at a bound from insignificance to what was, for an Englishman, the summit of greatness. In 1529, when the breach came, Gardiner already held the place of chief secretary, while Cranmer remained a poor Fellow of Jesus. Within four years he had been consecrated primate, and he had bought his preferment by swearing allegiance to the pope, though he knew himself promoted for the express purpose of violating his oath, by decreeing the divorce which should sever England from Rome. His qualities were all recognized by his contemporaries; his adroitness, his trustworthiness, and his flexibility. "Such an archbishop so nominated, and... so and in such wise consecrated, was a meet instrument for the king to work by... a meet cover for such a cup; neither was there ever bear-ward that might more command his bears than the king might command him." (41) This judgment has always been held by Churchmen to be no small claim to fame; Burnet, for example, himself a bishop and an admirer of his eminent predecessor, was clear that Cranmer's strength lay in that mixture of intelligence and servility which made him useful to those who paid him:—

"Cranmer's great interest with the king was chiefly grounded on some opinions he had of the ecclesiastical officers being as much subject to the king's power as all other civil officers were.... But there was this difference: that Cranmer was once of that opinion... but Bonner against his conscience (if he had any) complied with it." (42)

The genius of the archbishop as a courtier may be measured by the fate which overtook his contemporaries. He was the fourth of Henry's great ministers, of whom Cromwell, Norfolk, and Wolsey were the other three. Wolsey was disgraced, plundered, and hounded to death; Cromwell was beheaded, and Norfolk was on his way to the scaffold, when saved by the death of the man who condemned him. The priest alone, as Lutheran, or as worshipper of the miracle which he afterward denied, always kept the sunshine of favour. Burnet has described how readily he violated his oath by participating in the attempt to change the succession under Edward. "He stood firm, and said, that he could not subscribe it without perjury; having sworn to the observance of King Henry's will.... The king himself required him to set his hand to the will.... It grieved him much; but such was the love that he bore to the king, that in conclusion he yielded, and signed it." (43) Like the chameleon, he changed his colour to match the force which upheld him. Under Edward, he became radical as easily as he had sung the mass under the "Six Articles," or as, under Mary, he pleaded to be allowed to return to Rome. Nor did he act thus from cowardice, for when he went to the fire, not a martyr of the Reformation showed more constancy than he. With hardly an exception, Cranmer's contemporaries suffered because they could not entirely divest themselves of their scruples. Even Gardiner had convictions strong enough to lodge him in the Tower, and Bonner ended his days in the Marshalsea, rather than abjure again under Elizabeth, but no such weakness hampered Cranmer. At Oxford, before his execution, he recanted, in various forms, very many times, and would doubtless have gone on recanting could he have saved himself by so doing.

Unlike Gardiner, his convictions were evangelical, and he probably imbibed reformed principles quite early, for he married Ossiander's niece when in Germany, before he became archbishop. Characteristically enough, he voted for the "Six Articles" in deference to Henry, (44) although the third section of the act provided death and forfeiture of goods for any priest who might marry. Afterward, he had to conceal his wife and carry "her from place to place hidden from sight in a chest." (45) Cranmer alleged at his trial that he had stayed orthodox regarding the sacrament until Ridley had converted him, after Henry's death. But, leaving out of consideration the improbability of a man of Cranmer's remarkable acuteness being influenced by Ridley, the judgment of such a man as Foxe should have weight. Certainly, Foxe thought him a "gospeller" at the time of Lambert's trial, and nothing can give so vivid an idea of the lengths to which men of the Anglican type were ready to go, as the account given by Foxe of the martyrdom of this sectary:—

"Lambert: 'I answer, with Saint Augustine, that it is the body of Christ, after a certain manner.'
"The King: 'Answer me neither out of Saint Augustine, nor by the authority of any other; but tell me plainly, whether thou sayest it is the body of Christ, or no.'...
"Lambert: 'Then I deny it to be the body of Christ.'
"The King: 'Mark well! for now thou shalt be condemned even by Christ's own words, "Hoc est corpus meum."'
"Then he commanded Thomas Cranmer, Archbishop of Canterbury, to refute his assertion; who, first making a short preface unto the hearers, began his disputation with Lambert very modestly.... Then again the king and the bishops raged against Lambert, insomuch that he was not only forced to silence, but also might have been driven into a rage, if his ears had not been acquainted with such

taunts before.... And here it is much to be marvelled at, to see how unfortunately it came to pass in this matter, that... Satan (who oftentimes doth raise up one brother to the destruction of another) did here perform the condemnation of this Lambert by no other ministers than gospellers themselves, Taylor, Barnes, Cranmer, and Cromwell; who, afterwards, in a manner, all suffered the like for the gospel's sake; of whom (God willing) we will speak more hereafter.... Upon the day that was appointed for this holy martyr of God to suffer, he was brought out of the prison at eight o'clock in the morning unto the house of the lord Cromwell, and so carried into his inward chamber, where, it is reported of many, that Cromwell desired of him forgiveness for what he had done.... As touching the terrible manner and fashion of the burning of this blessed martyr, here is to be noted, that of all others who have been burned and offered up at Smithfield, there was yet none so cruelly and piteously handled as he. For, after that his legs were consumed and burned up to the stumps, and that the wretched tormentors and enemies of God had withdrawn the fire from him, so that but a small fire and coals were left under him, then two that stood on each side of him, with their halberts pitched him upon their pikes, as far as the chain would reach.... Then he, lifting up such hands as he had, and his finger's ends flaming with fire, cried unto the people in these words, 'None but Christ, none but Christ;' and so, being let down again from their halberts, fell into the fire, and there ended his life." (46)

In a hierarchy like the Anglican, whose function was to preach passive obedience to the representative of an opulent, but somewhat sluggish oligarchy, there could be no permanent place for idealists. With a Spanish invasion threatening them, an unwarlike ruling class might tolerate sailors like Drake, or priests like Latimer; but, in the long run, their interest lay in purging England of so dangerous an element. The aristocracy sought men who could be bought: but such were of a different type from Latimer, who, when they brought to him the fire, as he stood chained to the stake, "spake in this manner: 'Be of good comfort, master Ridley, and play the man. We shall this day light such a candle, by God's grace, in England, as I trust shall never be put out.'" And so, "after he had stroked his face with his hands, and as it were bathed them a little in the fire, he soon died."

Ecclesiastics like Latimer were apt to be of the mind of Knox, who held "that sîck as may and do brjdill the inordinatt appetyteis of Princes, cannot be accusit of resistance to the aucthoratie, quhilk is Godis gud ordinance." And as the interests of landed capital were bound up with the maintenance of the royal prerogative, such men had to be eliminated. After the death of Mary, the danger apprehended by the landed gentry was a Spanish invasion, coupled with a Catholic insurrection, and therefore the policy of statesmen like Cecil was to foster hostility to Rome. Until after the Armada, Anglicans were permitted to go all lengths towards Geneva; even as late as 1595 the "Lambeth Articles" breathed pure Calvinism. But with the opening of a new century, a change set in; as the power of Spain dwindled, rents rose, and the farmers grew restive at the precise moment when men of the heroic temperament could be discarded. Raleigh was sent to the Tower in 1603.

According to Thorold Rogers, "good arable land [which] let at less than a shilling an acre in the last quarter of the sixteenth century, was let at 5s. to 6s. at the end of the first quarter of the seventeenth," while rent for pasture doubled.(47) Rising rents, and prices tending to become stationary, caused suffering among the rural population, and with suffering came discontent. This discontent in the country was fomented by restlessness in the towns, for commerce had been strongly stimulated during the reign of Elizabeth by the Spanish wars, and the mercantile element began to rebel against legislation passed in the interest of the favoured class. Suddenly the dissatisfaction found vent; for more than forty years the queen's ministers had met with no serious opposition in Parliament; in 1601, without warning, their system of monopolies was struck down, and from that day to the revolution of 1688, the House of Commons proved to be unmanageable by the Crown. Even as early as the accession of James, the competition between the aristocracy and their victims had begun to glow with the heat which presages civil war.

Had the Tudor aristocracy been a martial caste, they would doubtless have organized an army, and governed by the sword; but they instinctively felt that, upon the field of battle, they might be at a disadvantage, and therefore they attempted to control the popular imagination through the priesthood. Thus the divine right of primogeniture came to be the distinguishing tenet of the Church of England. James felt the full force of the current which was carrying him onward, and expressed the situation pithily in his famous apothegm, "No bishop, no king." "I will have," said he, "one doctrine, one discipline, one religion in substance and ceremony;" and the policy of the interest he represented was laid down as early as 1604, at the conference at Hampton Court.

Passive obedience was to be preached, and the church filled with men who could be relied on by the oligarchy. Six weeks after the conference at Hampton Court, Whitgift died, and Bancroft, Bishop of London, was translated to Canterbury. Within a week he was at work. He had already prepared a Book of Canons with which to test the clergy, and this he had ratified by the convocation which preceded his consecration. In these canons the divine origin of episcopacy was asserted; a strange departure from the doctrine of Cranmer. In 1605 there are supposed to have been about fifteen hundred Puritan clergymen in England and Wales, and at Bancroft's first winnowing three hundred were ejected.

Among these Puritans was a certain John Robinson, the teacher of a small congregation of yeomen, in the village of Scrooby, in Nottinghamshire. The man's birth is unknown, his early history is obscure, but in him, and in the farmers who heard him preach, the long and bitter struggle against the pressure of the class which was destroying them, had bred that stern and sombre enthusiasm which afterward marked the sect. By 1607 England had grown intolerable to this congregation, and they resolved to emigrate. They had heard that in Holland liberty of conscience was allowed, and they fondly hoped that with liberty of conscience they might be content to earn their daily bread in peace. Probably with them, however, religion was not the cause, but the effect of their uneasiness, as the result proved.

After many trials and sorrows, these poor people finally assembled in Amsterdam, and thence journeyed to Leyden, where they dwelt some eleven years. But they found the struggle for life to be full as severe in the Low Countries as it had been at home, and presently the exiles began to long for some distant land where "they might more glorify God, do more good to their country, better provide for their posterity, and live to be more refreshed by their labours, than ever they could do in Holland." Accordingly, obtaining a grant from the Virginia Company, they sailed in the Mayflower in 1620, to settle in New England; and thus, by the eviction of the yeomen, England laid the foundation of one great province of her colonial empire.

Footnotes

(1) *Agriculture and Prices*, iv. 64.

(2) 6 Henry VIII., c. 5; 7 Henry VIII., c. 1.

(3) *Jewel of Joy*, Becon. Also *England in the Reign of Henry VIII.*, Early Eng. Text Soc., Extra Ser., No. xxxii. p. 75.

(4) *First Sermon before Edward VI. Sermons of Bishop Latimer*, Ed. of Parker Soc., 100, 101.

(5) 22 Henry VIII., c. 12.

(6) 27 Henry VIII., c. 25.

(7) 1 Edward VI., c. 3.

(8) Brit. Mus. Cole MS. xii. 41. Cited in *Henry VIII. and the English monasteries*, Gasquet, ii. 514, note.

(9) *Eccl. Mem.,* ii. pt. 1, 260.

(10) Sermon on Rebellion, Cranmer, *Miscellaneous Writings and Letters*, 194-6.

(11) Sermon on Rebellion, Cranmer, *Miscellaneous Writings and Letters*, 195, 196.

(12) *Cal.* ix. No. 193.

(13) *Eccl. Mem.*, ii. pt. 1, 152.

(14) 5 and 6 Edw. VI., c. 2.

(15) *Cromwell's Letters and Speeches*, Carlyle, Speech XI.

(16) Raleigh to Burleigh, *Life of Sir Walter Raleigh*, Edwards, ii. 76, letter xxxiv.

(17) *The Reformation of the Church of England,* ii. 68.

(18) *History of England*, v. 432.

(19) Gorham's *Reformation Gleanings*, 61.

(20) Ridley's disputation at Oxford in 1554, *Acts and Monuments*, vi. 474.

(21) *A Godly Letter to the Faithful, Works*, iii. 176.

(22) *Ibid.*, 177.

(23) *A Faithful Admonition, Works*, iii. 283.

(24) *Ibid.*, iii. 281, 282.

(25) *On True Obedience*, Heywood's ed., 73.

(26) *The Institution of a Christian Man*, Preface, *Formularies of Faith of Henry VIII.*, Lloyd, 26.

(27) See Burnett's *History of the Reformation, Records*, part I. book iii. quest 9.

(28) *S. P. Dom. Eliz.* vol. 176, No. 69.

(29) *Zurich Letters*, 1st Series, 287.

(30) *Towchinge the bill and the booke exhibited in the Parliament 1586 for a further reformation of the Churche, S. P. Dom. Eliz.* 199, No. 1.

(31) *History of the Non-jurors*, Lathbury, 50.

(32) See *History of the Reformation*, Burnet, Pocock's ed. *Records* part I. book iii. quest 9.

(33) *History of England*, ch. 1.

(34) *History of England*, ch. iii.

(35) *Ibid.*, ch. vi.

(36) *History of England*, ch. xiv.

(37) *Queen's conference upon Graunt of a Subsidy, etc.,* 1584. *State Papers, Dom. Eliz.*, 176, No. 69.

(38) *History of England*, ch. iii.

(39) *Cal.* x., No. 570.

(40) *Ambassades*, v. 150. Quotation from *History of the Church of England* Dixon, iv. 450.

(41) Pretended Divorce of Henry VIII., Harpsfield, Camden Society, 291.

(42) Burnet's *History of the Reformation*, Pocock's ed., i. 428.

(43) *Ibid.*, iii. 376.

(44) Blunt's *Reformation*, i. 475.

(45) *Anglican Schism*, Sander, Lewis' trans., 181. Also *Pretended Divorce of Henry VIII.*, Harpsield, 290.

(46) *Acts and Monuments*, v. 230.

(47) *Agriculture and Prices*, Rogers, v. 804.

Chapter X: Spain and India

IN the words of Mr. Froude: "Before the sixteenth century had measured half its course the shadow of Spain already stretched beyond the Andes; from the mines of Peru and the custom-houses of Antwerp the golden rivers streamed into her imperial treasury; the crowns of Aragon and Castile, of Burgundy, Milan, Naples, and Sicily, clustered on the brow of her sovereigns." (1) But with all their great martial qualities, the Spaniards seem to have been incapable of attaining the same velocity of movement as the races with which they had to compete. They never emerged from the imaginative period, they never developed the economic type, and in consequence they never centralized as the English centralized. Even as early as the beginning of the seventeenth century this peculiarity had been observed, for the Duke de Sully remarked that with Spain the "legs and arms are strong and powerful, but the heart infinitely weak and feeble."

Captain Mahan has explained the military impotence of the mighty mass which, scattered over two continents, could not command the sea, and in the seventeenth century an intelligent Dutchman boasted that "the Spaniards have publicly begun to hire our ships to sail to the Indies.... It is manifest that the West Indies, being as the stomach to Spain (for from it nearly all the revenue is drawn), must be joined to the Spanish head by a sea force"; (2) and the glory of the Elizabethan sailors lay not only in having routed this sea force, but in having assimilated no small portion of the nutriment which the American stomach should have supplied to the Spanish heart.

As Spain lingered long in the imaginative age, the priest and soldier there reigned supreme after the mercantile and sceptical type had begun to predominate elsewhere; and the instinct of the priest and soldier has always been to exterminate their rivals when pressed by their competition. In the Spanish peninsula itself the Inquisition soon trampled out heresy, but by the middle of the sixteenth century the Low Countries were a hotbed of Protestantism, and in Flanders these opposing forces fought out their battle to the death. The war which ruined Antwerp made England.

In 1576 Antwerp was sacked and burned; in 1585 the town was reduced to starvation by the Duke of Parma, and its commerce having been scattered by successive disasters, some of it migrated to Amsterdam, and some sought shelter in the Thames. In London the modern man was protected by the sea, and the crisis of the combat came in 1588, when the Spaniards, having decided to pursue their enemy to his last stronghold, sent the Armada to perish in the Channel. With that supreme effort the vitality of the great imaginative empire began to fail, disintegration set in, and on the ruins of Spain rose the purely economic centralization of Great Britain.

Like the Venetians, the British laid the basis of their high fortune by piracy and slaving, and their advantage over Spain lay not in mass, but in a superior energy, which gave them more rapid movement. Drake's squadron, when he sailed round the world, numbered five ships, the largest measuring only one hundred and twenty tons, the smallest twelve, but with these he succeeded because of their speed. For example, he overtook the Cacafuego, whose ballast was silver, and whose cargo gold and jewels. He never disclosed her value, but the Spanish government afterward proved a loss of a million and a half of ducats, beside the property of private individuals. In like manner the Armada was destroyed by little ships, which sailed round their clumsy enemy, and disabled him before he could strike a blow in self-defence.

The Spanish wars were halcyon days for the men of martial blood who had lost their land; they took to the sea by thousands, and ravaged the Spanish colonies with the energy and ferocity of vikings. For nearly a generation they wallowed in gold and silver and gems, and in the plunder of the American towns. Among these men Sir Francis Drake stood foremost, but, after 1560, the southern counties swarmed with pirates; and when, in 1585, Drake sailed on his raid against the West Indies, he led a force of volunteers twenty-five hundred strong. He held no commission, the crews of his twenty-five ships served without pay, they went as buccaneers to fatten on the commerce of the Spaniard. As it happened, this particular expedition failed financially, for the treasure fleet escaped, and the plunder of the three cities of Santiago, Saint Domingo, and Carthagena yielded only £60,000, but the injury done to Spain was incalculable.

No computation can be attempted of the spoil taken during these years; no reports were ever made; on the contrary, all concerned were anxious to conceal their doings, but certain prizes were too dazzling to be hidden. When Drake surprised three caravans on the Isthmus, numbering one hundred and ninety mules, each mule loaded with three hundred pounds of silver, the fact became known. No wonder Drake ate off "silver richly gilt, and engraved with his arms," that he had "all possible luxuries, even to perfumes," that he dined and supped "to the music of violins," and that he could bribe the queen with a diamond cross and a coronet set with splendid emeralds, and give the lord chancellor a service of plate. What he gave in secret he alone knew.

As Francis Drake was the ideal English corsair, so John Hawkins was the ideal slaver. The men were kinsmen, and of the breed which, when driven from their farms at the end of the Middle Ages, left their mark all over the world. Of course the two sailors were "gospellers," and Mr. Froude has quoted an interesting passage from the manuscript of a contemporary Jesuit, which shows how their class was esteemed toward the close of the sixteenth century: "The only party that would fight to the death for the queen, the only real friends she had, were the Puritans, the Puritans of London, the Puritans of the sea towns." (3) These the priest thought desperate and determined men. Nevertheless they sometimes provoked Elizabeth by their sermonizing. The story is told that one day after reading a letter of Hawkins to Burleigh she cried: "God's death! This fool went out a soldier, and has come back a divine."

Though both Drake and Hawkins possessed the predatory temperament, Hawkins had a strong commercial instinct, and kept closely to trade. He was the son of old William Hawkins, the first British captain who ever visited Brazil, and who brought from thence a native chief, whom he presented to Henry VIII. As a young man John had discovered at the Canaries "that negroes were a very good commodity in Hispaniola," (4) and that they might easily be taken on the coast of Guinea. Accordingly, in 1562, he fitted out three ships, touched at Sierra Leone, and "partly by the sword and partly by other means," he obtained a cargo, "and with that prey he sailed over the ocean sea" to Hispaniola, where he sold his goods at a large profit. The West India Islands, and the countries bordering the Gulf of Mexico, cannot be cultivated profitably by white labourers; therefore, when the Spaniards had, by hard usage, partially exterminated the natives, a fresh supply of field hands became necessary, and these could be had easily and cheaply on the coast of Africa.

At first Spain tried to exclude foreigners from this most lucrative traffic; but here again the English moved too quickly to be stopped. Wherever Hawkins went, he went prepared to fight, and, if prevented from trading peaceably, he used force. In his first voyage he met with no opposition, but subsequently, at Burburata, leave to sell was denied him, and, without an instant's hesitation, he marched against the town with "a hundred men well armed," and brought the governor to terms. Having supplied all the slaves needed at that port, Hawkins went on to Rio de la Hacha, where he, in like manner, made a demonstration with "one hundred men in armour," and two small guns, and in ten days he had disposed of his whole stock.

As at that time an able negro appears to have been worth about £160 in the West Indies, (5) a cargo of five hundred ought to have netted between seventy and eighty thousand pounds, for the cost of kidnapping was trifling. No wonder, therefore, that slaving flourished, and that, by the middle of the eighteenth century, England probably carried not far from one hundred thousand blacks annually from Africa to the colonies. The East offered no such market, and doubtless Adam Smith was right in his opinion that the commerce with India had never been so advantageous as the trade to America. (6)

Both slavers and pirates brought bullion to England, and presently this flow of silver began to stimulate at London a certain amount of exchange between the East and West. The Orientals have always preferred payment in specie, and, as silver has usually offered more profit than gold as an export, the European with a surplus of silver has had the advantage over all competitors. Accordingly, until Spain lost the power to protect her communications with her mines, the Spanish peninsula enjoyed almost a monopoly of the trade beyond the Cape; but as the war went on, and more of the precious metal flowed to the north, England and Holland began to send their silver to Asia, the Dutch organizing one East India Company in 1595, and the British another in 1600.

Sir Josiah Child, who was, perhaps, the ablest merchant of the seventeenth century, observed that in 1545 "the trade of England then was inconsiderable, and the merchants very mean and few." (7) Child's facts are beyond doubt, and the date he fixed is interesting because it coincides with the discovery of Potosi, whence most of the silver came which supplied the pirates and the slavers. Prior to 1545 specie had been scarce in London, but when the buccaneers had been scuttling treasure galleons for a generation, they found themselves possessed of enough specie to set them dreaming of India, and thus piracy laid the foundation of the British empire in Asia.

But robbing the Spaniards had another more immediate and more startling result, for it probably precipitated the civil war. As the city grew rich it chafed at the slow movement of the aristocracy, who, timid and peaceful, cramped it by closing the channels through which it reached the property of foreigners; and, just when the yeomanry were exasperated by rising rents, London began to glow with that energy which, when given vent, was destined to subdue so large a portion of the world. Perhaps it is not going too far to say that, even from the organization of the East India Company, the mercantile interest controlled England. Not that it could then rule alone, it lacked the power to do so for nearly a hundred years to come; but, after 1600, its weight turned the scale on which side soever thrown. Before the Long Parliament the merchants were generally Presbyterians or moderate Puritans; the farmers, Independents or Radicals; and Winthrop, when preparing for the emigration to Massachusetts, dealt not only with squires like Hampden, but with city magnates like Thomas Andrews, the lord mayor. This alliance between the rural and the urban Puritans carried through the Great Rebellion, and as their coalition crushed the monarchy so their separation reinstated it.

Macaulay has very aptly observed that "but for the hostility of the city, Charles the First would never have been vanquished, and that, without the help of the city, Charles the Second could scarcely have been restored." (8) At the Protector's death the Presbyterians abandoned the farmers, probably because they feared them. The army of the Commonwealth swarmed with men like Cromwell and Blake, warriors resistless alike on land and sea, with whom, when organized, the city could not cope. Therefore it scattered them, and, throwing in its lot with the Cavaliers, set up the king.

For about a generation after the Restoration, no single interest had the force to impose its will upon the nation, or, in other words, parties were equally balanced; but from the middle of the century the tide flowed rapidly. Capital accumulated, and as it accumulated the men adapted to be its instruments grew to be the governing class. Sir Josiah Child is the most interesting figure of this period.

His acquaintance remembered him a poor apprentice sweeping the counting-house where he worked; and yet, at fifty, his fortune reached £20,000 a year, a sum almost equal to the rent-roll of the Duke of Ormond, the richest peer of the realm. Child married his daughter to the eldest son of the Duke of Beaufort, and gave her £50,000, and his ability was so commanding that for years he absolutely ruled the East India Company, and used its revenues to corrupt Parliament. On matters of finance such a man would hardly err, and he gave it as his opinion that in 1635 "there were more merchants to be found upon the Exchange worth each one thousand pounds and upwards, than were in the former days, viz., before the year 1600, to be found worth one hundred pounds each."

"And now... there are more men to be found upon the Exchange now worth ten thousand pounds estates, than were then of one thousand pounds. And if this be doubted, let us ask the aged, whether five hundred pounds portion with a daughter sixty years ago, were not esteemed a larger portion than two thousand pounds is now; and whether gentlewomen in those days would not esteem themselves well clothed in a serge gown, which a chambermaid now will be ashamed to be seen in.... We have now almost one hundred coaches for one we had formerly. We with ease can pay a greater tax now in one year than our forefathers could in twenty. Our customs are very much improved, I believe above the proportion aforesaid, of six to one; which is not so much in advance of the rates of goods as by increase of the bulk of trade....

"I can myself remember since there were not in London used so many wharves or keys for the landing of merchants goods, by at least one third part, as now there are, and those that were then could scarce have employment for half what they could do; and now, notwithstanding one-third more used to the same purpose, they are all too little, in time of peace, to land the goods at, that come to London." (9)

Child estimated that, within twenty years, wages had risen one-third, and rents twenty-five per cent, while "houses new-built in London yield twice the rent they did before the fire."(10) Farms that "their grandfathers or fathers bought or sold fifty years past... would yield, one with another, at least treble the money, and in some cases, six times the money, they were then bought and sold for." (11) Macaulay has estimated the population of London in 1685 at half a million, and believed it to have then become the largest city in Europe.

The aristocracy were forced to tolerate men of the predatory type while they feared a Spanish invasion, but after the defeat of the Armada these warriors became dangerous at home, and the oligarchy, very naturally, tried to purge the island of a class which constantly menaced their authority. Persecution drove numbers of Nonconformists to America, and the story of Captain John Smith shows how hardly society then pressed on the race of adventurers, even where the bitterness of the struggle did not produce religious enthusiasm.

Smith lived a generation too late. Born in 1579, he was a child of nine when the Armada perished, and only sixteen when Drake and Hawkins died at sea. Smith's father had property, but when left an orphan his guardians neglected him, and at fifteen let him set out on his travels with only ten shillings in his pocket. At home no career was open to him, for the Cecils rather inclined to imprison and behead soldiers of fortune than to reward them. Accordingly he went abroad, and by twenty-five had seen service in most countries of the Continent, had been enslaved by the Turks, had escaped and wandered to Barbary, had fought the Spanish on a French man-of-war, and at last had learned that the dreams of his youth belonged to a past age, and that he must enter a new path. He therefore joined himself to a party bound for Virginia, and the hardship of the times may be gauged by the fact that out of a company of a hundred, fifty-two were gentlemen adventurers as needy as himself, none of whom sought exile for religion.

Smith's voyages to America brought him nothing but bitterness. He returned to England and passed his last years in obscurity and neglect, and perhaps the fate that awaited soldiers under James, has been nowhere better told than in Smith's own words. He spent five years and more than five hundred pounds in the service of Virginia and New England, yet "in neither... have I one foot of land, nor the very house I builded, nor the ground I digged with my own hands, nor ever any content or satisfaction at all, and though I see ordinarily those two countries shared before me by them that neither have them, nor know them but by my descriptions." (12)

As long as the Tudor aristocracy ruled, Great Britain afforded small comfort for men like Smith. That aristocracy had genius neither for adventure nor for war, and few Western nations have a sorrier military history than England under the Stuarts. Yet beneath the inert mass of the nobility seethed an energy which was to recentralize the world; and when capital had accumulated to a certain point, the men who gave it an outlet laid their grasp upon the State. In 1688 the commercial adventurers conquered the kingdom.

The change was radical; at once social, political, and religious. The stronghold of the Tories had been the royal prerogative. The victors lodged the power of the Crown in a committee chosen by the House of Commons. The dogma of divine right immediately vanished, and with it all that distinguished Anglicanism. Though perverted by the Tudors, this great tenet of the Church of Henry VIII. had been at least a survival of an imaginative age; and when the merchants swept it away, all trace of idealism departed. Thenceforward English civilization became a purely materialistic phenomenon.

In proportion as movement accelerates societies consolidate, and as societies consolidate they pass through a profound intellectual change. Energy ceases to find vent through the imagination, and takes the form of capital; hence as civilizations advance, the imaginative temperament tends to disappear, while the economic instinct is fostered, and thus substantially new varieties of men come to possess the world.

Nothing so portentous overhangs humanity as this mysterious and relentless acceleration of movement, which changes methods of competition and alters paths of trade; for by it countless millions of men and women are foredoomed to happiness or misery, as certainly as the beasts and trees, which have flourished in the wilderness, are destined to vanish when the soil is subdued by man.

The Romans amassed the treasure by which they administered their Empire, through the plunder and enslavement of the world. The Empire cemented by that treasure crumbled when adverse exchanges carried the bullion of Italy to the shore of the Bosphorus. An accelerated movement among the semi-barbarians of the West caused the agony of the crusades, amidst which Constantinople fell as the Italian cities rose; while Venice and Genoa, and with them the whole Arabic civilization, shrivelled, when Portugal established direct communication with Hindostan.

The opening of the ocean as a highroad precipitated the Reformation, and built up Antwerp, while in the end it ruined Spain; and finally the last great quickening of the age of steam, which centralized the world at London, bathed the earth in blood, from the Mississippi to the Ganges. Thus religions are preached and are forgotten, empires rise and fall, philosophies are born and die, art and poetry bloom and fade, as societies pass from the disintegration wherein the imagination kindles, to the consolidation whose pressure ends in death.

In 1688, when the momentum of England suddenly increased, the change was equivalent to the conquest of the island by a new race. Among the family of European nations, Great Britain rose as no people had risen since the Punic Wars. Almost instantly she entered on a career of conquest unparalleled in modern history. Of the hundred and twenty-five years between the Boyne and Waterloo, she passed some seventy in waging ferocious wars, from which she emerged victorious on land and sea, the mistress of a mighty empire, the owner of incalculable wealth, and the centre of the world's exchanges. Then, from this culminating point of expansion by conquest, she glided subtly, and almost imperceptibly, into the period of contraction, as Rome went before her under the Caesars.

Although abundant metallic currency does not, probably, of itself, create mercantile prosperity, such prosperity is hardly compatible with a shrinking stock of money; for when contraction sets in and prices fall, producers and debtors are ruined, as they were ruined in Italy under the later emperors. Toward the close of the seventeenth century Europe appeared to be on the brink of such a contraction, for though Peru had lavishly replenished the supply of the precious metals a hundred years previously, the drain to Asia and the increasing demands of commerce had been so considerable, that the standard coin had generally depreciated. From the reign of Augustus downward, commerce between Europe and Asia has usually favoured Asia, and this was particularly true of the seventeenth century, when the value of bullion fell in the West, and therefore encouraged lavish exports to the East, where it retained its purchasing power. According to Adam Smith, "the banks of Venice, Genoa, Amsterdam, Hamburg, and Nuremberg, seem to have been all originally established" to provide an ideal currency for the settlement of bills of exchange, and the money "of such banks, being better than the common currency of the country, necessarily bore an agio, which was greater or smaller, according as the currency was supposed to be more or less degraded below the standard of the State." (13)

Smith estimated the depreciation at Hamburg at fourteen per cent, and at Amsterdam, early in the previous century, at nine per cent; in short, all European countries suffered, but in England the evil reached a climax through the inertia of the new aristocracy.

In England, silver had always been the standard, and by the third year of Elizabeth the coin had been restored to its proper fineness, which thenceforward was scrupulously maintained. But though the metal was not degraded by the government, the stock of bullion, if not constantly replenished from without, tended to diminish in proportion to the growth of the country and the export of specie to Asia. After the discovery of America, the value of silver in relation to gold fell, in Europe, to about fourteen or fifteen to one, while in China or India it stood pretty steady at from ten to twelve to one. Consequently from 1600 downward, silver remained the most profitable cargo which could be sent round the Cape of Good Hope, and, unhappily for British prosperity, at the very moment when the East India Company came into being, piracy ceased. The chief supply of bullion being thus cut off, the strain of the export trade fell upon the coin, and within a little more than a generation the effect become apparent in a degeneration of the currency.

To make good her position as a centre of exchanges, England had no choice but to supply her necessities by force. Cromwell understood the situation perfectly, and had hardly assumed the office of Protector when he laid plans to cut the evil at the root by conquering Spanish America, and robbing Spain of her mines. To this end he fitted out his great expedition against Saint Domingo, which was to serve him as his base; but for once his military genius failed him, his commanders blundered, the attack miscarried, and the island of Jamaica was all that came of the campaign.

Meanwhile, however, that no time might be lost while fighting for the mines themselves, Cromwell sent Blake to intercept the treasure ships off the coast of Spain. At first Blake also had ill-luck. In 1655 the plate fleet escaped him, but the next year, though forced himself to go to port for supplies, he detached Captain Stayner, with six sail, to cruise off Cadiz, and on September 19, General Montague was able to report that his "hart [was] very much warmed with the apprehension of the singular providence of God," who had permitted Stayner to meet, "with the Kinge of Spain's West India fleete," and take among other prizes "a gallion reported to have in her two million pieces of plate." (14) If the "plate" were Mexican "pieces of eight" at four shillings and sixpence, the cargo was worth £450,000, or considerably more than the whole annual export to the East at the beginning of the eighteenth century. Had the Protector lived, there can be little doubt that, by some such means as this, he would have fostered British resources, and maintained the integrity of British coin; but in less than two years from the date of Montague's dispatch, Cromwell was dead, and the inertia of the Tory landlords paralyzed the nation for another generation. No foreigner was robbed, and the stock of domestic silver dwindled from year to year, until at the Revolution the golden guinea, which, from its first issue in 1662 down to the accession of William and Mary, had been nominally current for twenty shillings, actually sold in the market for thirty shillings of the money in use.

"This diminishing and counterfeiting the money was at this time so excessive, that what was good silver was worth scarcely one-half of its current value, whilst a great part of the coins was only iron, brass, or copper plated, and some no more than washed over." (15)

One of the first acts of the new government was a complete recoinage, which was finished in 1699; but the measure failed of its purpose, for the reason that the exports of silver regularly exceeded the imports.

In 1717, a committee of the House of Lords considered the condition of the currency, and Lord Stanhope then explained very lucidly the cause of the scarcity of silver. Among other papers he produced a report from the Custom House, by which it appeared that, in the year 1717, "the East India Company had exported near three million ounces of silver, which far exceeding the imports of the bullion in that year, it necessarily followed that vast quantities of silver specie must have been melted down, both to make up the export, and to supply the silversmith." (16) For the decade from 1711 to 1720 the annual export of bullion by the East India Company averaged £434,000. (17) At the accession of George III., in 1760, Lord Liverpool estimated that shillings had lost one-sixth, and sixpences one-quarter of their original weight, while the crown-piece had almost wholly disappeared. (18) Even Adam Smith admitted that because of this outflow silver had risen in value, and probably purchased "a larger quantity both of labour and commodities" than it otherwise would. (19)

In this emergency the British merchants showed the resource which has always been their characteristic, and, in default of an adequate supply of specie, relieved the strain upon their currency by issuing paper. Mediæval banking had gone no further than the establishment of reserves of coin, to serve as a medium for clearing bills of exchange; the English took the great step of accelerating the circulation of their money, by using this reserve as a basis for a paper currency which might be largely expanded. The Bank of England was incorporated in 1694, the Bank of Scotland in 1695, and the effect was unquestionably considerable. Adam Smith has thus described the impetus received by Glasgow:—

"The effects of it have been precisely those above described. The business of the country is almost entirely carried on by means of the paper of those different banking companies, with which purchases and payments of all kinds are commonly made. Silver very seldom appears except in the change of a twenty shillings bank note, and gold still seldomer. But though the conduct of all those different companies has not been unexceptionable... the country, notwithstanding, has evidently derived great benefit from their trade. I have heard it asserted, that the trade of the city of Glasgow doubled in about fifteen years after the first erection of the banks there; and that the trade of Scotland has more than quadrupled since the first erection of the two public banks at Edinburgh." (20)

But although by this means a certain degree of relief was given, and though prices rose slowly throughout the first half of the eighteenth century, the fundamental difficulty remained. There was insufficient silver for export, exchanges were adverse, and that stock of coined money was lacking which is the form in which force clothes itself in highly centralized communities. How England finally supplied her needs is one of the most dramatic pages of history.

As Jevons has aptly observed, Asia is "the great reservoir and sink of the precious metals." From time immemorial the Oriental custom has been to hoard, and from the Mogul blazing with the diamonds of Golconda, to the peasant starving on his wretched pittance, every Hindoo had, in former days, a treasure stored away against a day of trouble. Year by year, since Pizarro had murdered the Inca Atahualpa for his gold, a stream of bullion had flowed from America to Europe, and from Europe to the East: there it had vanished as completely though once more buried in the bowels of the mine. These hoards, the savings of millions of human beings for centuries, the English seized and took to London, as the Romans had taken the spoil of Greece and Pontus to Italy. What the value of the treasure was, no man can estimate, but it must have been many millions of pounds—a vast sum in proportion to the stock of the precious metals then owned by Europeans. Some faint idea of the booty of the conqueror may be drawn from Macaulay's description of the first visit of an English soldier to an Oriental treasure chamber:—

"As to Clive, there was no limit to his acquisitions but his own moderation. The treasury of Bengal was thrown open to him. There were piled up, after the usage of Indian princes, immense masses of coin, among which might not seldom be detected the florins and byzants with which, before any European ship had turned the Cape of Good

Hope, the Venetians purchased the stuffs and spices of the East. Clive walked between heaps of gold and silver, crowned with rubies and diamonds, and was at liberty to help himself." (21)

The lives of few men are better known than those of Clive and Hastings, and yet there are few whose influence upon the fate of mankind has had such scant appreciation. It is not too much to say that the destiny of Europe hinged upon the conquest of Bengal. Robert Clive was of the same stock as Drake and Hawkins, Raleigh, Blake, and Cromwell; he was the eldest son of one of those small farmers whose ancestors had held their land ever since the Conquest, and who, when at last evicted and driven out to sea, had fought and conquered on every continent and on every ocean. Among the throng of great English adventurers none is greater than he.

He was born in 1725, and from childhood displayed those qualities which made him pre-eminent on the field of battle; fighting was his delight, and so fierce was his temper that his family could not control him. At last, when eighteen, his father gladly sent him to Madras as a clerk in the service of the East India Company; and there, in a torrid climate which shattered his health, poor and neglected, lonely and forlorn, he pined, until in melancholy he twice attempted suicide. But he was destined to found an empire, and at last his hour came.

When Clive went to India, the Company was still a purely commercial concern, holding only the land needed for its warehouses, and having in their pay a few ill-disciplined sepoys. In the year 1746, when Clive was twenty-one, the war of the Austrian Succession was raging, and suddenly a French fleet, commanded by Labourdonnais, appeared off Madras, and attacked Fort Saint George. Resistance was hopeless, the place surrendered, and the governor and chief inhabitants were taken to Pondicherry. Clive, however, managed to escape, and, volunteering, received an ensign's commission, and began his military career.

Shortly after, peace was made in Europe, but in India the issue of the struggle lay undecided between the French and English, the prize being the peninsula. Dupleix, the French governor of Pondicherry, was a man of commanding intellect, who first saw the possibility of constructing a European empire in Hindostan by controlling native princes. Following up his idea, he mixed in a war of succession, and having succeeded in establishing a sovereign of the Deccan, he made imself master of Southern India. The Nizam's treasure was thrown open to him, and beside many jewels of price, he is said to have appropriated two hundred thousand pounds in coin. This was the man whom Clive, when only a clerk of twenty-five, without military education or experience, attacked and overthrew.

Clive began his campaigns by the capture and defence of Arcot, one of the most daring deeds of a generation given over to perpetual war. Aided by their native allies, the French had laid siege to Trichinopoly, and Clive represented to his superiors that with the fate of Trichinopoly was bound up the fate of the whole peninsula. He recommended making a diversion by assaulting Arcot, the capital of the Carnatic; his plan met with approval, and, with two hundred Europeans and three hundred sepoys, he marched to fight the greatest power in the East. He succeeded in surprising and occupying the town without loss, but when within the city his real peril began. Arcot had neither ditches nor defensible ramparts, the English were short of provisions, and the Nabob hurried forward ten thousand men to relieve his capital. With four officers, one hundred and twenty British, and two hundred sepoys, Clive held the town for fifty days, and when the enemy assaulted for the last time he served his own guns. He won a decisive victory, and from that hour was recognized as among the most brilliant officers of the world.

Other campaigns followed, but his health, undermined by the tropics, gave way, and at twenty-seven he returned home to squander his money and contest an election to

Parliament. He soon reached the end of his resources, and, just before the opening of the Seven Years' War, he accepted a lieutenant-colonel's commission, and set sail to take command in Hindostan. The Company appointed him governor of Fort Saint David, a settlement near Madras; but he had hardly assumed his office before an event occurred which caused the conquest of Bengal. The Nabob of Bengal captured Calcutta, and imprisoned one hundred and forty-six of the English residents in the "Black Hole," where, in a single night, one hundred and twenty-three perished.

Clive was summoned, and acted with his usual vigour. He routed the Nabob's army, recovered Calcutta, and would have taken vengeance at once had not the civilians, who wanted to be restored to their places, interfered.

Long and tortuous negotiations followed, in which Clive displayed more than Oriental cunning and duplicity, ending in a march into the interior and the battle of Plassey. There, with one thousand English and two thousand sepoys, he met and crushed the army of the Nabob, sixty thousand strong. On June 23, 1757, one of the richest provinces of Asia lay before him defenceless, ripe for plunder. Eight hundred thousand pounds were sent down the Hooghly to Calcutta, in one shipment; Clive himself took between two and three hundred thousand pounds.

Like Drake and Hawkins, Clive had done great things for England, but he was a military adventurer, one of the class in whom the aristocracy recognized an enemy; and though in London he was treated with outward respect, and even given an Irish peerage, the landed interest hated him, and tried to destroy him, as in the next generation it tried to destroy Hastings.

Upon the plundering of India there can be no better authority than Macaulay, who held high office at Calcutta when the administration of Hastings was still remembered; and who less than any of the writers who have followed him, was a mouth-piece of the official class. (22) He has told how after Plassey "the shower of wealth" began to fall, and he has described Clive's own gains: "We may safely affirm that no Englishman who started with nothing has ever, in any line of life, created such a fortune at the early age of thirty-four." (23) But the takings of Clive, either for himself or for the government, were trifling compared to the wholesale robbery and spoliation which followed his departure, when Bengal was surrendered a helpless prey to a myriad of greedy officials. These officials were absolute, irresponsible, and rapacious, and they emptied the private hoards. Their only thought was to wring some hundreds of thousands of pounds out of the natives as quickly as possible, and hurry home to display their wealth.

"Enormous fortunes were thus rapidly accumulated at Calcutta, while thirty millions of human beings were reduced to the extremity of wretchedness." "The misgovernment of the English was carried to a point such as seems hardly compatible with the very existence of society. The Roman proconsul, who, in a year or two, squeezed out of a province the means of rearing marble palaces and baths on the shores of Campania, of drinking from amber, of feasting on singing birds, of exhibiting armies of gladiators and flocks of camelopards; the Spanish viceroy, who, leaving behind him the curses of Mexico or Lima, entered Madrid with a long train of gilded coaches, and of sumpterhorses trapped and shod with silver, were now outdone." (24)

Thus treasure in oceans flowed into England through private hands, but in India the affairs of the Company went from bad to worse. Misgovernment impoverished the people, the savings of long years of toil were exhausted, and when, in 1770, a drought brought famine, the resources of the people failed, and they perished by millions: "the very streets of Calcutta were blocked up by the dying and the dead." Then came an outbreak of wrath from disappointed stockholders; the landed interest seized its opportunity to attack Clive in Parliament; and the merchants chose Hastings to develop the resources of Hindostan.

As Sheridan said, the Company "extended the sordid principles of their origin over all their successive operations; connecting with their civil policy, and even with their boldest achievements, the meanness of a pedlar and the profligacy of pirates." In Hastings the Company found a man fitted to their hands, a statesman worthy to organize a vast empire on an economic basis. Able, bold, cool, and relentless, he grasped the situation at a glance, and never faltered in his purpose. If more treasure was to be wrung from the natives, force had to be used systematically. Though Bengal might be ruined, the hoards of the neighbouring potentates remained safe, and these Hastings deliberately set himself to drain. Macaulay has explained the policy and the motives which actuated him:—

"The object of his diplomacy was at this time simply to get money. The finances of his government were in an embarrassed state, and this embarrassment he was determined to relieve by some means, fair or foul. The principle which directed all his dealings with his neighbours is fully expressed by the old motto of one of the great predatory families of Teviotdale, 'Thou shalt want ere I want.' He seems to have laid it down, as a fundamental proposition which could not be disputed, that, when he had not as many lacs of rupees as the public service required, he was to take them from anybody who had. One thing, indeed, is to be said in excuse for him. The pressure applied to him by his employers at home, was such as only the highest virtue could have withstood, such as left him no choice except to commit great wrongs, or to resign his high post, and with that post all his hopes of fortune and distinction." (25)

How he obtained his money, the pledges he violated, and the blood he spilt, is known as few passages of history are known, for the story has been told by Macaulay and by Burke. How he robbed the Nabob of Bengal of half the income the Company had solemnly promised to pay, how he repudiated the revenue which the government had covenanted to yield to the Mogul as a tribute for provinces ceded them, and how, in consideration of four hundred thousand pounds, he sent a brigade to slaughter the Rohillas, and placidly saw "their villages burned, their children butchered, and their women violated," has been described in one of the most popular essays in the language. At Hastings' impeachment, the heaviest charge against him was that based on his conduct toward the princesses of Oude, whom his creature, Asaph-ul-Dowlah, imprisoned and starved, whose servants he tormented, and from whom he wrung at last twelve hundred thousand pounds, as the price of blood. By these acts, and acts such as these, the treasure which had flowed to Europe through the extermination of the Peruvians, was returned again to England from the hoards of conquered Hindoos.

Footnotes

(1) *History of England*, viii. 425.

(2) *Influence of the Sea Power upon History*, Mahan, 41.

(3) *English Seamen of the Sixteenth Century*, 6.

(4) Anderson's *History of Commerce*, i. 400.

(5) *S. P. Dom. Eliz.*, 53.

(6) *Wealth of Nations*, book 4, ch. i.

(7) *Discourse of Trade*, Child, ed. 1775, 8.

(8) *History of England*, ch. iii.

(9) *Discourse of Trade*, Josiah Child, ed. 1775, 8, 9, 10.

(10) *Ibid.* Pref. xxxi.

(11) *Ibid.*, 41.

(12) *American Biography*, Sparks, ii. 388.

(13) *Wealth of Nations*, bk. iv. c. 3, pt. 1.

(14) Thurloe's *State Papers*, v. 433, 434.

(15) *Annals of the Coinage of Britain*, Ruding, iii. 378.

(16) *Annals of the Coinage*, Ruding, iii. 470.

(17) *Investigations in Currency and Finance*, Jevons, 140.

(18) *Annals of the Coinage*, Ruding, iv. 26.

(19) *Wealth of Nations*, bk. iv. c. 1.

(20) *Wealth of Nations*, bk. ii. c. 2.

(21) *Lord Clive.*

(22) Macaulay's essays have been the subject of much recent adverse criticism; but, in regard to the plundering of Hindostan, nothing of consequence has been brought forward against him. All recent historical work relating to India must be taken with suspicion. The whole official influence has been turned to distorting evidence in order to make a case for the government.

(23) *Lord Clive.*

(24) *Lord Clive.*

(25) *Warren Hastings.*

Chapter XI: Modern Centralization

IN discussing the phenomena of the highly centralized society in which he lived, Mill defined capital "as the accumulated stock of human labour." In other words, capital may be considered as stored energy; but most of this energy flows in fixed channels, money alone is capable of being transmuted immediately into any form of activity. Therefore the influx of the Indian treasure, by adding considerably to the nation's cash capital, not only increased its stock of energy, but added much to its flexibility and the rapidity of its movement.

Very soon after Plassey the Bengal plunder began to arrive in London, and the effect appears to have been instantaneous, for all authorities agree that the "industrial revolution," the event which has divided the nineteenth century from all antecedent time, began with the year 1760. Prior to 1760, according to Baines, the machinery used for spinning cotton in Lancashire was almost as simple as in India; (1) while about 1750 the English iron industry was in full decline because of the destruction of the forests for fuel. At that time four-fifths of the iron in use in the kingdom came from Sweden.

Plassey was fought in 1757, and probably nothing has ever equalled the rapidity of the change which followed. In 1760 the flying-shuttle appeared, and coal began to replace wood in smelting. In 1764 Hargreaves invented the spinning-jenny, in 1779 Crompton contrived the mule, in 1785 Cartwright patented the power-loom, and, chief of all, in 1768 Watt matured the steam-engine, the most perfect of all vents of centralizing energy. But though these machines served as outlets for the accelerating movement of the time, they did not cause that acceleration. In themselves inventions are passive, many of the most important having lain dormant for centuries, waiting for a sufficient store of force to have accumulated to set them working. That store must always take the shape of money, and money not hoarded, but in motion.

Thus printing had been known for ages in China before it came to Europe; the Romans probably were acquainted with gunpowder; revolvers and breechloading cannon existed in the fifteenth and sixteenth centuries, and steam had been experimented upon long before the birth of Watt. The least part of Watt's labour lay in conceiving his idea; he consumed his life in marketing it. Before the influx of the Indian treasure, and the expansion of credit which followed, no force sufficient for this purpose existed; and had Watt lived fifty years earlier, he and his invention must have perished together. Considering the difficulties under which Matthew Boulton, the ablest and most energetic manufacturer of his time, nearly succumbed, no one can doubt that without Boulton's works at Birmingham the engine could not have been produced, and yet before 1760 such works could not have been organized. The factory system was the child of the "industrial revolution," and until capital had accumulated in masses capable of giving solidity to large bodies of labour, manufactures were necessarily carried on by scattered individuals, who combined a handicraft with agriculture. Defoe's charming description of Halifax about the time Boulton learned his trade, is well known:—

"The nearer we came to Halifax, we found the houses thicker, and the villages greater, in every bottom;...for the land being divided into small enclosures, from two acres to six or seven each, seldom more, every three or four pieces of land had an house belonging to them.

"In short, after we had mounted the third hill, we found the country one continued village, tho' every way mountainous, hardly an house standing out of a speaking distance from another; and, as the day cleared up, we could see at every house a tenter, and on almost every tenter a piece of cloth, kersie, or shalloon; which are the three articles of this countries labour....

"This place then seems to have been designed by providence for the very purposes to which it is now allotted.... Nor is the industry of the people wanting to second these advantages. Tho' we met few people without doors, yet within we saw the houses full of lusty fellows, some at the dye vat, some at the loom, others dressing the cloths; the women and children carding, or spinning; all employed from the youngest to the oldest; scarce anything above four years old, but its hands were sufficient for its own support. Not a beggar to be seen, nor an idle person, except here and there in an alms-house, built for those that are antient, and past working. The people in general live long; they enjoy a good air; and under such circumstances hard labour is naturally attended with the blessing of health, if not riches." (2)

To the capitalist, then, rather than to the inventor, civilization owes the steam engine as a part of daily life, and Matthew Boulton was one of the most remarkable of the race of producers whose reign lasted down to Waterloo. As far back as tradition runs the Boultons appear to have been Northamptonshire farmers, but Matthew's grandfather met with misfortunes under William, and sent his son to Birmingham to seek his fortune in trade. There the adventurer established himself as a silver stamper, and there, in 1728, Matthew was born. Young Boulton early showed both energy and ingenuity, and on coming of age became his father's partner, thenceforward managing the business. In 1759, two years after the conquest of Bengal, the father died, and Matthew, having married in 1760, might have retired on his wife's property, but he chose rather to plunge more deeply into trade. Extending his works, he built the famous shops at Soho, which he finished in 1762 at an outlay of £20,000, a debt which probably clung to him to the end of his life.

Boulton formed his partnership with Watt in 1774, and then began to manufacture the steam-engine, but he met with formidable difficulties. Before the sales yielded any return, the outlay reduced him to the brink of insolvency; nor did he achieve success until he had exhausted his own and his friends' resources.

"He mortgaged his lands to the last farthing; borrowed from his personal friends; raised money by annuities; obtained advances from bankers; and had invested upwards of forty thousand pounds in the enterprise before it began to pay." (3)

Agriculture, as well as industry, felt the impulsion of the new force. Arthur Young remarked in 1770, that within ten years there had been "more experiments, more discoveries, and more general good sense displayed in the walk of agriculture than in an hundred preceding ones"; and the reason why such a movement should have occurred seems obvious. After 1760 a complex system of credit sprang up, based on a metallic treasure, and those who could borrow had the means at their disposal of importing breeds of cattle, and of improving tillage, as well as of organizing factories like Soho. The effect was to cause rapid centralization. The spread of high farming certainly raised the value of land, but it also made the position of the yeomanry untenable, and nothing better reveals the magnitude of the social revolution wrought by Plassey, than the manner in which the wastes were enclosed after the middle of the century. Between 1710 and 1760 only 335,000 acres of the commons were absorbed; between 1760 and 1843, nearly 7,000,000. In eighty years the yeomanry became extinct. Many of these small farmers migrated to the towns, where the stronger, like the ancestor of Sir Robert Peel, accumulated wealth in industry, the weaker sinking into factory hands. Those who lingered on the land, toiled as day labourers.

Possibly since the world began, no investment has ever yielded the profit reaped from the Indian plunder, because for nearly fifty years Great Britain stood without a competitor. That she should have so long enjoyed a monopoly seems at first mysterious, but perhaps the condition of the Continent may suggest an explanation. Since Italy had been ruined by the loss of the Eastern trade, she had ceased to breed the economic mind; consequently no class of her population could suddenly and violently accelerate their movements. In Spain the priest and soldier had so thoroughly exterminated the sceptic, that far from centralizing during the seventeenth century, as England and France had done, her empire was in full decline at the revolution of 1688. In France something similar had happened, though in a much less degree. After a struggle of a century and a half, the Church so far prevailed in 1685 as to secure the revocation of the Edict of Nantes. At the revocation many Huguenots went into exile, and thus no small proportion of the economic class, who should have pressed England hardest, were driven across the Channel, to add their energy to the energy of the natives. Germany lacked capital. Hemmed in by enemies, and without a seacoast, she had been at a disadvantage in predatory warfare; accordingly she did not accumulate money, and failed to consolidate until, in 1870, she extorted a treasure from France. Thus, in 1760, Holland alone remained as a competitor, rich, maritime, and peopled by Protestants. But Holland lacked the mass possessed by her great antagonist, beside being without minerals; and accordingly, far from accelerating her progress, she proved unable to maintain her relative rate of advance.

Thus isolated, and favoured by mines of coal and iron, England not only commanded the European and American markets, at a time when production was strained to the utmost by war, but even undersold Hindoo labour at Calcutta. In some imperfect way her gains may be estimated by the growth of her debt, which must represent savings. In 1756, when Clive went to India, the nation owed £74,575,000, on which it paid an interest of £2,753,000. In 1815 this debt had swelled to £861,000,000, with an annual interest charge of £32,645,000. In 1761 the Duke of Bridgewater finished the first of the canals which were afterward to form an inland water-way costing £50,000,000, or more than two-thirds of the amount of the public debt at the outbreak of the Seven Years' War. Meanwhile, also, steam had been introduced, factories built, turnpikes improved, and bridges erected, and all this had been done through a system of credit extending throughout the land. Credit is the chosen vehicle of energy in centralized societies, and no sooner had treasure enough accumulated in London to offer it a foundation, than it shot up with marvellous rapidity.

From 1694 to Plassey, the growth had been relatively slow. For more than sixty years after the foundation of the Bank of England, its smallest note had been for £20, a note too large to circulate freely, and which rarely travelled far from Lombard Street. Writing in 1790, Burke mentioned that when he came to England in 1750 there were not "twelve bankers' shops" in the provinces, though then, he said, they were in every market town.(4) Thus the arrival of the Bengal silver not only increased the mass of money, but stimulated its movement; for at once, in 1759, the bank issued £10 and £15 notes, and, in the country, private firms poured forth a flood of paper. At the outbreak of the Napoleonic wars, there were not far from four hundred provincial houses, many of more than doubtful solvency. Macleod, who usually does not exaggerate such matters, has said, that grocers, tailors, and drapers inundated the country with their miserable rags. (5)

The cause of this inferiority of the country bankers was the avarice of the Bank of England, which prevented the formation of joint stock companies, who might act as competitors; and, as the period was one of great industrial and commercial expansion, when the adventurous and producing classes controlled society, enough currency of some kind was kept in circulation to prevent the prices of commodities from depreciating relatively to coin. The purchasing power of a currency is, other things being equal, in proportion to its quantity. Or, to put the proposition in the words of Locke, "the value of money, in general, is the quantity of all the money in the world in proportion to all the trade." (6) At the close of the eighteenth century, many causes combined to make money plentiful, and therefore to cheapen it. Not only was the stock of bullion in England increased by importations from India, but, for nearly a generation, exports of silver to Asia fell off. From an average of £600,000 annually between 1740 and 1760, the shipments of specie by the East India Company fell to £97,500 between 1760 and 1780; nor did they rise to their old level until after the close of the administration of Hastings, when trade returned to normal channels. After 1800 the stream gathered volume, and between 1810 and 1820 the yearly consignment amounted to £2,827,000, or to nearly one-half of the precious metals yielded by the mines.

From the crusades to Waterloo, the producers dominated Europe, the money-lenders often faring hardly, as is proved by the treatment of the Jews. From the highest to the lowest, all had wares to sell; the farmer his crop, the weaver his cloth, the grocer his goods, and all were interested in maintaining the value of their merchandise relatively to coin, for they lost when selling on a falling market. By degrees, as competition sharpened after the Reformation, a type was developed which, perhaps, may be called the merchant adventurer; men like Child and Boulton, bold, energetic, audacious. Gradually energy vented itself more and more freely through these merchants, until they became the ruling power in England, their government lasting from 1688 to 1815. At length they fell through the very brilliancy of their genius. The wealth they amassed so rapidly, accumulated, until it prevailed over all other forms of force, and by so doing raised another variety of man to power. These last were the modern bankers.

With the advent of the bankers, a profound change came over civilization, for contraction began. Self-interest had from the outset taught the producer that, to prosper, he should deal in wares which tended rather to rise than fall in value, relatively to coin. The opposite instinct possessed the usurer; he found that he grew rich when money appreciated, or when the borrower had to part with more property to pay his debt when it fell due, than the cash lent him would have bought on the day the obligation was contracted. As, toward the close of the eighteenth century, the great hoards of London passed into the possession of men of the latter type, the third and most redoubtable variety of the economic intellect arose to prominence, a variety of which perhaps the most conspicuous example is the family of Rothschild.

In one of the mean and dirty houses of the Jewish quarter of Frankfort, Mayer Amschel was born in the year 1743. The house was numbered 152 in the Judengasse, but was better known as the house of the Red Shield, and gave its name to the Amschel family. Mayer was educated by his parents for a rabbi; but, judging himself better fitted for finance, he entered the service of a Hanoverian banker named Oppenheim, and remained with him until he had saved enough to set up for himself. Then for some years he dealt in old coins, curiosities and bullion, married in 1770, returned to Frankfort, established himself in the house of the Red Shield, and rapidly advanced toward opulence. Soon after he gave up his trade in curiosities, confining himself to banking, and his great step in life was made when he became "Court Jew" to the Landgrave of Hesse. By 1804 he was already so prosperous that he contracted with the Danish Government for a loan of four millions of thalers.

Mayer had five sons, to whom he left his business and his wealth. In 1812 he died, and, as he lay upon his death-bed, his last words were, "You will soon be rich among the richest, and the world will belong to you." (7) His prophecy came true. These five sons conceived and executed an original and daring scheme. While the eldest remained at Frankfort, and conducted the parent house, the four others migrated to four different capitals, Naples, Vienna, Paris, and London, and, acting continually in consort, they succeeded in obtaining a control over the money market of Europe, as unprecedented as it was lucrative to themselves.

Of the five brothers, the third, Nathan, had commanding ability. In 1798 he settled in London, married in 1806 the daughter of one of the wealthiest of the English Jews, and by 1815 had become the despot of the Stock Exchange;

"peers and princes of the blood sat at his table, clergymen and laymen bowed before him." He had no tastes, either literary, social, or artistic; "in his manners and address he seemed to delight in displaying his thorough disregard of all the courtesies and amenities of civilized life"; and when asked about the future of his children he said, "I wish them to give mind, soul, and heart, and body—everything to business. That is the way to be happy." (8) Extremely ostentatious, though without delicacy or appreciation, "his mansions were crowded with works of art, and the most gorgeous appointments." His benevolence was capricious; to quote his own words, "Sometimes to amuse myself I give a beggar a guinea. He thinks it is a mistake, and for fear I shall find it out off he runs as hard as he can. I advise you to give a beggar a guinea sometimes. It is very amusing." (9)

Though an astonishingly bold and unscrupulous speculator, Nathan probably won his chief successes by skill in lending, and, in this branch of financiering, he was favoured by the times in which he lived. During the long wars Europe plunged into debt, contracting loans in depreciated paper, or in coin which was unprecedentedly cheap because of the abundance of the precious metals.

In the year 1809, prices reached the greatest altitude they ever attained in modern, or even, perhaps, in all history. There is something marvellously impressive in this moment of time, as the world stood poised upon the brink of a new era. To the contemporary eye Napoleon had reached his zenith. Everywhere victorious, he had defeated the English in Spain, and forced the army of Moore to embark at Corunna; while at Wagram he had brought Austria to the dust. He seemed about to rival Cæsar, and establish a military empire which should consolidate the nations of the mainland of Europe. Yet in reality one of those vast and subtle changes was impending, which, by modifying the conditions under which men compete, alter the complexion of civilizations, and which has led in the course of the nineteenth century to the decisive rejection of the martial and imaginative mind.

In April 1810 Bolivar obtained control at Caracas, and, with the outbreak of the South American revolutions, the gigantic but imaginative empire of Spain passed into the acute stage of disintegration. On December 19 of the same year, the Emperor Alexander opened the ports of Russia to neutral trade. By so doing Alexander repudiated the "continental system" of Napoleon, made a breach with him inevitable, and thus brought on the campaign of Moscow, the destruction of the Grand Army, and the close of French military triumphs on the hill of Waterloo. From the year 1810, nature has favoured the usurious mind, even as she favoured it in Rome, from the death of Augustus.

Moreover, both in ancient and modern life, the first symptom of this profound economic and intellectual revolution was identical. Tacitus has described the panic which was the immediate forerunner of the rise of the precious metals in the first century; and in 1810 a similar panic occurred in London, when prices suddenly fell fifteen per cent,(10) and when the most famous magnate of the Stock Exchange was ruined and killed. The great houses of Baring and of Goldsmid had undertaken the negotiation of a government loan of £14,000,000. To the surprise of these eminent financiers values slowly receded, and, in September, the death of Sir Francis Baring precipitated a crisis; Abraham Goldsmid, reduced to insolvency, in despair committed suicide; the acutest intellects rose instantaneously upon the corpses of the weaker, and the Rothschilds remained the dictators of the markets of the world. From that day to this the slow contraction has continued, with only the break of little more than twenty years, when the gold of California and Australia came in an overwhelming flood; and, from that day to this, the same series of phenomena have succeeded one another, which eighteen hundred years ago marked the emasculation of Rome.

At the peace, many causes converged to make specie rise; the exports of bullion to the East nearly doubled; America grew vigorously, and mining was interrupted by the revolt of the Spanish colonies. Yet favourable as the position of the creditor class might be, it could be improved by legislation, and probably no financial policy has ever been so ably conceived, or so adroitly executed, as that masterpiece of state-craft which gave Lombard Street control of the currency of Great Britain.

Under the reign of the producers, values had generally been equalized by cheapening the currency when prices fell. In the fourteenth, fifteenth, and sixteenth centuries, the penny had been systematically degraded, to keep pace with the growing dearth of silver. When the flood of the Peruvian bullion had reached its height in 1561, the currency regained its fineness; but in 1601 the penny lost another half-grain of weight, and, though not again adulterated at the mint, the whole coinage suffered so severely from hard usage that, under the Stuarts, it fell to about two-thirds of its nominal value. A re-coinage took place under William, but then paper came in to give relief, and the money in circulation continued to degenerate, as there was no provision for the withdrawal of light pieces. By 1774, the loss upon even the guinea had become so great that Parliament intervened, and Lord North recommended "that all the deficient gold coin should be called in, and re-coined" and also that the "currency of the gold coin should, in future, be regulated by weight as well as by tale... and that the several pieces should not be legal tender, if they were diminished, by wearing or otherwise, below a certain weight, to be determined by proclamation." (11)

By such means as this, the integrity of the metallic money was at length secured; but the emission of paper remained unlimited, and in 1797 even the Bank of England suspended cash payments. Then prices advanced as they had never advanced before, and, during the first ten years of the nineteenth century, the commercial adventurers reached their meridian. From 1810 they declined in power; but for several preceding generations they had formed a true aristocracy, shaping the laws and customs of their country. They needed an abundant currency, and they obtained it through the Bank. On their side the directors recognized this duty to be their chief function, and laid it down as a principle that all legitimate commercial paper should always be discounted. If interest rose, the rise proved a dearth of money, and they relieved that dearth with notes.

Lord Overstone has thus explained the system of banking which was accepted, without question, until 1810: "A supposed obligation to meet the real wants of commerce, and to discount all commercial bills arising out of legitimate transactions, appears to have been considered as the principle upon which the amount of the circulation was to be regulated." (12) And yet, strangely enough, even the adversaries of this system admitted that it worked well. A man as fixed in his opinions as Tooke, could not contain his astonishment that "under the guidance of maxims and principles so unsound and of such apparently mischievous tendency, as those professed by the governors and some of the directors of the Bank in 1810, such moderation and... such regularity of issue should, under chances and changes in politics and trade, unprecedented in violence and extent, have been preserved, as that a spontaneous readjustment between the value of the gold and the paper should have taken place, as it did, without any reduction of their circulation." (13)

With such a system the currency tended to fall rather than to rise in value, in comparison with commodities, and for this reason the owners of the great hoards were at a disadvantage. What powerful usurers, like Rothschild, wanted, was a legal tender fixed in quantity, which, being unable to expand to meet an increased demand, would rise in price. Moreover, they needed a circulating medium sufficiently compact to be controlled by a comparatively small number of capitalists, who would thus, under favourable conditions, hold the whole debtor community at their mercy.

If the year 1810 be taken as the point at which the energy stored in accumulations of money began to predominate in England, the revolution which ended in the overthrow of the producers, advanced, with hardly a check, to its completion by the "Bank Act" of 1844. The first symptom of approaching change was the famous "Bullion Committee," appointed on the motion of Francis Horner in 1810. This report is most interesting, for it marks an epoch, and in it the struggle for supremacy between the lender and the borrower is brought out in full relief. To the producer, the commodity was the measure of value; to the banker, coin. The producer sought a currency which should retain a certain ratio to all commodities, of which gold was but one. The banker insisted on making a fixed weight of the metal he controlled, the standard from which there was no appeal.

A distinguished merchant, named Chambers, in his evidence before the Committee, put the issue in a nutshell:—

Q. "At the Mint price of standard gold in this country, how much gold does a Bank of England note for one pound represent?

A. "5 dwts. 3 grs.

Q. "At the present market price of standard gold of £4 12. per ounce, how much gold do you get for a Bank of England note for one pound?

A. "4 dwts. 8 grs.

Q. "Do you consider that a Bank of England note for one pound, under these present circumstances, is exchangeable in gold for what it represents of that metal?

A. "I do not conceive gold to be a fairer standard for Bank of England notes than indigo or broadcloth."

Although the bankers controlled the "Bullion Committee," the mercantile interest still maintained itself in Parliament, and the resolutions proposed by the chairman in his report were rejected in the Commons by a majority of about two to one. The tide, however, had turned, and perhaps the best index of the moment at which the balance of power shifted, may be the course of Peel. Of all the public men of his generation, Peel had the surest instinct for the strongest force. Rarely, if ever, did this instinct fail him, and after 1812 his intuition led him to separate from his father; as, later in life, it led him to desert his party in the crisis of 1845. The first Sir Robert Peel, the great manufacturer, who made the fortune of the family, had the producer's instinct and utterly opposed contraction. In 1811 he voted against the report of the Bullion Committee, and then his son voted with him. After 1816, however, the younger Peel became the spokesman of Lombard Street, and the story is told that when the bill providing for cash payments passed in July, 1819, the old man, after listening to his son's great speech, said with bitterness: "Robert has doubled his fortune, but ruined his country." (14)

Probably Waterloo marked the opening of the new era, for after Waterloo the bankers met with no serious defeat. At first they hardly encountered opposition. They began by discarding silver. In 1817 the government made 123 $^{274}/_{1000}$ grs. of gold the unit of value, the coin representing this weight of metal ceasing to be a legal tender when deficient by about half a grain. The standard having thus been determined, it remained to enforce it. By this time Peel had been chosen by the creditor class as their mouthpiece, and in 1819 he introduced a bill to provide for cash payments. He found little resistance to his measure, and proposed 1823 as the time for the return; as it happened, the date was anticipated, and notes were redeemed in gold from May 1, 1821. As far as the coinage was concerned, this legislation completed the work, but the task of limiting discounts remained untouched, a task of even more importance, for, as long as the Bank continued discounting bills, and thus emitting an unlimited quantity of notes whenever the rate of interest rose, debtors not only might always be able to face their obligations, but the worth of money could not be materially enhanced. This question was decided by the issue of the panic of 1825, brought on by the Resumption Act.

At the suspension of 1797, paper in small denominations had been authorized to replace the coin which disappeared, but this act expired two years after the return to specie payments. Therefore, as time elapsed, the small issues began to be called in, and, according to Macleod, the country circulation, by 1823, had contracted about twelve per cent. The Bank of England also withdrew a large body of notes in denominations less than five pounds, and, to fill the gap, hoarded some twelve million sovereigns, a mass of gold about equal to the yield of the mines for the preceding seven or eight years. This gold had to be taken from the currency of Europe, and the sudden contraction caused a shock which vibrated throughout the West.

In France gold coinage almost ceased, and prices dropped heavily, declining twenty-four per cent between 1819 and 1822. Yet perhaps the most vivid picture of the distress caused by this absorption of gold, is given in a passage written by Macleod, to prove that Peel's act had nothing to do with the catastrophe:—

"There was one perfectly satisfiictory argument to show that the low prices of that year had nothing to do with the Act of 1819, namely, that prices of all sorts of agricultural produce were equally depressed all over the continent of Europe from the same cause. The fluctuations, indeed, on the continent were much more violent than even in England.... The same phenomena were observed in Italy. A similar fall, but not to so great an extent, took place at Lisbon. What could the Act of 1819 have to do with these places?" (15)

The severe and protracted depression, while affecting all producers, bore with peculiar severity upon the gentry, whose estates were burdened with mortgages and all kinds of settlements, so much so that frequently properties sank below their encumbrances, and the owners were beggared. At the opening of Parliament, both Houses were overwhelmed with petitions for aid. Among these petitions, one of the best known was presented to the Commons in May, 1822, by Charles Andrew Thompson, of Chiswick, which serves to show the keenness of the distress among debtors owning land.

Thompson stated, in substance, that in 1811 he and his father, being wealthy merchants, purchased an estate in Hertfordshire for £62,000, and afterward laid out £10,000 more in improvements. That in 1812 they entered into a contract for another estate, whose price was £60,000, but, a question having arisen as to the title, a lawsuit intervened, and, before judgment, the petitioner and his father had experienced such losses that they could not pay the sum adjudged due by the court. Thereupon, to raise money, they mortgaged both estates for £65,000. In July, 1821, both estates were offered for sale, but they failed to bring the amount for which they were mortgaged. Estates in other counties which cost £33,166, had been sold for £12,000, and through the depression of trade the petitioners had become bankrupt. In 1822 the petitioner's father died of a broken heart; and he himself remained a ruined man, with seven children of his own, ten of his brother's, and seven of his sister's all depending on him.(16)

The nation seemed upon the brink of some convulsion, for the gentry hardly cared to disguise their design of effecting a readjustment of both public and private debts. Passions ran high, and in June, 1822, a long debate followed upon a motion, made by Mr. Western, to inquire into the effects produced by the resumption of cash payments. The motion was indeed defeated, but defeated by a concession which entailed a catastrophe up to that time unequalled in the experience of Great Britain. To save the "Resumption Act" the ministry in July brought in a bill to respite the small notes until 1833, a measure which at once quieted the agitation, but which produced the most far-reaching and unexpected results.

According to Francis, the country banks augmented their issues fifty per cent between 1822 and 1825,(17) nor was this increase of paper the only or the most serious form taken by the inflation. The great hoard of sovereigns, accumulated by the Bank to replace its small notes, was made superfluous; and, in a memorandum delivered by the directors to the House of Commons, no less than £14,200,000 were stated to have been thrown on their hands in 1824 by this change of policy.(18) The effect was to create a veritable glut of gold in the United Kingdom; prices rose abnormally—fifteen per cent—between 1824 and 1825.

As values tended upward, a frenzy of speculation seized upon a people who had long suffered from the grinding of contraction, and meanwhile the Bank, adhering to its old policy, freely discounted all the sound bills brought them. In 1824 prices rose above the Continental level, and gold, being cheaper in London than in Paris, began to flow thither. The Bank reserve steadily fell. In March, 1825, the fever reached its height, and a decline set in, while the directors, anxious at the condition of their reserve in May, attempted to restrict their issues. The consequence was sharp contraction, and in November the crash came. Mr. Huskisson stated, in the House of Commons, that for forty-eight hours it was impossible to convert even government securities into cash. Exchequer bills, bank stock, and East India stock were alike unsalable, and many of the richest merchants of London walked the streets, not knowing whether on the morrow they might not be insolvent. "It is said" the Bank itself "must have stopped payment, and that we should have been reduced to a state of barter, but for a box full of old one and two-pound notes which was discovered by accident." (19) What happened in the Bank parlour during those days is unknown. Probably the pressure of the mercantile classes became too sharp to be withstood, perhaps even the strongest bankers were alarmed; but, at all events, the financial policy changed completely. Contraction was abandoned, the Bank reverted to the system of 1810, and in an instant relief came. "We lent by every possible means, and in modes we had never adopted before;... we not only discounted outright, but we made advances on deposit of bills of exchange to an immense amount." The Bank emitted five millions in notes in four days, and "this audacious policy was crowned with the most complete success, the panic was stayed almost immediately." (20)

With an expansion of the currency sufficient to furnish the means of paying debts, the panic passed away, but the disaster gave the bankers their opportunity; they seized it, and thenceforward their hold upon the community never, even for an instant, relaxed. The administration fell into discredit, and turned for assistance to the only men who promised to give them effective support: these were the capitalists of Lombard Street, whose first care was to obtain a statute prohibiting the small notes, which, they alleged, were the cause of the misfortune of 1825. The act they demanded passed in 1826, and about this time Samuel Loyd rose into prominence, who was, perhaps, the greatest financier of modern times. Cautious and sagacious, though resolute and bold, gifted with an amazing penetration into the complex causes which control the competition of modern life, he swayed successive administrations, and crushed down the fiercest opposition. Apparently he never faltered in his course, and down to the day of his death he sneered at the panic-stricken directors, who only saved themselves from bankruptcy by accidentally remembering and issuing a "parcel of old discarded one-pound notes... drawn forth from a refuse cellar in 1825." (21)

Loyd's father began life somewhat humbly as a dissenting minister in Wales, but, after his marriage, he entered a Manchester firm, and subsequently founded in London the house of Jones, Loyd and Co., afterward merged in the London and Westminster Bank, one of the largest concerns in the world. Samuel did not actually succeed his father until 1844, but much earlier he had grown to be the recognized chief of the monied interest, and Sir Robert Peel long served as his lieutenant. Loyd was the man who conceived the Bank Act of 1844, who succeeded in laying his grasp upon the currency of the kingdom, and in whose words, therefore, the policy of the new governing class is best stated:—

"A paper-circulation is the substitution of paper... in the place of the precious metals. The amount of it ought therefore to be equal to what would have been the amount of a metallic circulation; and of this the best measure is the influx or efflux of bullion." (22)

"By the provisions of that Act [the Bank Act of 1844] it is permitted to issue notes to the amount of £14,000,000 as before—that is, with no security for the redemption of the notes on demand beyond the legal obligation so to redeem them. But all fluctuations in the amount of notes issued beyond this £14,000,000 must have direct reference to corresponding fluctuations in the amount of gold." (23)

Thus Loyd's principle, which he embodied in his statute, was the rigid limitation of the currency to the weight of gold available for money. "When... notes are permitted to be issued, the number in circulation should always be exactly equal to the coin which would be in circulation if they did not exist." (24) In 1845 the Bank Act was extended to Scotland, except that there small notes were still tolerated; the expansion of provincial paper was prohibited, and England reverted to the economic condition of Byzantium,—a condition of contraction in which the debtor class lies prostrate, for, the legal tender being absolutely limited, when creditors choose to withdraw their loans, payment becomes impossible.

Perhaps no financier has ever lived abler than Samuel Loyd. Certainly he understood as few men, even of later generations, have understood, the mighty engine of the single standard. He comprehended that, with expanding trade, an inelastic currency must rise in value; he saw that, with sufficient resources at command, his class might be able to establish such a rise, almost at pleasure; certainly that they could manipulate it when it came, by taking advantage of foreign exchanges. He perceived moreover that, once established, a contraction of the currency might be forced to an extreme, and that when money rose beyond price, as in 1825, debtors would have to surrender their property on such terms as creditors might dictate.

Furthermore, he reasoned that under pressure prices must fall to a point lower than in other nations, that then money would flow from abroad, and relief would ultimately be given, even if the government did not interfere; that this influx of gold would increase the quantity of money, by so doing would again raise prices, and that, when prices rose, pledges forfeited in the panic might be resold at an advance. He explained the principle of this rise and fall of values, with his usual lucidity, to a committee of the House of Lords, which investigated the panic of 1847:—

"Monetary distress tends to produce fall of prices; that fall of prices encourages exports and diminishes imports; consequently it tends to promote an influx of bullion. I can quote a fact of rather a striking character, which tends to show that a contracting operation upon the circulation tends to cheapen the cost of our manufactured productions, and therefore to increase our exports." He then stated that during the panic he had received a letter "from a person of great importance in Lancashire," begging him to use his influence with the ministry "to be firm in maintaining the act,—to be firm in resisting these applications for relaxation," because in Lancashire the manufacturers were struggling to "resist the improperly high price of the raw material of cotton." "That letter reached me the very morning that the letter of the government was issued [suspending the act], and almost immediately the raw cotton rose in price."

Q. "The writer of that letter was probably a man of considerable substance, a very wealthy man, with abundant capital to carry on his business?

A. "He had recently retired from business. I can state another circumstance that occurred in London corroborative of the same results. Within half an hour of the time that the notes summoning the Court of Directors... were issued, parties, inferring probably... that a relaxation was about to take place, sent orders to withdraw goods from a sale which was then going on." (25)

The history of half a century has justified the diagnosis of this eminent financier. As followed out by his successors, Loyd's policy has not only forced down prices throughout the West, but has changed the aspect of civilization. In England the catastrophe began with the passage of the Bank Act.

No sooner had this statute taken effect than it necessarily caused a contraction of the currency at a time when gold was rising because of commercial expansion. Between 1839 and 1849 there was a fall in prices of twenty-eight per cent, and, severe as may have been the decline, it seems moderate considering the conditions which then prevailed. The yield of the mines was scanty, and of this yield India absorbed annually an average of £2,308,000, or somewhat more than one-sixth.

America was growing with unprecedented vigour, industrial competition sharpened as prices fell, and the year of the "Bank Act" was the year in which railway building began to take the form of a mania.

The peasantry are always the weakest part of every population, and therefore agricultural prices are the most sensitive. But the resources of a peasantry are seldom large, and, as the value of their crops shrinks, the margin of profit on which they live dwindles, until they are left with only a bare subsistence in good years, and with famine facing them in bad. The Irish peasants were the weakest portion of the population of Great Britain when Lord Overstone became supreme, and when the potato crop failed in 1845 they starved.

Although the landlords had lost their command over the nation in 1688, they yet, down to the last administration of Peel, had kept strength enough to secure protection from Parliament against foreign competition. By 1815 the yeomanry had almost disappeared, the soil belonged to a few rich families whose revenue depended on rents, and the value of rents turned on the price of the cereals. To sustain the market for wheat became therefore all-important to the aristocracy, and when, with the peace, prices collapsed, they obtained a statute which prohibited imports until the bushel should fetch ten shillings at home.

This statute, though frequently amended to make it more effective, partially failed of its purpose. A contracting currency did its resistless work, prices dropped, tenants went bankrupt, and, as the value of money rose, encumbered estates passed more frequently into the hands of creditors. Thus when Peel took office in 1841, the Corn Laws were regarded by the gentry as their only hope, and Peel as their chosen champion; but only a few years elapsed before it became evident that the policy of Lombard Street must precipitate a struggle for life between the manufacturers and the landlords. In the famine of 1846 the decisive moment came, and when Sir Robert sided, as was his wont, with the strongest, and abandoned his followers to their fate, he only yielded to the impulsion of a resistless force.

As a class both landlords and manufacturers were debtors, and, by 1844, cheap bread appeared to be as vital to the one as dear corn was to the other. With a steadily falling market the manufacturers saw their margin of profit shrink, and at last Manchester and Birmingham believed themselves to be confronted with ruin unless wages fell proportionately, or they could broaden the market for their wares by means of international exchanges. The Corn Laws closed both avenues of relief; therefore there was war to the death between the manufacturers and the aristocracy. The savageness of the attack can be judged by Cobden's jeers at gentlemen who admitted that free corn meant insolvency:—

"Sir Edward Knatchbull could not have made a better speech for the League than that which he made lately, even if he were paid for it. I roared so with laughter that he called me specially to order, and I begged his pardon, for he is the last man in the world I would offend, we are all so much obliged to him. He said they could not do without this Corn Law, because, if it were repealed, they could not pay the jointures, charged on their estates. Lord Mountcashel, too (he's not over-sharp) said that one half the land was mortgaged, and they could not pay the interest unless they had a tax upon bread. In Lancashire, when a man gets into debt and can't pay, he goes into the *Gazette*, and what is good for a manufacturer is, I think, good for a landlord." (26)

In such a contest the gentry were overmatched, for they were but nature's first effort toward creating the economic type, and they were pitted against later forms which had long distanced them in the competition of life. Bright and Cobden, as well as Loyd and Peel, belonged to a race which had been driven into trade, by the loss of their freeholds to the fortunate ancestors of the men who lay at their mercy in 1846. Peel himself was the son of a cotton-spinner, and the grandson of a yeoman, who, only in middle life, had quitted his hand-loom to make his fortune in the "industrial revolution."

In modern England, as in ancient Italy, the weakest sank first, and the landed gentry succumbed, almost without resistance, to the combination which Lombard Street made against them. Yet, though the manufacturers seemed to triumph, their exultation was short, for the fate impended over them, even in the hour of their victory, which always overhangs the debtor when the currency has been seized by the creditor class. By the "Bank Act" the usurers became supreme, and in 1846 the potato crop failed even more completely than in 1845. Credit always is more sensitive in England than in France, because it rests upon a narrower basis, and at that moment it happened to be strained by excessive railway loans. With free trade in corn, large imports of wheat were made, which were paid for with gold. A drain set in upon the Bank, the reserve was depleted, and by October 2, 1847, the directors denied all further advances. Within three years of the passage of his statute, the event Loyd had foreseen arrived. "Monetary distress" began to force down prices. The decision of the directors to refuse discounts created "a great excitement on the Stock Exchange. The town and country bankers hastened to sell their public securities, to convert them into money. The difference between the price of consols for ready money and for the account of the 14th of October showed a rate of interest equivalent to 50 per cent per annum. Exchequer bills were sold at 35s. discount.".... "A complete cessation of private discounts followed. No one would part with the money or notes in his possession. The most exorbitant sums were offered to and refused by merchants for their acceptances." (27)

Additional gold could only be looked for from abroad, and as a considerable time must elapse before specie could arrive in sufficient quantity to give relief, the currency actually in use offered the only means of obtaining legal tender for the payment of debts. Consequently hoarding became general, and, as the chancellor of the exchequer afterward observed, "an amount of circulation which, under ordinary circumstances, would have been adequate, became insufficient for the wants of the community." Boxes of gold and bank-notes in "thousands and tens of thousands of pounds" were "deposited with bankers." The merchants, the chancellor said, begged for notes: "Let us have notes;... we don't care what the rate of interest is.... Only tell us that we can get them, and this will at once restore confidence." (28)

But, after October 2, no notes were to be had, money was a commodity without price, and had the policy of the "Bank Act" been rigorously maintained, English debtors, whose obligations then matured, must have forfeited their property, since credit had ceased to exist and currency could not be obtained wherewith to redeem their pledges.

The instinct of the usurer has, however, never been to ruin suddenly the community in which he has lived: only by degrees does he exhaust human vitality. Therefore, when the great capitalists had satisfied their appetites, they gave relief. From the 2d to the 25th of October, contraction was allowed to do its work; then Overstone intervened, the government was instructed to suspend the "act," and the community was promised all the currency it might require.

The effect was instantaneous. The letter from the cabinet, signed by Lord John Russell, which recommended the directors of the Bank to increase their discounts, "was made public about one o'clock on Monday, the 25th, and no sooner was it done so than the panic vanished like a dream! Mr. Gurney stated that it produced its effect in ten minutes! No sooner was it known that notes might be had, than the want of them ceased!"(29) Large parcels of notes were "returned to the Bank of England cut into halves, as they had been sent down into the country."

The story of this crisis demonstrates that, by 1844, the money-lenders had become autocratic in London. The ministry were naturally unwilling to suspend a statute which had just been enacted, and the blow to Sir Robert Peel was peculiarly severe; but the position of the government admitted of no alternative. At the time it was said that the private bankers of London intimated to the chancellor of the exchequer that, unless he interfered forthwith, they would withdraw their balances from the Bank of England. This meant insolvency, and to such an argument there was no reply. But whether matters actually went so far or not, there can be no question that the cabinet acted under the dictation of Lombard Street, for the chancellor of the exchequer defended his policy by declaring that the "act" had not been suspended until "those conversant with commercial affairs, and least likely to decide in favour of the course which we ultimately adopted," unanimously advised that relief should be given to the mercantile community. (30)

There was extreme suffering throughout the country, which manifested itself in all the well-known ways. The revenue fell off, emigration increased, wheat brought but about five shillings the bushel, while in England and Wales alone there were upwards of nine hundred thousand paupers. Discontent took the form of Chartism, and a revolution seemed imminent. Nor was it Great Britain only which was convulsed: all Europe was shaken to its centre, and everything portended some dire convulsion, when nature intervened and poured upon the world a stream of treasure too bountiful to be at once controlled.

In 1849 the first Californian gold reached Liverpool. In four years the supply of the precious metals trebled, prices rose, crops sold again at a profit. As the farmers grew rich, the demand for manufactures quickened, wages advanced, discontent vanished, and though values never again reached the altitude of 1809, they at least attained that level of substantial prosperity which preceded the French Revolution. Nevertheless, the fall in the purchasing power of money, and the consequent ability of debtors to meet their obligations, did not excite that universal joy which had thrilled Europe at the discovery of Potosi, for a profound change had passed over society since the buccaneers laid the foundations of England's fortune by the plunder of the Peruvian galleons.

To the type of mind which predominated after 1810, the permanent rise of commodities relatively to money was unwelcome, and, almost from the opening of the gold discoveries, a subtle but resistless force was working for contraction—a force which first showed itself in the movement for an uniform gold coinage, and afterwards in general gold monometallism. The great change came with the conquest of France by Germany. Until after the middle of the nineteenth century, Germany held only a secondary position in the economic system of Europe, because of her poverty. With few harbours, she had reaped little advantage from the plunder of America and India, exchanges had never centred within her borders, and her accumulated capital had not sufficed to stimulate high consolidation. The conquest of France suddenly transformed these conditions. In 1871 she acquired an enormous booty, and the effect upon her was akin to the effect on England of the confiscations in Bengal; the chief difference being that, unlike England, Germany passed almost immediately into the period of contraction.

The spoliation of India went on for twenty years, that of France was finished in a few months, and, while in England the "industrial revolution" intervened between Plassey and the adoption of the gold standard, in Germany the bankers dominated from the outset. The government belonged to the class which desired an appreciating currency, and in 1873 the new empire followed in the steps of Lombard Street, and demonetized silver.

Germany's action was decisive. Restrictions were placed on the mints of the Latin Union and of the United States, and thus, by degrees, the whole stress of the trade of the West was transferred from the old composite currency to gold alone. In this way, not only was the basis of credit in the chief commercial states cut in half, but the annual supply of metal for coinage was diminished. In 1893 the gold mined fell nearly nine per cent short of the value of the gold and silver produced in 1865, and yet, during those twenty-eight years, the demand for money must have increased enormously, if it in any degree corresponded with the growth of trade.

The phenomena which followed the adoption of the gold standard by Western countries were precisely those which had been anticipated by Loyd. Lord Overstone had explained them to an earlier generation. In one of his letters on the "Bank Charter," as early as 1855, he developed the whole policy of the usurers:—

"If a country increases in population, in wealth, in enterprise, and activity, more circulating medium will probably be required to conduct its extended transactions. This demand for increased circulation will raise the value of the existing circulation; it will become more scarce and more valuable,... in other words — gold will rise...." (31)

By the action of Germany, Overstone's policy was extended to the whole Western world, with the results he had foreseen. Gold appreciated, until it acquired a purchasing power unequalled since the Middle Ages, and while in the silver-using countries prices remained substantially unchanged and the producers accordingly prospered, prostration supervened in Europe, the United States, and Australia. As usual the rural population suffered most, and the English aristocracy, who had been respited by the gold discoveries, were the first to succumb. They not only drew their revenues from farming land, but, standing at the focus of competition, they were exposed to the pressure of Asia and America alike. The harvest of 1879 was one of the worst of the century, land depreciated hopelessly, and that year may probably be taken as marking the downfall of a class which had maintained itself in opulence for nearly three hundred and fifty years.

This Tudor aristocracy, which sprang up at the Reformation, was one of the first effects of the quickened movement which transferred the centre of exchanges from Italy to the North Sea. They represented sharpening economic competition, and they prospered because of an intellectual gift, an aptitude they enjoyed, of absorbing the lands of the priests and soldiers amidst whom they dwelt. These soldiers were the yeomen who, when evicted, became pirates, slavers, commercial adventurers, religious colonists, and conquerors, and who together poured the flood of treasure into London which, transmuted into movement, made the "industrial revolution." When by their efforts, toward the beginning of the nineteenth century, sufficiently vast reservoirs of energy in the shape of money had accumulated, a new race rose to prominence, fitted to give vent to this force—men like Nathan Rothschild and Samuel Loyd, probably endowed with a subtler intellect and a keener vision than any who had preceded them, financiers beside whom the usurers of Byzantium, or the nobles of Henry VIII., were pigmies.

These bankers conceived a policy unrivalled in brilliancy, which made them masters of all commerce, industry, and trade. They engrossed the gold of the world, and then, by legislation, made it the sole measure of values. What Samuel Loyd and his followers did to England, in 1847, became possible for his successors to do to all the gold standard nations, after 1873. When the mints had been closed to silver, the currency being inelastic, the value of money could be manipulated like that of any article limited in quantity, and thus the human race became the subjects of the new aristocracy, which represented the stored energy of mankind.

From the moment this aristocracy has determined on a policy, as, for example the "Bank Act" or monometallism, resistance by producers becomes most difficult. Being debtors, producers are destroyed when credit is withdrawn, and, at the first signs of insubordination, the bankers draw in their gold, contract their loans, and precipitate a panic. Then, to escape immediate ruin, the debtor yields.

Since 1873 prices have generally fallen, and the mortgage has tended to engulf the pledge; but, from time to time the creditor class feels the need of turning the property it has acquired from bankrupts into gold, and then the rise explained by Overstone takes place. The hoards are opened, credit is freely given, the quantity of currency is increased, values rise, sales are made, and new adventurers contract fresh obligations. Then this expansion is followed by a fresh contraction, and liquidation is repeated on an ever-descending scale.

For many years farming land has fallen throughout the West, as it fell in Italy in the time of Pliny. Everywhere, as under Trajan, the peasantry are distressed; everywhere they migrate to the cities, as they did when Rome repudiated the denarius. By the census of the United

Kingdom taken in 1891, not only did it appear that over seventy-one per cent of the inhabitants of England and Wales lived in towns, but that, while the urban districts had increased above fifteen per cent since the last census, the population of the purely agricultural counties had diminished. (32)

Moreover, within a generation, there has been a marked loss of fecundity among the more costly races. The rate of increase of the population has diminished. In the United States it is generally believed that the old native American blood is hardly reproducing itself; but, in all social phenomena, France precedes other nations by at least a quarter of a century, and it is, therefore, in France that the failure of vitality is most plainly seen. In 1789 the average French family consisted of 4.2 children. In 1891 it had fallen to 2.1,(33) and, since 1890, the deaths seem to have equalled the births.(34) In 1889 legislation was attempted to encourage productiveness, and parents of seven children were exempted from certain classes of taxes, but the experiment failed. Levasseur, in his great work on the population of France, has expressed himself almost in the words of Tacitus: "It can be laid down as a general law that, if in such a social condition as that of the French of the nineteenth century, the number of children is small, it is because the majority of parents wish it should be small." (35)

Such signs point to the climax of consolidation. And yet, even the rise of the bankers is not the only or the surest indication that centralization is culminating. The destruction, wrought by accelerated movement, of the less tenacious organisms, is more evident below than above, is more striking in the advance of cheap labour, than in the evolution of the financier.

Footnotes

(1) *History of the Cotton Manufacture*, 115.

(2) *A Tour Thro' the whole Island of Great Britain*, ed. 1753, iii. 136, 137.

(3) *Lives of Boulton and Watt*, Smiles, 484.

(4) *First Letter on a Regicide Peace.*

(5) *Theory and Practice of Banking*, i. 507.

(6) *Considerations of the Lowering of Interests. Works*, ed. 1823, v. 49.

(7) *The Rothschilds*, Reeves, 51.

(8) *The Rothschilds*, Reeves, 192, 199.

(9) *Ibid.*, 200.

(10) Wherever reference is made to comparative prices of commodities, the authority used has been the tables published by W. S. Jevons in *Investigations in Currency and Finance*, 144.

(11) *Annals of the Coinage*, Ruding, iv. 37.

(12) *Overstone Tracts*, 49.

(13) *History of Prices*, i. 158.

(14) *Political Life of Sir Robert Peel*, Doubleday, i. 218, note.

(15) *Theory and Practice of Banking*, Macleod, ed. 1893, ii. 103.

(16) See Hansard, New Series, viii. 189.

(17) *History of the Bank of England*, i. 348.

(18) *History of the Bank of England*, i. 347.

(19) *History of the Currency*, Maclaren, 161.

(20) *Theory and Practice of Banking*, Macleod, ii. 117, 118.

(21) *Overstone Tracts*, 325.

(22) *Ibid.*, 191.

(23) *Ibid.*, 318.

(24) *Theory and Practice of Banking*, ii. 147.

(25) *Overstone Tracts*, 573, 574.

(26) *Cobden and the League*, Ashworth, 174.

(27) *Theory and Practice of Banking*, Macleod, ii. 169, 170.

(28) Hansard, Third Series, xcv. 399.

(29) *Theory and Practice of Banking*, ii. 170.

(30) Hansard, Third Series, xcv. 398.

(31) *Overstone Tracts*, 319.

(32) See *Journal of Roy. Stat. Soc.*, liv. 464.

(33) Dénombrement de 1891, 261.

(34) *Annuaire de l'Économie Politique*, 1894, Block, 18.

(35) *La Population Française*, ii. 214.

Chapter XII: Conclusion

APPARENTLY nature needs to consume about three generations in perfecting the selection of a new type. Accordingly the money-lenders did not become absolute immediately after Waterloo, and a period of some sixty years followed during which the adventurers kept up a struggle, wherein they were aided by the discoveries of gold near the middle of the century. Seemingly they met their final defeat at Sedan, for the decay of the soldier, which had been in progress since the fall of Napoleon, reached a point, after the collapse of the Second Empire, even lower than after the consolidation of Rome.

From Alaric to Napoleon the soldier had served as an independent vent to energy. Often, even when opposed to capital, he had been victorious, and the highest function of a leader of men had been, in theory at least, military command. The ideal statesman had been one who, like Cromwell, Frederic the Great, Henry IV., William III., and Washington, could lead his followers in battle, and, on the Continent, down to 1789, the aristocracy had professedly been a military caste. In France and Germany the old tradition lasted to within a generation. Only after 1871 came the new era, an era marked by many social changes. For the first time in their history the ruler of the French people passed admittedly from the martial to the monied type, and everywhere the same phenomenon appeared; the whole administration of society fell into the hands of the economic man. Nothing so radical happened at Rome, or even at Byzantium, for there the pressure of the barbarians necessitated the retention of the commander at the head of the State; in Europe he lost this importance. Since the capitulation of Paris the soldier has tended to sink more and more into a paid official, receiving his orders from financiers with his salary, without being allowed a voice even in questions involving peace and war. The same fate has overtaken the producing classes; they have failed to maintain themselves, and have become subjects of the possessors of hoarded wealth. Although the conventions of popular government are still preserved, capital is at least as absolute as under the Caesars, and, among capitalists, the money-lenders form an aristocracy. Debtors are in reality powerless, because of the extension of that very system of credit which they invented to satisfy their needs. Although the volume of credit is gigantic, the basis on which it rests is so narrow that it may be manipulated by a handful of men. That basis is gold; in gold debts must be paid; therefore, when gold is withdrawn, the debtor is helpless and becomes the servant of his master. The elasticity of the age of expansion has gone.

The aristocracy which wields this autocratic power is beyond attack, for it is defended by a wage-earning police, by the side of which the legions were a toy; a police so formidable that, for the first time in history, revolt is hopeless and is not attempted. The only question which preoccupies the ruling class is whether it is cheaper to coerce or to bribe. On looking back over long periods of time, the sequence of causes may be followed which have led to this result. First, inventions from the East facilitated trade; then, the perfection of weapons of attack made police possible, and individual bravery unnecessary; on this followed the abasement of the martial and exaltation of the economic type; and finally that intense acceleration of movement by machinery supervened, which, in annihilating space, has destroyed the protection that the costly races long enjoyed against the competition of simpler organisms.

Roman civilization was less complex than modern because of the relative inflexibility of the Latin mind. Unable to quicken his motions by inventions, the ancient Italian failed to discover America or absorb India, and, for the same reason, collapsed without an effort under the insidious attack of Asiatic and African labour. No industrial expansion followed the influx of bullion under Caesar, and therefore, when the value of cereals fell, the evicted farmer either sank into slavery or begged for bread from the magnates of the Senate. In modern times an industrial period has intervened; the evicted long found employment in the factories of the towns, and it has only been as contraction has reduced the demand for merchandise, by diminishing the purchasing power of the agricultural population, that those stagnant pools of the unemployed have collected, which exactly correspond to the proletariat. But, as each special faculty which, for a time, enables its possessor to excel in competition, seems to bear with it the seeds of its own decay, so the inventive, which once enabled the Western races to undersell the Eastern in their homes seems destined to reduce all to a common economic level, as Rome sank to the level of Egypt.

For nearly a century the inventions of Hargreaves, of Crompton, of Cartwright, and of Watt, enabled Lancashire to supply Bombay and Calcutta with fabrics, as, in the seventeenth century, Surat and Calicut had supplied London, and this superiority appeared assured until Orientals should acquire the momentum necessary for machinery. One effect in Europe was the rapid increase of a population congregated in towns, and bearing a marked resemblance to the "humiliores" of Rome in their disinclination for war. True to their instincts, the adventurers ever quickened their movements, ever extended the sphere of their enterprises, and, finally, just as the Second Empire verged upon its fall, they opened the Suez Canal in 1869. The consequences of this great engineering triumph have probably equalled in gravity the establishment of the gold standard, but the two phenomena had this marked difference. The producers saw their danger and resisted to the utmost the contraction of the currency, whereas the Canal was a case of suicide. Thenceforward grain, raised by the most enduring labour of the world, could be thrown without limit on the European market, and, agricultural competition once established, industrial could only be a question of time. The Canal made the importation and the reparation of machinery cheap throughout Asia.

From a period, perhaps, as remote as Clive's victories, the Hindoos had experienced a certain impulsion from contact with the British, but it was not until the building of railroads, under Lord Dalhousie, that the severer phases of competition opened among the inhabitants of India. Lord Dalhousie became Governor General in 1848, and, that the acceleration of the next nine years culminated in a catastrophe seems certain, for nothing can be plainer than that the Mutiny of 1857 was an outbreak of a martial Mohammedan population crushed under an intolerable pressure.

The locality of the disturbance alone is enough to demonstrate the accuracy of this inference. Dalhousie's last act was the annexation of the Kingdom of Oude. Of this province Lucknow is the capital, and while Lucknow was one focus of the insurrection, Delhi, the capital of the ancient Mogul empire, was the other. Once subdued by the British, and reduced to an economic equality with subtler races, the old Moslem gentry rapidly disappeared. Since 1857 these families, which had maintained themselves for six or seven hundred years, have rapidly fallen into ruin, and their estates have been bought by their creditors, the rising usurer class.

Under immemorial native custom the money-lender, generally speaking, had no forcible means of collecting debt; he relied on public opinion and conducted himself accordingly. On the other hand, unrestricted alienation of land was not usually incidental to proprietorship, and thus the tenant for life, as he would be called in English law, could only pledge his crops; he could not sell the succession. With centralization came full ownership, and with it summary process for debt. Following her immutable law, nature, having changed the form of competition, proceeded to select a quality of mind to correspond with the new conditions of life. She demanded improved vents for her energy. Forthwith, under the pressure of accelerated movement and advancing consolidation, the trammels of caste relaxed, the population fused, and a new aristocracy arose, composed of the strongest economic types culled from all the peoples who inhabit the plains south of the Himalayas. This aristocracy is a strange mixture of blood, an amalgam of the most diverse elements, of Parsees, Brahmins, Bunniahs of different races, with gifted individuals from other castes, like the leather-workers or the goldsmiths; but among them all the most ruthless, the corruptest, the most hated, and the most successful, are the Marwaris, who have been thus described by a British commission:—

"The average Marwari money-lender is not a pleasant character to analyze; his most prominent characteristics are love of gain and indifference to the opinions or feelings of his neighbour. He has considerable self-reliance and immense industry, but the nature of his business and the method by which it is pursued would tend to degrade and harden even a humane nature, which his is not. As a landlord he follows the instincts of the usurer, making the hardest terms possible with his tenant, who is also his debtor and often little better than his slave." (1)

The effect of the selection of such a type as a dominant class must be destructive to a martial population, whether it be French or English, Mohammedan or Hindoo. The social revolution which swept over Oude after its annexation has been referred to, but the fate which overtook the famous Mahratta nation is even more tragic and impressive.

When, toward the close of the last century, the British were pushing their conquests inland, the most formidable enemy they met were the Mahrattas; and, perhaps, the most renowned battle, next to Plassey, ever fought by Europeans against natives, was Assaye, where Wellesley defeated Sindhia in 1803. These Mahrattas were tribes of Hindoo farmers, who inhabited the mountainous country about one hundred miles to the east of Bombay; a territory of which Poona has always been considered the capital. Mounted on their hill ponies, these bold and hardy spearmen were always ready to follow their chiefs to battle, and, in the eighteenth century, became the terror not only of the Mohammedans of the Deccan, but of the Mogul himself, at Delhi. Even the English respected and feared them, and only subdued them in 1818 after desperate fighting. Then they were disarmed and subjected to the combined action of peace and English law.

Soon after this conquest an inflow of Marwaris began. As early as 1854, in Dalhousie's administration, Captain Anderson stated that "two-thirds of the ryots [were] in the hands of the Marwaris, and that the average debt of each individual [was] not less than Rs. 100."(2) Competition continued unchecked as time flowed on, and in 1875 disturbances broke out in certain villages near Poona, serious enough to cause the government to appoint a commission of inquiry. After full investigation this commission reported that up to 1872 or 1873 the peasantry had seemed relatively prosperous, but that afterward "prices fell quickly," and that this fall had been accompanied by a rise in taxation of somewhat more than fifty per cent.(3) Under this double pressure the peasantry had rapidly sunk into insolvency, and the whole real estate of the Deccan was passing into the hands of usurers, while the farmers had become serfs toiling on the soil they had once owned, to satisfy an inextinguishable debt. Precisely like the *colonus*, the delinquent was not evicted, but remained, "recorded as occupier of his holding, and responsible for the payment of revenue assessed on it, but virtually reduced by pressure of debt to a tenant-at-will,... sweated by his Marwari creditor. It is in that creditor's power to eject him any day;... and if allowed to hold on, it is only on condition of paying over to his creditor all the produce of his land not absolutely necessary for next year's seed grain or for the support of life. He is indebted on an average to the extent of sixteen or seventeen years' payment of the government revenue. He has nothing to hope for, but lives in daily fear of the final catastrophe." (4)

Since Assaye three generations have passed away, and the Mahratta spearmen have vanished. The Western

Ghats are now tilled by a sluggish race whom the British officers deem unworthy of their cavalry, and in the place of those renowned and daring chiefs Sivaji and Holkar, stands the Marwari under whom no ryots can prosper save those "who having received some education are able to combat the sowkars with their own weapons, fraud, chicanery, and even forgery." (5) Apparently the same destiny awaits every people which requires more than the minimum of nutriment, or which is not gifted with the economic mind, (6) for the "money-lenders sweep off the crops as soon as harvested, only leaving with the ryots barely sufficient to eke out a subsistence till the following year." (7) That allowance, in the Deccan, is estimated at about a dollar a month in silver—too little to sustain any but the most tenacious organisms, even among Asiatics. Consequently, though the population of India is increasing rapidly, the increase lies chiefly among the aboriginal tribes who form the lowest castes, or in other words among the non-martial or servile races. Men who, though enslaved by the Aryan invaders of prehistoric times, and who have always been subjected to extremest hardship, have been gifted, like the Egyptian fellah, with an endurance which has enabled them to survive.(8)

Herein, likewise, may be plainly perceived the destructive effects of the policy of the Western usurers upon the population subject to them. By enhancing the value of their own money they have nearly doubled the intensity of this Asiatic competition. In India, silver has substantially retained its purchasing power, therefore the ryot now, as in the days of Captain Cunningham, can exist on two rupees a month, but he cannot live on less. Accordingly, the severity of his competition with Europeans must be measured by the value of his wages when reckoned on the European scale. In 1854 the ryot's two rupees were worth one dollar; now, through the appreciation of gold, they are worth about sixty cents, and the effect is the same as though the tenacity of life of the Asiatic had been increased four-sixths. Everything the Indian or Chinese peasant produces with his hands, whether on the farm or in the factory, has been reduced in price, in relation to Western peoples, in the ratio of six to ten.

The cheapest form of labour is thus being bred on a gigantic scale, and this labour is being accelerated by an industrial development which is stimulated by eviction of the farmers, as the "industrial revolution" was stimulated in England one hundred and thirty years ago. For many years the cotton mills of Bombay have undersold Lancashire in the coarser fabrics, and when, by means of a canal to the Pacific, American cotton can be imported cheaply, they will spin the finer also. Moreover, Hindostan is full of iron and coal which has never been utilized because of the immense difference in the rapidity of European and Asiatic labour, but the steadily falling range of Western prices must force the cheapest product on the market, and when the Indian railways have been assumed by the government, a new era will have opened. The same causes are affecting China and Japan, and, under precisely similar conditions, the centre of exchanges passed from the Tiber to the Bosphorus sixteen hundred years ago.

Such uniformity of development in the most distant times, and among the most divergent peoples, points to a progressive law of civilization, each stage of progress being marked by certain intellectual, moral, and physical changes. As the attack in war masters the defence, and the combative instinct becomes unnecessary to the preservation of life, the economic supersedes the martial mind, being superior in breadwinning. As velocity augments and competition intensifies, nature begins to sift the economic minds themselves, culling a favoured aristocracy of the craftiest and the subtlest types; choosing, for example, the Armenian in Byzantium, the Marwari in India, and the Jew in London. Conversely, as the costly nervous system of the soldier becomes an encumbrance, organisms, which can exist on less, successively supplant each other, until the limit of endurance is reached. Thus the Slavs exterminated the

Greeks in Thrace and Macedonia, the Mahrattas and the Moslems dwindle before the low caste tribes of India, and the instinct of self-preservation has taught white races to resist an influx of Chinese. When nature has finished this double task, civilization has reached its zenith. Humanity can ascend no higher.

In view of this possible extermination of the martial blood in the higher stages of civilization, the attention necessarily becomes concentrated on what is, perhaps, the main point of divergence between ancient and modern society,—the presence and the absence of a supply of barbaric life. All the evidence points to the conclusion that the infusion of vitality which Rome ever drew from territories beyond her borders, was the cause both of her strength and of her longevity. Without such aid she could never have consolidated the world. On the other hand, the lack of this resource has been the weakness of modern nations. One after another they have dreamed of universal conquest, and one after another they have fallen through exhaustion in war.

Spain levied never a pikeman in America, and her colonies were a source of debility in so far as they drained her of her youth. Had Rome been similarly situated, she could hardly have carried the eagles beyond the Bosphorus and the Alps. Perhaps Caesar's army was the best an ancient general ever put in the field, and yet it was filled with barbarians. All his legions were raised north of the Po, and most of them, including the tenth, north of the Alps. (9) When pitted against this force native Italians broke in rout, and one of the most striking pages of Plutarch is the story of the gradual awakening of Pompey to a sense of the impotence of Romans. Pompey himself was a commander of high ability, and, until he split upon the rock of the pure martial blood, battle had been with him synonymous with victory.

At first he felt such confidence, he laughed at the suggestion of an attack within the Rubicon. With the conviction of the conqueror he said: "Whenever I stamp with my foot in any part of Italy, there will rise up forces enough in an instant, both horse and foot." (10) A very short experience of the men of the north sufficed to sober him; for, though Caesar's command amounted to only twenty-two thousand, and his to twice as many, he not only declined an action, but took what care he could to keep the threats of the Gauls from his men, "who were out of heart and despondent, through terror at the fierceness and hardiness of their enemies, whom they looked upon as a sort of wild beasts." (11) Pharsalia stunned him. When the tenth legion routed his left wing, he went to his tent and sat speechless until the invasion of the camp; then he walked away "softly afoot, taken up altogether with thoughts such as probably might possess a man that for the space of thirty-four years together had been accustomed to conquest and victory, and was then at last, in his old age, learning for the first time what defeat and flight were." (12)

Thus, in reality, barbarians consolidated the ancient world, and the force which created the Empire, afterward upheld it. With each succeeding century the drafts of centralized society upon the blood of the country beyond the Danube and the Rhine increased, but the supply proved limitless; and, when the Western provinces disintegrated, a new imaginative race poured over Italy and France, creating a new religion, a new art, a new literature, and new institutions. Among modern nations the Russians alone have developed this power of absorbing kindred conquered peoples; and yet, obviously, Napoleon would have fought his campaigns under very different circumstances, and, perhaps, brought them to a different end, had he, like Cæsar, had an exhaustless supply of the best soldiers, altogether independent of the population of France.

Religious phenomena become explicable when viewed from the same standpoint. Unquestionably scepticism has been to the full as rife in Paris since 1789 as it ever was in Rome, and yet no new religion has been born. Supposing, however, that a vast and highly emotional emigration flowed annually into France, the aspect of life would be completely changed. Christian saints and martyrs were not begotten by the usurers of Constantinople or of Rome, but by barbarian soldiers and Asiatic serfs, and Christianity could hardly have become a State religion had the composition of society, as it existed under Trajan, remained unaltered. Even in the reign of Justinian the aristocracy carped at faith, and Byzantine architecture did not bloom until the invasions of Alaric and Attila.

If, then, although nature never precisely repeats herself, she operates upon the human mind according to immutable laws, it should be possible by comparing a living civilization with a dead, to estimate in some degree the course which has been run. For such an attempt an infinite variety of standards might be suggested, but few, perhaps, are more suitable than the domestic relations which lie at the basis of the reproduction of life.

In a martial and imaginative age, where energy vents itself through fear, and every man must be a soldier, the family generally forms a unit; the women and children being under the control of the father, as they were under the control of the patriarchs in the Bible, or of the paterfamilias in Rome. In such periods the woman is sought after by the man, and even commands a high money value; "And Shechem said unto her father,... Ask me never so much dowry and gift, and I will give according as ye shall say unto me: but give me the damsel to wife."(13) The Homeric heroes bought their wives, and, moreover, were very fond of them—an affection the women returned, for in all classical literature there are few more charming legends than that of Penelope. Divorce was unknown to Hector and Agamemnon, Ulysses and Achilles. Marriage, in these simple ages, is usually a rite half sacred, half warlike. When Abraham's servant found Rebekah at the well, he bowed his head, and blessed the Lord God of his master Abraham, which had led him in the right way. A Roman wedding was a solemn religious function accompanied by prayer and sacrifice, and, at the end, the bride was carried to her husband's house, where she was violently torn from her mother's arms.

Aristotle, with his unerring acumen, made this observation: "That all warlike races are prone to the love of women," and also that they tend to "fall under the dominion of their wives." (14) Undoubtedly this is the instinct of the soldier, and, in martial ages, women are idealized. When a foreigner asked the wife of Leonidas, "Why do you Lacedaemonian wives, unlike all others, govern your husbands?" the Spartan answered, "Because we alone are the mothers of men." When at Rome Tiberius killed the male serpent, thereby devoting himself to death to save Cornelia, Plutarch, telling the story, remarked, "that Tiberius seemed to all men to have done nothing unreasonable, in choosing to die for such a woman; who, when King Ptolemy himself proffered her his crown, and would have married her, refused it, and chose rather to live a widow." (15)

In the Middle Ages, that greatest of martial and imaginative epochs, marriage developed into the most solemn of sacraments, and the worship of women became the popular religion. In France, especially, the centre of thought, enthusiasm, and war, from the mighty fane of Paris downward, the churches were dedicated to Mary, and the vow of chivalry bound the knight to fight for God and for his lady.

"It hath bene through all ages ever scene
That with the praise of armes and chevalrie
The prize of beautie still hath ioyned beene." (16)

It might almost be said that the destinies of France have been moulded by men's love for women, and that this influence still prevailed down to the advent of the usurers after the rout of Waterloo. On the other hand, nature bred a type of woman fit to mate with the imaginative man. The devotion of Saint Clara to Saint Francis is one of the most exquisite lyrics of the Church, and for six hundred years

Héloïse remained an ideal of the West. Perhaps, indeed, that strange blending of tenderness and enthusiasm, which was peculiar to the mediaeval mind, never found more refined and exalted expression than in the simple hymn which Héloïse is said to have composed and sung at the grave of Abélard:—

"Tecum fata sum perpessa;
Tecum dormiam defessa,
Et in Sion veniam.
Solve crucem,
Duc ad lucem
Degravatam animam."

In primitive ages children are not only a source of power, but of wealth, and therefore the highest merit of the woman is fecundity. "And they blessed Rebekah, and said unto her,... be thou the mother of thousands of millions." Also maternity is then a glory, and childlessness a shame; and Rachel said, "Give me children, or else I die." "And she conceived and bare a son; and said, God hath taken away my reproach." That she might live for her boys, Cornelia refused a crown; and when they grew up, she would upbraid them because "the Romans as yet rather called her the daughter of Scipio than the mother of the Gracchi." But Cornelia's father was the conqueror of Hannibal, and her son was an agrarian agitator, whom the monied oligarchy murdered for reviving the Licinian Laws. Apparently, one of the first signs of advancing civilization is the fall in the value of women in men's eyes. Not very long after the siege of Troy, husbands must have ceased paying for their wives; for, at a comparatively early date, they demanded a price for wedding them. Euripides, born in 480 B.C., made Medea complain that women had to buy their husbands for great sums of money. In other words, the custom of the wedding portion had come to prevail.

As the pressure of economic competition intensifies with social consolidation, the family regularly disintegrates, the children rejecting the parental authority at a steadily decreasing age; until, finally, the population fuses into a compact mass, in which all individuals are equal before the law, and all are forced to compete with each other for the means of subsistence. When at length wealth has accumulated sufficiently to find vent through capitalistic methods of farming and manufacture, children lose all value, for then hiring labour is always cheaper than breeding. Thenceforward, among the more extravagant races, the family dwindles, as in ancient Rome or modern France, and marriage, having become a luxury, decreases. Moreover, the economic instinct impels parents to reduce the number of possible inheritors of their property, that its bulk may not shrink.

Upon women the effect of these changed conditions is prodigious. Their whole relation to society is altered. From a religious sacrament marriage is metamorphosed into a civil contract, dissoluble, like other contracts, by mutual consent; and, as the obligations of maternity diminish, the relation of husband and wife resolves itself into a sort of business partnership, tending always to become more ephemeral. Frequent as divorce now is, it was even more so under the Antonines.

On men the action of natural selection is, at least, as drastic. The change wrought in Roman character in about three hundred years has always been one of the problems of history. In the words of Aristotle, the primitive Roman "was prone to the love of women." Strong in his passions, austere in his life, fierce in his jealousy, he set the undisputed possession of the female as his supreme happiness. Virginius slew his daughter to keep her from Appius Claudius, and his comrades in the legions washed out his wrong in the Decemvir's blood; while among the stirring ballads of the fabled time which were sung at the farmer's fireside, none roused such emotion as the tale of the vengeance wreaked on Tarquin for Lucretia's death. Compare this virile race with the aristocracy of the middle Empire. By the second century female purity weighed light against money. Marcus Aurelius is said to have condensed the whole economic moral code in one short sentence. His wife, Faustina, was accused, by scandal, of being the most abandoned woman of her generation, more notorious even than had been Messalina. When the philosopher was urged to repudiate her, he replied, "Then I should have to surrender her portion" (the Empire); and he not only lived with her, but built a temple to her memory. Even if the story be false, it reflects none the less truly the temper of the age.

The minds of noble Romans of the third and fourth centuries, under the same impulsion, worked differently from those of their primitive ancestors; they lacked the martial and the amatory instincts. As a general rule one salient characteristic of the later reigns was a sexual lassitude yielding only to the most potent stimulants. The same phenomena were noticed among Frenchmen at the collapse of the Empire, since when like symptoms have become notorious in London.

Taking history as a whole, women seem never to have more than moderately appealed to the senses of the economic man. The monied magnate seldom ruins himself for love, and chivalry would have been as foreign to a Roman senator under Diocletian, as it would be now to a Lombard Street banker. On the other hand, in proportion as women's influence has declined when measured by their power over men, it has increased when measured by the economic standard. In many ways the female seems to serve as a vent for the energy of capital almost as well as men; in the higher planes of civilization they hold their property in severalty, and, by means of money, wield a power not unlike Faustina's. If unmarried, the economic woman competes with the man on nearly equal terms, and everywhere, and in all ages, the result is not dissimilar. The stronger and more fortunate members of the sex have grown rich and have bought social and political power. Roman politics under Septimius Severus and Caracalla was much in the hands of women, and Julia Massa, who was enormously wealthy, carried through a most famous intrigue by purchasing the throne for Elagabalus.

In Rome, however, there was always a strong admixture of barbaric blood, and, to the last, the barbarians married for love. Justinian was an example. Born of an obscure race of barbarians in the desolate Bulgarian country, he fell uncontrollably in love with Theodora, who had scandalized even the theatres of Constantinople. His mother died of shame; but Justinian persevered, and, while she lived, his devotion to his wife never wavered.

In Rome and in Byzantium such women were the stronger or the more fortunate; their counterparts are easily to be found in any economic age. The fate of the weaker there was slavery; now they are forced by competition into the ranks of the cheapest labour,—a lot, perhaps, hardly preferable.

And yet art, perhaps, even more clearly than religion, love, or war, indicates the pathway of consolidation; for art reflects with the subtlest delicacy those changes in the forms of competition which enfeeble or inflame the imagination. Of Greek art, in its zenith, little need be said; its great qualities have been too fully recognized. It suffices to point out that it was absolutely honest, and that it formed a vehicle of expression as flexible as the language itself. A temple apparently of marble, was of marble; a colonnade apparently supporting a portico, did support it; and, while the ornament formed an integral part of the structure, the people read it as intelligently as they read the poems of Homer. Nothing similar ever flourished in Rome.

Unlike the Greeks, the Romans were never sensitive or imaginative. Properly speaking, they had nothing which they could express through art; they were utilitarian from the outset, and their architecture finally took shape in the most perfect system of materialistic building which, probably, has ever existed. Obviously such a system could only be matured in a capitalistic society, and, accordingly,

Roman architecture only reached perfection somewhat late, perhaps, toward the close of the first century.

The Romans, though vulgar and ostentatious, understood business. They knew how to combine economy and even solidity with display. As Viollet-le-Duc has observed, "They were rich, and they wanted to appear so," (17) but they strove to attain their end without waste. Therefore they first ran up a cheap core of rubble, bricks, and mortar, which could be put together by rude slave labour under the direction of an engineer and a few overseers; and their squalid interior they afterward veneered with marble, adding, by way of ornament, tier above tier of Greek columns ranged against the walls. That gaudy exterior had nothing whatever to do with the building itself, and could be stripped off without vital injury. From the Greek standpoint nothing could be falser, more insulting to the intelligence, or, in a word, more plutocratic; but the work was sound and durable, and, to a certain degree, imposing from its mass. This system lasted, substantially unimpaired, even to Constantine or until the final migration of capital to the Bosphorus, the only difference between the monuments of the fourth century and the first being that the former are somewhat coarser, just as the coins of Diocletian are coarser than those of Nero. Yet, although the monied aristocracy remained supreme down to the final disintegration of the West, emigration began very early to modify the base of society, by the injection of a considerable amount of imaginative blood; and, as early as the reign of Claudius, this new store of energy made its presence felt through the outlet of Christianity. The converts were, of course, the antipodes of the ruling class. They were "humiliores," poor people, below the notice of a rich man like Tacitus; "quos,... vulgus Christianos appellabat." (18)

These Christians held a position analogous to that of Nihilists now, whom they resembled save in respect to violence. They were socialists living under a monied despotism, and they openly prayed for the end of the world; therefore they were thought "haters of the human race," (19) and they suffered the penalty. Primitive Christianity was incompatible with the existence of Roman society, against which it was a protest, for it "fully accepted the idea that the rich, if he did not surrender his superfluity, kept what belonged to another." (20) By right the Kingdom of Heaven was closed to the wealthy.

Probably very few of these early Christians were Italians; most of them were from the Levant, and that they were intensely emotional is proved by their lust for martyrdom— they voluntarily sought death as a means of glorifying God. One day Arrius Antoninus, proconsul of Asia, having ordered certain Christians arrested, saw all the faithful of the town present themselves before his tribunal, demanding to share the fate of those chosen for martyrdom. He dismissed them in wrath, telling them that if they were so in love with death they might commit suicide; (21) and Renan's account of the persecutions under Nero shows an incredible exaltation. (22)

Almost at once the effect of this emotional temperament became perceptible. The paintings in the catacombs are, perhaps, the oldest example of Christian art, and of these M. Vitet thus spoke many years ago:—

"These decorations, made with the hand raised, in secret, hurriedly, and more for pious reasons than for love of the beautiful, nevertheless reveal to the most rebellious eyes and in spite of strange negligence and incorrectness, I know not what of animation, of youth, of fecundity, and, so to speak, a real transformation of that very art which, in the service of paganism, seemed then, we are all agreed, dying of exhaustion." (23)

As the world disintegrated, and the imagination everywhere acquired power, and with power wealth and the means of expression, an entirely new architecture sprang up in the East, whose growth closely followed upon the barbarian invasions and the progressive failure of the Roman blood. The system of construction was Asiatic modified by Greek influences,(24) and with this new construction came an equally new decoration, a decoration which once more served as a language.

Mosaics of stone had long been used, but mosaics of glass, which give such an incomparable lustre to the dome, were the invention of Levantine Christians, and seem to have come into general use toward the beginning of the fifth century. But the fifth century was the period of the great invasions of Alaric, Attila, and Theoderic, and during this period the population of Italy, Macedonia, and Thrace must have undergone profound changes. In Italy the whole fabric of consolidated society crumbled; south of the Danube it survived, but survived in a modified form, a form on which the recent migrations left an unmistakable imprint. Galla Placidia, the first great patron of the pure Byzantine school, died in 450, after an eventful life largely passed among the barbarians, one of whom she married. She began to embellish Ravenna, and a comparison of these remains with those of France and Italy of the eleventh, twelfth, and thirteenth centuries, exposes the difference in the forces which moulded these three civilizations.

With all its grace and refinement the characteristic of Ravenna was not religious ecstasy, but rather an absence of fear of the unknown, and a respect for wealth. There is nothing mysterious or terrible about these charming buildings, which are manifestly rather a glorification of the Empire on the Bosphorus, than of the Kingdom of Heaven.

At San Vitale it is Justinian, with an aureole about his head and surrounded by his courtiers, carrying a gift to the shrine; or Theodora, blazing with jewels, and followed by the magnificent ladies of her household. At San Apollinare the long procession of saints are richly clad and bear crowns, while the Virgin herself, seated on a throne and revered as a sovereign, is as far removed from the vulgar as Theodora herself. "Byzantine etiquette no longer permits her to be approached directly; four angels surround her and separate her from humanity."(25) The terrifying was scrupulously avoided. "By a most significant scruple, the artist, in reproducing various episodes of the Passion, avoided the most painful, the Crucifixion." (26)

Saint Sophia offers every indication of having been expressly contrived to provide the large light spaces needful for such functions as those depicted in San Vitale, and the account given by Procopius of its erection sustains this supposition. According to Procopius, Saint Sophia was a hobby of Justinian, who not only selected the architect Anthemius because he was the most ingenious mechanic of his age, but who also supplied the funds and "assisted it by the labour and powers of his mind."(27) The dome, "from the lightness of the building... does not appear to rest upon a solid foundation, but to cover the place beneath as though it were suspended from heaven by the fabled golden chain"; and the interior "is singularly full of light and of sunshine; you would declare that the place is not lighted by the sun from without, but that the rays are produced within itself, such an abundance of light is poured into this church."(28) Of the decorations it is impossible to speak with certainty, since it is probable that the mosaics which now exist were of a later period.

Perhaps, however, the most significant phenomenon about the church is its loneliness; nothing like it was built elsewhere, and the reason seems plain. There was but one imperial court which needed so superb a setting, and but one emperor who could pay for it. Herein lies the radical divergence between the East and West; the great tabernacle of Constantinople stood alone because it represented the wealth, the pomp, and the imagination of the barbarian shepherd who had been raised by fortune to be the chief of police of the city where the world's wealth had centralized. In France every diocese had a temple magnificent according to its means, some of which exceeded in majesty that of Paris; and the cause was that, in France, the artistic and imaginative caste formed a theocracy, who were not hired by king or emperor, but who were themselves the strongest force in all the land. In the East, the imaginative inroad was not strong enough to cause disintegration, and the artists always remained wage-earners. In the West, society fell back a thousand years, and consolidation began afresh. Six centuries intervened between the death of Galla Placidia and the famous dream of the monk Gauzon which contained the revelation of the plan of the Abbey of Cluny, and yet six hundred years by no means represented the gap between the Franks and the Burgundians, and the Eastern Empire, even when it sank lowest under Heraclius. To Justinian the building of Saint Sophia was a matter of time and money; to Saint Hugh the church of Cluny was a miracle.

In France the churches long were miracles; the chronicles are filled with the revelations vouchsafed the monks; and none can cross the threshold of one of these noble monuments and fail to grasp its meaning. They are the most vigorous of all expressions of fear of the unseen. The Gothic architect heeded no living potentate; he held kings in contempt, and oftener represented them thrust down into hell than seated on their thrones. With the enemy who lurked in darkness none but the saints could cope, and them he idealized. No sculpture is more terrible than the demons on the walls of Rheims, none more majestic and pathetic than that over the door of the Virgin at Paris, while no colour ever equalled the windows of Saint Denis and Chartres.

With the thirteenth century came the influx of the Eastern trade and the rise of the communes. Immediately the glory of the Gothic began to fade; by the reign of Saint Louis it had passed its prime, and under Philip the Fair it fell in full decline. The men who put dead cats in shrines were not likely to be inspired in religious sculpture. The decay, and the reasons for it, can be readily traced in colour.

The monks who conceived the twelfth century windows, or painted the pictures of the saints, only sought to render an emotion by a conventional symbol which should rouse a response. Consequently they used marvellous combinations of colours, in which blue was apt to predominate, and they harmonized their colours with gold.

Viollct-le-Duc has elaborately explained how this was done. (29) But such a system was not pretentious, and was incompatible with perspective. The mediaeval burgher, like the Roman, was rich, and wanted to appear so. He demanded more for his money than a solemn portrait of a saint. He craved a picture of himself, or of his guild, and above all he insisted on display. The fourteenth century was the period when the reds and yellows superseded the blues, and when the sense of harmony began to fail. Furthermore, the burgher was realistic and required a representation of the world he saw about him. Hence came perspective, the abandonment of gold, and the final degradation of colour, which sank into a lost art. For hundreds of years it has been impossible to imitate the work of the monks of Saint Denis. In Italy, the economic phenomena were yet more striking; for Italy, even in the Middle Ages, was always a commercial community, which looked on art with the economic eye. One example will suffice,—the treatment of the dome.

Placed between the masterpieces of the East and West, and having little imagination of his own, the Florentine banker conceived the idea of combining the two systems and embellishing them in a cheap and showy manner. Accordingly on Gothic arches he placed an Eastern dome, and instead of adorning his dome with mosaics, which are costly, he had his interior painted at about one-quarter of the price. The substitution of the fresco for the mosaic is one of the most typical devices of modern times.

Before the opening of the economic age, when the imagination glowed with all the passion of religious enthusiasm, the monks who built the abbeys of Cluny and Saint Denis took no thought of money, for it regarded them not. Sheltered by their convents, their livelihood was assured; their bread and their robe were safe; they pandered to no market, for they cared for no patron. Their art was not a chattel to be bought, but an inspired language in which they communed with God, or taught the people, and they expressed a poetry in the stones they carved which far transcended words. For these reasons Gothic architecture, in its prime, was spontaneous, elevated, dignified, and pure.

The advent of portraiture has usually been considered to portend decay, and rightly, since the presence of the portrait demonstrates the supremacy of wealth. A portrait can hardly be the ideal of an enthusiast, like the figure of a god, for it is a commercial article, sold for a price, and manufactured to suit a patron's taste; were it made to please the artist, it might not find a buyer. When portraits are fashionable, the economic period must be well advanced. Portraiture, like other economic phenomena, blossomed during the Renaissance, and it was then also that the artist, no longer shielded by his convent or his guild, stood out to earn his living by the sale of his wares, like the Venetian merchants whom he met on the Rialto, whose vanity he flattered, and whose palaces he adorned. From the sixteenth century downward, the man of imagination, unable to please the economic taste, has starved.

This mercenary quality forms the gulf which has divided the art of the Middle Ages from that of modern times—a gulf which cannot be bridged, and which has broadened with the lapse of centuries, until at last the artist, like all else in society, has become the creature of a commercial market, even as the Greek was sold as a slave to the plutocrat of Rome. With each invention, with each acceleration of movement, prose has more completely supplanted poetry, while the economic intellect has grown less tolerant of any departure from those representations of nature which have appealed to the most highly gifted of the monied type among successive generations. Hence the imperiousness of modern realism.

Thus the history of art coincides with the history of all other phenomena of life; for experience has demonstrated that, since the Reformation, a school of architecture, like the Greek or Gothic, has become impossible. No such school could exist in a society where the imagination had decayed, for the Greek and Gothic represented imaginative ideals. In an economic period, like that which has followed the Reformation, wealth is the form in which energy seeks expression; therefore, since the close of the fifteenth century, architecture has reflected money.

Viollet-le-Duc has said of the Romans, that, like all parvenus, the true expression of art lay, for them, rather in lavish ornament than in purity of form, (30) and what was true of the third century is true of the nineteenth. The type of mind being the same, its operation must be similar, and the economic, at once ostentatious and parsimonious, produces a cheap core fantastically adorned. The Romans perched the travesty of a Grecian colonnade upon the summit of a bath or an amphitheatre, while the Englishman, having pillaged weaker nations of their imaginative gems, delights to cover with coarse imitations the exterior of banks and counting-houses.

And yet, though thus alike, a profound difference separates Roman architecture from our own; the Romans were never wholly sordid, nor did they ever niggle. When they built a wall, that wall was solid masonry, not painted iron; and, even down to Constantine, one chord remained which, when struck, would always vibrate. Usurers may have sat in the Senate, but barbarians filled the legions, and, as long as the triumph wound its way through the Forum, men knew how to raise triumphal arches to the victor. Perhaps, in all the ages, no more serious or majestic monument has been conceived to commemorate the soldier than the column of Trajan, a monument which it has been the ambition of our century to copy.

In Paris an imitation of this trophy was erected to the greatest captain of France, and the column of the Place Vendôme serves to mark the grave of the modern martial blood. Raised in 1810, almost at the moment when Nathan Rothschild became despot of the London Stock Exchange, the tide from thence ran swiftly, and, since Sedan, the present generation has drained to the lees the cup of realism.

No poetry can bloom in the arid modern soil, the drama has died, and the patrons of art are no longer even conscious of shame at profaning the most sacred of ideals. The ecstatic dream, which some twelfth-century monk cut into the stones of the sanctuary hallowed by the presence of his God, is reproduced to bedizen a warehouse; or the plan of an abbey, which Saint Hugh may have consecrated, is adapted to a railway station.

Decade by decade, for some four hundred years, these phenomena have grown more sharply marked in Europe, and, as consolidation apparently nears its climax, art seems to presage approaching disintegration. The architecture, the sculpture, and the coinage of London at the close of the nineteenth century, when compared with those of the Paris of Saint Louis, recall the Rome of Caracalla as contrasted with the Athens of Pericles, save that we lack the stream of barbarian blood which made the Middle Age.

Footnotes

(1) *Report of the Commission appointed in India to enquire into the Causes of the Riots which took place in the year 1875, in the Poona and Ahmednagar Districts of the Bombay Presidency*, 12.

(2) *Report of the Commission appointed in India to enquire into the Causes of the Riots which took place in the year 1875, in the Poona and Ahmednagar Districts of the Bombay Presidency*, 159.

(3) *Report of the Commission, etc.*, 25, 26.

(4) *Ibid.*, 167.

(5) *Report of the Commission, etc.*, 168.

(6) See *Musulmans and Money-lenders in the Punjab*, Thorburn.

(7) *Report of the Commission, etc.*, 168.

(8) See *Brief History of the Indian Peoples*, Hunter, 50.

(9) See *History of the Romans*, ed. of 1852, Merivale, ii. 81, where the authorities are collected.

(10) Plutarch's *Lives*, Clough's trans., iv. 123.

(11) *Ibid.*, 298.

(12) *Ibid.*, 142.

(13) Genesis xxxiv. 11, 12.

(14) Aristotle, *Pol.*, ii. 9.

(15) Plutarch's *Lives*, Clough's trans., iv. 507.

(16) *Faery Queene*, Spenser, iv. 5, 1.

(17) *Entretiens sur l'Architecture*, i. 102.

(18) *Ann.*, xv. 44.

(19) *Ann.*, xv. 44.

(20) *Marc-Aurèle.*, Renan, 600.

(21) Tertullian, *Ad Scapulam*, 5.

(22) *L'Antechrist*, 163 *et seq.*

(23) *Études sur l'Histoire de l'Art*, Vitet, i. 200.

(24) *L'Art de Batir chez les Byzantins*, Choisy, 5, 6.

(25) *Recherches pour servir à l'Histoire de la Peinture et de la Sculpture Chrétiennes en Orient*, Bayet, 99.

(26) *Ibid.*, 99.

(27) *Buildings of Justinian*, Procopius, trans. by Stewart, i. 1.

(28) *Ibid.*

(29) *Dictionnaire de l'Architecture*, Art. "Peinture."

(30) *Entretiens*, i. 102.

CPSIA information can be obtained
at www.ICGtesting.com
Printed in the USA
LVHW081332021219
639170LV00014B/339/P

9 781533 262448